DESIGNING YOUR OWN CLASSICAL CURRICULUM

LAURA M. BERQUIST

Designing Your Own Classical Curriculum

A Guide to Catholic Home Education

THIRD EDITION

IGNATIUS PRESS   SAN FRANCISCO

Cover design by Roxanne Mei Lum

Contents

* The author advises the reader to refer to the chapter on "The High School Years" (pp. 108–204) before proceeding with the ninth grade curriculum.

Foreword

THIS BOOK is a treasure for Catholic parents. It provides a guide to something they may have thought no longer existed: a way to raise their children in a Catholic culture.

A culture is a natural accretion, built up over centuries out of faith expressed in the ordinary and extraordinary events of life: the love of God, scholarly reflection, the language of prayer, Sacred Scripture and sacred music, of domestic customs, memories of saints and heroes, repentant sinners and answered prayers, legends of courage and loyalty, honor and charity. Catholic culture reached its highest development within Western civilization, but in the past thirty years that culture in which most Catholics lived and which seemed to them to be simply the unchangeable *given* of life has collapsed in a vast secularizing implosion. Catholics who were formed by this culture, and intended to transmit it to their children, have discovered that they are opposed, not only by external enemies (an opposition they expected and were prepared to meet), but also by an emerging managerial class within the Church, apparently devoted to accommodation and surrender.

In consequence, the old culture has vanished from most Catholic institutions, but it has not died. It is still alive in faithful Catholic families, not only those of aging believers who refuse to relinquish the past, but also in young families who are consciously reclaiming it. These young parents recognize that their most sacred obligation to their children, after giving them life, is to educate them so that they can save their souls. They are doing what the monasteries did for Catholic culture in an earlier Dark Age—preserving it and passing it on.

Designing Your Own Classical Curriculum has been written for those who are schooling their children at home. Homeschooling is one of the phenomena that give striking witness to the vitality of Christian culture. In the early years of the current crisis—the late 1960s and early 1970s—scattered groups of Catholic parents tried to establish a network of academies independent of control by the Church bureaucracy, but the concurrent demands of fund-raising, administration, state regulations, insurance expenses and clashes of opinion about educational philosophy proved too much for most of them. The homeschooling movement has since then largely eclipsed those efforts to build a lay-directed school system. It was initiated a few years later by parents searching for some other workable alternative to the decaying Catholic schools, much as Catholics in previous generations had inaugurated the parochial school system itself as an alternative to Protestant-dominated public schools. A few desperate Catholic parents first turned for help to the vigorous young evangelical homeschool programs already being developed by concerned Protestant parents. Though grateful for the example, encouragement and useful text materials provided by these Protestant pioneers, the Catholics soon grew troubled about the anti-Catholic flavor of some texts. Before long the first Catholic correspondence schools opened, and Catholic homeschooling began to acquire its own identity. It has grown exponentially over the past decade.

Still, not every parent alarmed about the condition of Catholic schools has yet ventured to take up homeschooling. Almost all the doubters wonder whether home education would not constitute over-protection of their children or deprive them of essential "socialization". Some hesitate to add the role of educator to that of parent, lest the two somehow conflict. Some are daunted by their ignorance of what skills ought to be taught at each grade level; others think they could shelter their children from much of the world's corruption by teaching them at home but doubt that they could give them a really excellent college preparatory education. Still others may have been overwhelmed by the flood of paper that a correspondence curriculum entails or may want a more flexible approach for their children. In *Designing Your Own Classical Curriculum*, Mrs. Berquist addresses such questions in ways that will not only quiet their fears about homeschooling but fire them with eagerness to begin.

Drawing upon many years' experience as a homeschool teacher, Laura Berquist has written a book that is not merely an argument for the virtues of such education. What it offers is an overview of the natural stages of intellectual development, informed by her understanding of the way they conform to the divisions of the classical Trivium, the first steps in a liberal education. Thus, it is not a *program* but a *method*, perfectly adaptable to the needs of every child. As the child progresses through this kind of education, the subject matter grows more difficult, but the method remains constant. At each level, Mrs. Berquist provides specific practical information about appropriate materials, essential facts and even discussion questions. But her most important contribution is the understanding that education has to do with teaching the child how to think, providing him with the tools for independent analysis and learning, not simply requiring him to accumulate a mountain of facts.

When the idea of homeschooling was first presented to me twenty-five years ago, it sounded like a manifestation of romantic counter-culturalism, admirable in its daring but probably imprudent and certainly illegal. As the disintegration of American society proceeded, parental pressure forced its legalization, and I came to see that it was absolutely essential that Christians become countercultural. Home-schooling then seemed to be an important defense against the growing evils in the world. What I did not understand until I saw its fruits in the lives of my own grandchildren was that it is a superior kind of education, so compatible with the healthy formation of the child's character and intellect, so reinforcing of virtue, and fostering such respect between parents and children, that I conclude it must be what God has always intended.

The homeschooled child escapes the common agonies that go by the name of "socialization"—the petty cruelties of the playground, the scalding classroom snickers at his mistakes, his infirmities or even mere differences. At home, he is taught by those who love him and know him best, who know the weaknesses he needs to overcome and the strengths he might be too shy to display in public, and whose deepest desire is for him to become all he is capable of becoming, in both his intellectual and his spiritual development, so that he will become a saint. Adolescence is more manageable in a home setting, where there is no appeal beyond the parents, than in the classroom milieu, where the child newly testing his limits is abetted by an army of rebels. Homeschooled children retain their appealing innocence long after their contemporaries at the local junior high have been turned into precocious, and often foul-mouthed, cynics. One of the most striking qualities of homeschooled families is their marvelous harmony, their obvious delight in their younger brothers and sisters.

An appetite for achievement is built into human nature. What men and women seek is not a life of easy luxury but a lifework deserving the expenditure of all their gifts. I believe this book can help Catholic parents—especially mothers—to find that kind of joy in the work of leading their children to God within the shelter of a living Catholic culture.

Donna Steichen
Author of *Ungodly Rage*
September 9, 1994

Acknowledgments

M ANY PEOPLE have contributed to this book. My children come to mind first of all. Margaret, Theresa, John, Rachel, James and Richard, thank you for your patience and cooperation. Sarah Kaiser, Maria Kaiser, Austin Ferrier, Katy Finley, Rosie Finley, Andrew DeSilva and Thomas O'Reilly have been delightful guinea pigs, helping me arrive at the curriculum here displayed. Thank you.

There are others who have more than earned my gratitude. My husband, Mark, my most valuable ally, has helped and encouraged me, proofread my material and made excellent suggestions. My mother, Donna Steichen, has made this her project as well as mine. I could not have done it without her help. My father, Roy, and sister Peggy have given me reassurance when I needed it and made suggestions that were constructive.

Mike Paietta has made most valuable suggestions for needed clarifications, and his concern for this project is much appreciated.

Kathy Ferrier is responsible for many of the lists and study guides in this book, and her invaluable suggestions have helped me raise my children. God bless you, Kathy.

Laura Berquist

Introduction

Designing Your Own K–12 Classical Curriculum

WHEN I BEGAN homeschooling fourteen years ago, I read many "how to" books and articles. One of the articles was "The Lost Tools of Learning", by Dorothy Sayers.[1] It was very impressive.

The most impressive of the many things Miss Sayers said was that the goal of education should be to teach children how to think; we want them to learn the art of learning. Then they will be equipped for life; whether or not they learn all the subjects possible in school, they will be able to learn any subject when it becomes necessary or desirable, *if* they know how to learn.

In fact, she goes on to say, learning subjects in school is of very secondary importance. What matters is the method of learning. Miss Sayers then directs our attention to the Trivium and Quadrivium of a classical education.

When I read this, I agreed immediately and wholeheartedly with what she said about learning the art of learning. But I was not clear enough about teaching or the development of children to understand how the method of the Trivium should fit into my curriculum. I set aside, you might say "lost", the "Lost Tools of Learning" and proceeded to experiment on my six children, particularly my oldest child, and the children of some (rash) friends and neighbors. You will be relieved to know that my three oldest children, at any rate, have survived. Two of them are presently attending Thomas Aquinas College, where my eldest daughter graduated this spring!

[1] Sources for items followed by a number in parentheses may be found at the back of the book in the list of suppliers. These resources will be discussed in greater depth in the following sections.

13

My experiments were surprisingly fruitful. I began to write various grade-level curricula and share them with friends. Eventually I was asked to give conference talks to help others design their own curricula.

While preparing for those talks, I reread "The Lost Tools of Learning" and discovered that the particular advice of Miss Sayers with respect to the Trivium of the classical curriculum was exactly what I had stumbled on by trial and error! What she suggests from an understanding of medieval education I came to by using what worked.

In this book I hope to introduce you to a method that will help you construct your own classical curriculum, a curriculum that will teach your children how to think and not just accumulate facts. It will not be something you accomplish all at once, but this method will guide you in incorporating different skills and courses at appropriate ages. The method first involves thinking clearly and in some detail about what you want to achieve in the education of your children.

The first step in constructing your curriculum is to do some background reading. There are a number of books available that will help you clarify what you want to achieve educationally in your homeschool. "The Lost Tools of Learning" (21) should certainly be read. *For the Children's Sake*, by Susan Schaeffer Macaulay (21), is very good. I recommend it highly to all parents, not only to homeschoolers. It presents a view of what education is and how to achieve it in a way that will encourage lifelong learning. *Homeschooling for Excellence*, by Micki and David Colfax (20), gives you a good look at a successful homeschool family and much valuable advice. Raymond Moore's books (20) remind one that in some cases late is better than early, and Marva Collins' book *Marva Collins' Way* (30) tells of her experiences teaching children; it also gives great lists of materials that she thinks work well. *Catholic Education: Homeward Bound*, by Kimberly Hahn and Mary Hasson (25), and *Catholic Homeschooling*, by Mary Kay Clark (49), are specifically Catholic books on homeschooling in general. All of these books are useful, not only for general information, but also because they give some knowledge of methods and list materials that have been found to work with children.

The second step is to acquire lists of other people's curricula. I recommend the curriculum lists of Seton Home Study (49), Our Lady of the Rosary (41), Kolbe Academy (28), Calvert Correspondence Course (9), and your own state's general requirements. Designing your own curriculum involves seeing what other people have used successfully.

Once you have acquired all this information, you will need to reduce it from a potential to an actual curriculum. This is where you use the background reading you have done. Think about the cause of causes, the end. Ask yourself, "What do I want for my children? What do I want them to achieve academically? Where are their interests? And what are their capabilities?"

This is the heart of designing your own curriculum, classical or otherwise. You need to be explicit about the ends you want to achieve. I would like to tell you about my own goals so that you can see an example of how defining those goals will direct your choice of curriculum, giving you a plan to be implemented over the course of a number of years. Perhaps some of my reflections will also help you in more particular ways, by suggesting materials or methods that will be useful to you in designing the curriculum that fits your particular homeschooling situation.

While I was designing my curriculum I knew that I wanted ultimately what we all want, the eternal salvation of my children. Academically I wanted a truly Catholic intellectual formation. I hoped to instill a lifelong love of learning and to give my children the tools to pursue that learning.

More proximately, I wanted my children to be able to go to an academically excellent Catholic college and do well there. The ultimate end would more likely be achieved this way. Further, I was concerned that they receive a classical education at college, one that would incorporate the seven liberal arts and the disciplines to which they are ordered, philosophy and theology. This kind of education is discussed in the essay by Dorothy Sayers that I mentioned earlier, "The Lost Tools of Learning".

There was a time when the excellence of liberal arts education was generally recognized; it was the education every informed person in Western civilization received. Even now in homeschooling circles such an education is usually aimed for, sometimes under the title of liberal arts and sometimes not. Whatever it is called, what is desired is that each child be formed well in all the most important intellectual areas. Most of us want our children to study mathematics and English, science and religion, whatever our own special interests might be. I will talk in more detail about what is involved in such an education because I think most of us use something like this in determining our educational goals.

Most proximately, I wanted to teach the appropriate disciplines at the right ages for each child to reap the maximum benefit.

In the light of the ultimate end, I knew that first importance must be given to spiritual formation. This would mean that the Church would have to be at the center of our lives as a family. We would go to daily Mass whenever possible, say the family Rosary and talk about the faith and its practical applications on a daily basis. While this is not an academic goal, it has an academic corollary. Our curriculum would always, at all levels, teach the doctrine of the faith clearly. After all, you cannot apply what you do not know.

Further, I wanted to instill an attitude about learning that would lead to real interest in all parts and aspects of God's creation. I wanted my children to think that a new book or a new subject or a new project would be likely to be interesting. And I wanted them to get the best out of their scholastic endeavors, even when the material or the teaching might have some flaws. I thought, and I still think, that the best way to achieve this is to have that attitude yourself. Talk to your children about their academic work. Conversation with you is the most formative part of their intellectual life.

I think our family has succeeded in this. I do not mean that my children always think that this or that particular project is the most fun they could possibly be having. What they do think is that it is worthwhile, something they are glad to have done when it is finished, because they learned from it.

A case in point comes to mind. Not long ago, I had my ninth graders read *The Red Badge of Courage*, by Stephen Crane (6). It is an introspective book and not all that easy to read. There was a certain amount of complaining about the book as we read and discussed it. However, when we finished the book, I asked my two children what they thought about using it for their siblings. "Was it worth reading?" Both children said yes. My son said he learned something about how to deal with fear that he was glad to know, and my daughter said she found the war discussions interesting! (It is not the kind of thing she ordinarily reads.) I was happy that even though it was not simply enjoyable for them, they were able to get something valuable from reading and discussing it.

I also knew I wanted a curriculum that would demand a certain amount of rigor, something challenging enough to be stimulating. At the same time I knew that I would have to be careful to ensure some success for each child. Children, like all the rest of us, do not like to do what they are not good at.

And finally, I knew that the moral virtues would have to become habits, both in me and in the children, because one has to be disciplined and docile, obedient and willing, to learn well. I found that out in college, when I spent most of my first year learning how to study and learning to get my work done on time. For this reason I do have some deadlines for the children's work, usually for bigger projects like papers. Unlike some teachers, however, I will accept a reasonable excuse, like "But, Mom, while you were writing your talk, I did laundry and made dinner."

Which brings me to the next consideration. It seems to me likely that good Catholic colleges resemble one another in essentials; if a student is well prepared for one, he ought to be well prepared for the others. The curriculum at such a college should include those studies that are called (or used to be called) "general requirements", or liberal arts.

Traditionally, liberal arts education meant the education of a free man. A free man was understood to be one who could direct his own life (and the common life of the community) and live a life of intrinsic and specifically human value (as opposed to the life of an animal or an instrument). The seven liberal arts were the introduction to such an education. These arts comprised the "Trivium": grammar, rhetoric and logic, and the "Quadrivium": arithmetic, geometry, music, astronomy. These arts are ordered to the disciplines of philosophy and theology. Such an education is devoted to what is intrinsically worth knowing, for a man and for a Christian, whatever his way of life may be. Thus, to prepare for such an academic program is to prepare for any further learning one may intend and to prepare for a reasonable and Christian life for those who do not continue on to college.

Any particular interests that a child has can be taken into account as well. That can be done either by emphasizing the area of interest, if it is one of the subjects that ordinarily falls into such a general educational plan, or by adding a somewhat more specialized field. Two of my daughters like history very much, and so I allow them to read more in that area and do papers that deal with some aspect of history. In other words, for them I emphasize something that we would be doing anyway. My oldest son, on the other hand, enjoys computers. That was not originally part of my curriculum plan. Because of his interest, however, we do include some time with the computer in his daily work.

In general our curriculum has been designed with a liberal arts education in mind. Miss Sayers, in "The Lost Tools of Learning" (21), directs our attention particularly to the arts of the Trivium: grammar, logic and rhetoric. She points out that two, at any rate, of these subjects are not subjects at all. They are methods of dealing with subjects. Grammar is a subject, in the sense that it means learning about a language, but language is a medium in which thought is expressed. In fact, the whole of the Trivium is intended to teach the tools of learning: methods of thinking, arguing and expressing one's conclusions that will be applied to subjects. Now there must be subjects for these methods to be practiced upon. One cannot learn grammar without learning a language, or learn to argue and orate without arguing and orating about something. But the subjects are of secondary importance until the tools of learning have been refined.

The grammatical stage of learning is the first that follows the acquisition of the basic skills of reading, writing and arithmetic. Once your child can do those, his attention should be turned to the "grammar" of each subject he studies. This entails using his faculties for observation and memory in each subject. Studying the grammar of language means learning an inflected language like Latin and practicing the chants. "Amo, amas, amat" is much like "eeny, meeny, miney, mo". This is what children do naturally at this stage; channel it into something constructive. In the other subjects, memorize. Train the imagination to retain information: fill the memory with a store of rich and varied images.

The next stage of the Trivium, the dialectical or logical, involves the discursive reason. The time to move into this level is when the student is able to appreciate and construct an intellectual argument. It seems to occur at about seventh grade for most children. At this point discussion and analysis become the heart of the curriculum.

The last stage of the Trivium is the rhetorical. This occurs somewhere around ninth grade and overlaps with the dialectical on one end and the movement to subjects as subjects on the other. It seems to be characterized in the student both by the discovery that he needs to know more and by a resulting interest in and capacity for acquiring information. There is a new enjoyment of the poetical in literature, music and art. This combination of information and poetry gives the child an ability to express himself in elegant and persuasive language. In other words, he will need to have writing at the center of his curriculum.

In all three of these stages of the Trivium the student must have matter to work upon. The subjects should be chosen with a view to the disciplines of the liberal arts curriculum. In some cases this means doing what disposes the student to these studies; in other cases, it means making a beginning in them. These are the kinds of considerations you make in setting up your curriculum. You say, "I want my children eventually to have this kind of formation. What needs to be done to achieve it? Do I start teaching the subject itself now, or do I do something that will enable them to do that subject well later on?"

In terms of disposing children to these disciplines, there are two ways to go. One is to remove the obstacles to learning. Concentration on areas that might be trouble spots, such as grammar, music and mathematics, would be a good idea. Many who are otherwise good students have trouble with these subjects in college.

Even if one is not planning on a program of schooling that includes Latin in college, there is still a case to be made for studying Latin. Latin is an inflected language, where the endings of the words clearly indicate their function in a sentence. This means that the nature of the parts of speech is seen more clearly in Latin than in English. For this reason it is a good language to use in teaching grammar. It makes English grammar easier to understand.

With mathematics, the children should be skilled enough in all the ordinary operations so that they are able simply to concentrate on what is specifically new and challenging in their college classes. In a traditional liberal arts program, Euclidean geometry is studied. It is a theoretical discipline, well suited to the awakening intellectual power of a new college student. It is better to be able to make these universal considerations unhindered by purely technical difficulties.

Similarly, mathematical astronomy will proceed more smoothly if the operations of mathematics are second nature. For these reasons, our curriculum places emphasis on consistent application of mathematical skills, and I insist every problem be reworked until it is right.

Preparation for the study of music is twofold. Mathematical ratios form much of the basis for discussion in the discipline. Clearly, mathematics is a preparation for this class. But so is the practical knowledge of how to read notes and tell what key a piece of music is in. Therefore, our curriculum includes some music. We use workbooks like *Music Reading, Ready to Use Activities Kit,* by Loretta Mitchell (21), and play recorder and piano. Also, because music is a wonderful thing in itself and something children will appreciate if exposed to, we always include music appreciation in the curriculum. There is a nice program called The Music Masters series (21).

Since there are a number of papers required regularly in every college, writing skills are important. It is better to learn these early in one's educational career and then be able to concentrate on the subject matter of one's paper, not having difficulties because of inadequate powers of expression. To acquire facility in writing, the important thing, it seems to me, is that the children write regularly and at some length. In the light of this consideration, I have chosen an area each year in school that involves extensive writing. It is usually religion or history. In the high school years, writing becomes the heart of the curriculum, but for that to happen there should be writing practice from the beginning. I have found that book reports make my children unhappy and tend to deaden their interest in the book they have read, whereas a retelling of it, as for example, a description of the encounter of David and Goliath from the Philistine's point of view, or the story of St. Louis' crusade, is exciting.

Communication skills are very important in college. One needs to be able to speak clearly as well as write clearly. This means that it is helpful to have lots of experience in discussion. This is an area where busy homeschooling moms with pleasant, competent children need to decide firmly to do what is time consuming but very important. Even if your children are able to go off, read their assignments and do their lessons without your help, it is important that they converse with you, important that you guide their understanding of the part of reality they encounter in their reading.

I use both Scripture readings and literature readings for discussion, and I encourage the children to state and defend their answers to the questions I ask. This is easier for them if their reading has been reflective. If they ask themselves some questions as they move through the book, anticipating a discussion where they will need to be able to present the heart of the position, they will be much better readers. I have found that having young children retell the story, and having older children prepare to discuss it, helps to produce reflective reading. It also helps them do better with factual questions.

The other way of preparing for the education at college involves the two disciplines to which the seven liberal arts are ordered. Our curriculum includes certain kinds of background information that will make the theology courses more immediately knowable, allowing the children to get involved right away in the heart of the matter. I have found that the *Baltimore Catechism* (21) is excellent preparation for theology because it is St. Thomas distilled. Pick a topic, see what the *Baltimore Catechism* says, and then compare it with the relevant article in the *Summa Theologiae*. St. Thomas is much more complete, but the basic position is in the catechism. Therefore, it seems to me that using the *Baltimore Catechism* in the early years makes St. Thomas much easier. One is already familiar with the terms and the general outline of the argument. And the format in the catechism is perfect for little children, who can memorize so much more easily than we can. Once learned, it stays with them for life.

Bishop John Myers said in a recent article, "Memorization of this sort allows a child to have a permanent space in mind and heart set aside for and dedicated to the things of God and of the Church. These essential elements are permanent acquisitions for the child, to refer to wherever he goes. He or she can retrieve them and ponder them from different aspects and in different life settings." Another preparation for theology is a familiarity with Sacred Scripture. St. Thomas and the other Fathers and Doctors of the Church most often use one part of Scripture to clarify and explain what is in another. All their theological works are full of scriptural references. So I have included Sacred Scripture in my curriculum at nearly every level.

And lastly, the more advanced discussions of Catholic doctrine and practice found in books like *Of Sacraments and Sacrifice,* by Fr. Clifford Howell (31), and the Fr. John Laux high school series (53) provide a familiarity with the context within which theology must be understood.

Another discipline that I think you can prepare for in some measure is philosophy. Two different approaches help. Some acquaintance with philosophic terms is useful. The Seton Junior and Senior High School

Religion courses do this. The other, and more important, approach is to provide your child with life experience.

To do philosophy well you need to have the beginning of wisdom, which enables you to make good judgments. Experience is essential and can be gained directly, in the obvious manner of doing many (appropriate) things. This would include natural history. Science has always seemed to me something to be learned in detail later on; in the early years we emphasize natural history. This is a good area for field trips; both the zoo and natural history museums are a pleasant change from school books.

Philosophy can also be prepared for indirectly by reading good books, both historical and fictional. In our curriculum I have included many books and allowed large chunks of time for reading. There are a number of resources for book lists of varying degrees of excellence. One is *Honey for a Child's Heart,* by Gladys Hunt (21), and another is *Catholic Authors* (11), both the 4-sight and Crown editions. *A Mother's List of Books*, by Theresa Fagan (21), is also very helpful. More specifically historical texts can be found in *Books Children Love,* by Elizabeth Wilson (21), and the short but first-rate journal *In Review: Living Books Past and Present,* published by Bethlehem Books (7). The catalogue of Greenleaf Press (22) also has many interesting texts in this field.

Through an examination of the ultimate end I desired for my children's education, and the more particular end of going to college, a curriculum began to take shape. It would include Latin and English grammar, mathematics, literature, history, music, some philosophy, the *Baltimore Catechism,* and Sacred Scripture.

We would have discussions, and I would endeavor to infuse those discussions with the sense of wonder and reverence for truth that could shape the attitudes of my children toward learning in general. I would require regular papers on subjects that would really be of interest.

Not all of these subjects would be covered every year, and not all would be covered in the same depth, but these would be the disciplines I would incorporate in my program. I would remember the method of the Trivium at each appropriate stage. With such a general plan we could make what we did do each year count in the overall intellectual formation of the children. You do not have to be so anxious about finishing each book (though it is certainly good to do so if possible) if you know that all of your efforts are coordinated and directed to a goal that is larger than accumulated knowledge in an individual subject.

You can see that my reflections on the ends I wanted to achieve guided my choice of subjects and methods. There were still further particular considerations to be made about what level was right for each subject and what method was appropriate. Those judgments can be made by examining the curriculum lists I mentioned earlier and by a certain amount of trial and error.

Additionally, you will need to consider state requirements. To acquire your own state's general requirements, write to your state's department of education. Consult your telephone book. If the department is not listed, you can call your local school district or the library for the address.

There was substantial general agreement among those lists with respect to what subjects were to be taught at what level. I would like to hit the highlights, without going into too much detail.

Virtually all the lists included mathematics, reading, memorization, beginning writing skills and formative stories in the first three grades. This would be the very beginning of the future facility in mathematics, language arts, philosophy and theology that we wanted to achieve. I am inclined to the view that it is better to learn a little really well than a great deal superficially. For this reason I decided to concentrate on a thorough basic formation.

In kindergarten we try to become thoroughly familiar with numbers. We use dominoes, dot-to-dot workbooks, the hundreds chart and even a computer mathematics game or two. I use the A Beka math program (1 or 8) in the earliest grades. They have worked very well for us, and my children generally find themselves ready to do the *Saxon 65* (48) in fourth grade. I think this is because of the solid, sequential presentation of basic operations. Nevertheless, there are other good mathematics programs, some emphasizing a more manipulative approach, using Cuisenaire rods, for example. Some children need to handle materials in order to learn; others can reason abstractly. Find out which kind of learner you are dealing with, and use the appropriate kind of program. But whatever approach you choose, make sure the operations become second nature.

For beginning reading, in kindergarten, I use *Teach Your Child to Read in 100 Easy Lessons*, by Engelmann, Haddox and Bruner (21), for about half of the book and then move on to *Sound Beginnings*, by Julia Fogassy (40), or *The Writing Road to Reading*, by Romalda Spalding (21). The main point about what you select for reading is that it be phonetic in its approach. Using phonics will allow the child to read much more difficult material at an earlier age. It also helps with spelling and Latin. My husband, who has taught Latin for many years, says that all students in his experience who have had trouble reading and pronouncing Latin had been taught to read by the whole word method. He has made an informal study of the subject. When someone consistently stumbles over Latin pronunciation and his spelling is "original", my husband discreetly asks what kind of reading instruction he has had. In such a case, the answer has never been phonics.

This early schooling is the stage Dorothy Sayers refers to as the "poll-parrot" stage, and it is a good time to begin the memorization of the questions and answers of the catechism. It is also a wonderful opportunity to introduce poetry. We pick a poem, work on it, say it for an obliging friend or relative, and then write it in a notebook reserved exclusively for that purpose. The child may illustrate it or not, depending on his inclination. We usually start with the poems of Robert Louis Stevenson, because they are so accessible to children. Then we move on to more difficult material. Two books, *Favorite Poems Old and New* (21) and *The Harp and Laurel Wreath: Poetry and Dictation for the Classical Curriculum* (25), have good collections of poetry.

The poetry notebook is great fun as the children get older, because they have a book of their own making, filled with the poems they learned all through grade school, and they love it. It also helps them review without coercion, because they get to reminiscing. I leave those notebooks in an accessible place, and every so often one of the children will pick a notebook up and leaf through it. They say, "Oh, I really liked this poem. Do you remember it?" And in that way they review the poems.

It is at this early stage that the child's broadest views of the world are being worked out. We all want our children to be clear about the difference between good and evil, truth and falsity. I think the things you pick to read to them and that you pick for their early reading are very important for this reason. Fairy tales, where there are clearly good guys and bad guys, are good for children. Books like *The Outlaws of Ravenhurst*, by S. Mary Wallace (37), instill a healthy respect for the

Eucharist. Tales of King Arthur and his knights teach concepts of nobility and sacrifice. Stories of the saints are very important in these formative years because they present the supernatural end as the most compelling motivation.

History in these first grades seems to me best taught in somewhat the same mode as literature. That is, use materials that emphasize heroism and individual accomplishment. Some of the books in the book lists I mentioned earlier are of this sort. Also, *Stories of Great Americans for Little Americans*, by Edward Eggleston (32), is very good. It deals with outstanding individuals and the difference their contributions made to the founding of our country.

We also read Bible stories in this early period. *The Children's Bible* (Golden Press) (21) is an easy-to-understand version of this genre and has kept the integrity of the stories. Whatever you use, emphasizing the goodness of particular individuals is important.

As I said earlier, science has always seemed to me something best learned in detail later on. The early years should be spent developing a love of nature. The zoo and natural history museums, as well as neighborhood walks, will encourage a real interest in natural history.

I mentioned earlier that for writing we prefer to pick a subject area and concentrate on writing in that area, rather than have writing as a separate subject. We often do Bible history this way, retelling the story after reading it. This exercise seems to strengthen the children's ability to see the story as a whole and to remember it. They like to illustrate their stories, too.

In the middle years, fourth through seventh grade, the child becomes capable of mastering certain subjects and of coping with increasingly difficult material in others. All the lists I have looked at think that grammar should be taught with some rigor in this period. I myself find that sixth grade is the place to work intensely on grammar. Children seem to have matured enough at this point to enjoy parsing and diagraming, which are analytical skills.

Latin is also well suited to this stage. Here, too, it seems that mastery of the fundamentals is most important. Vocabulary and forms can be taught and memorized in fourth and fifth grades, using Memoria Press' *Latina Christiana I* (34). Another book, *Basic Language Principles through Latin Background*, by Ruth Wilson (21), works well in seventh grade. It consolidates English grammar from the year before and teaches the first conjugation and first and second declensions very clearly. In the earlier years there are some texts that prepare the student for the study of Latin. *English from the Roots Up*, by Joegil Lundquist (21), gives a background in both Latin and Greek roots. This text can be used in second or third grade and will be the beginning of a lifetime of interest in words.

With respect to religion in these middle years, I use a combination of things, all of which are ordered to those further goals I have already spoken about. Each year is divided into three parts: doctrine, Church history or Sacred Scripture, and lives of the saints. I continue to use the *Baltimore Catechism,* moving from the No. 1, which I have used in first through third grades, one section per grade, to the No. 2, which I use again one section per grade. In addition to the catechism, I use some form of Bible history: Bishop Knecht's *Child's Bible History* (53), or Fr. Ignatius Schuster's *Bible History* (53), or Sacred Scripture itself, with discussion questions of my own making. In fourth grade, the lives of the saints are also read and reported on, and in fifth grade I use the Faith and Life Catechism *Credo: I Believe* (25), which is excellent. In seventh grade I also use a Church history that all of my children have enjoyed, *The Story of the Church,* by Fr. George Johnson, Fr. Jerome Hannan and Sr. M. Dominica (53).

For writing in these middle years, the important thing, it seems to me, is that the children write regularly and at some length. *Intermediate Language Lessons*, by Emma Serl (32), and *Learning Language Arts through Literature* (16) have some good ideas for creative writing. Retelling historical events has always been popular in my house. In sixth grade my oldest daughter wrote a history book that she greatly enjoyed, and she has kept it all these years. She read about different ancient civilizations and wrote down what she remembered in a notebook. She illustrated it with maps and made a cover for the front. That project made a major difference in her intellectual life. A friend's child decided to make a play about William the Conqueror. It was six pages, with many battle scenes. His whole family learned about that period of history from his writing effort. It matters more that there are some such writing exercises in your curriculum than that the children are always working on such a project. Pick a subject where you discern a lively interest and make that the focus of your writing curriculum.

Memorization at this stage can be more involved. Speeches from

Shakespeare can be learned, and perhaps, with other homeschooling families, whole sections of Shakespeare's plays can be done. There is a book called *Shakespeare in the Classroom: Plays for the Intermediate Grades,* by Albert Cullum (21), that edits the plays while retaining the flavor and much of the language and makes it easy for a group of children to put on a Shakespeare play. If you are a purist, you can keep the original language, but use this book as a guideline for cutting down the action. My children recently participated in a production of *A Midsummer Night's Dream*, which was the joint effort of three homeschooling families. It was fun for them, and they still enjoy quoting from the play.

There is a good science textbook series available called *Concepts and Challenges in Science* (43). It has clear descriptions and an easy-to-follow format. A more hands-on approach is the *Tops* series (21). Each topic is covered by having the child do experiments involving only easily obtained materials. The unit on the balance is one of the more successful courses we have had. All of my older children are quite clear about the balance beam and how it works.

History is a subject that can be fascinating, or it can be deadly dull. Using a textbook with unit tests has a way of engaging the short-term memory and nothing else. What works better is reading a chapter in a history text and then reading other books, real books rather than textbooks, that cover that period of history. Then the information seems to come alive and stay with you. Even in the later years, in high school, we have followed the same general procedure with history. *Books Children Love,* by Elizabeth Wilson (21), and the issues of *In Review*, published by Bethlehem Books (7), are both good sources for books of this kind. Also the catalogue of Greenleaf Press has many important texts in this field. We acknowledge the cyclical nature of history teaching and study American history in third, fifth and ninth grades. In fourth grade we study the exploration of the New World. Sixth and seventh grades are given to ancient civilizations, with an emphasis on Greece and Rome. In high school we study ancient history again, in more depth, and European history, concentrating on England and Spain, since these are the two that most directly affect our country.

Ecce Romani (3) is a series of books that incorporates the nature method of teaching Latin and analytic grammar, and it seems to work well at an eighth or ninth grade level. The text encourages learning the vocabulary from context as well as memorizing vocabulary lists. Seton

Home Study offers a good Latin program, which I have used for my high school curriculum.

In the later years, we concentrate more on reading well. Our religion, literature, art and science classes all incorporate some discussion of more difficult points, retelling or making a synopsis of major issues, and some factual research—locating the place in the book where the author makes his point. It is in these subjects, about once a week for each, that I spend time with my older children. They do the preparation for the discussion on their own, and they do the other subjects they have on their own. I correct work and tests and discuss with them. I have always tried to work one-on-one with my children only in the areas where they need that kind of instruction.

I have a friend who homeschooled her oldest son through ninth grade. In tenth grade he went to a local high school. His mother watched him anxiously through the first week and then asked, "Josh, how is it?" He said, "It's so unbelievably easy. They tell you everything! I go to algebra class, and they say, 'Watch while I do this problem.' Then they put another one on the board and make sure you know how to do it. Then you do the rest of the problems in class, and they'll answer any questions. School was never so simple before." I think Josh's experience is probably typical for homeschoolers. They are used to working on their own, at least as older students, and figuring things out. They are more independent learners and do not need constant instruction. Our teaching role is more that of guidance and correction.

In this role, you should arouse interest in intellectual subjects by selecting good materials. Good literature and challenging texts are your best allies. I have found that a number of the Seton Home Study courses in tenth through twelfth grades are of real help. One is not required to be a full-time student with Seton; one can just select the courses that seem useful.

We have found Seton's English programs for all three years to be outstanding. Their science courses are difficult but can be done. The Saxon mathematics can be done without their program, which simply consists of tests on the material. You can purchase the homeschool packet for the Saxon texts, along with the solution manuals, and do just as well on your own. As I mentioned earlier, Seton has a Latin program that we like, and it is nice to have someone else correcting the tests.

It is a good idea to meet the homeschoolers in your area. It is helpful to have the support of like-minded people. Often in talking over your successes and failures with others you will discover that your difficulty is a common one and, perhaps, that someone has discovered a solution. Or that your success is a solution to someone else's problem. In any case you will know you are not alone. *The Catholic Home Educator* is compiling a list of homeschoolers across the country. Their address is listed in the back of this book under suppliers (12).

I have some general advice about curriculum that is the result of my own mistakes over the years, which I hope you won't mind my adding. I love curricula, and I am always interested in new products; nevertheless, I've learned to stick with what works. If you have successfully taught your children to read using *Alphaphonics* (45), for example, don't abandon it because a friend is ecstatic about *Sing, Spell, Read and Write* (45). You already know how to use your program, and it works for you! On the other hand, throw out what does not work; sell it to a friend, it could be just what she needs. Or save it, maybe it will work for your next child. Each family, each child and each teacher is unique. You cannot tell for sure what is going to work for you except by trying it. When you find what does work, thank God for His blessings, and stick with it.

Evaluate your progress and success year by year, not moment by moment. Both you and your children will have ups and downs. Do not throw out good materials or despair of your ability because of a few bad days.

I have found that when those bad days are too frequent over too long a period of time, there are several corrective measures that might be considered. For one, easier materials can encourage success and a positive attitude. Challenge is important, but so is success. The right timing is also very important. Children mature at different rates, and that does not in itself tell you much about innate ability. If you are trying a new concept or subject and it doesn't "take", wait and try again in a few months. I have a friend whose child taught himself to read at the age of three. My son of the same age learned to read when he was five and a half years of age. By the time they were six and a half, there was no difference in their comprehension or reading ability. Another friend had a son who could not read well until he was nine. All three of these boys, by the time they were fourteen, were reading at the same level and read the same material. A late reader may have a certain number of classics to catch up on, but that is no problem.

Aristotle says that virtue is a mean between moral extremes. For example, courage is neither rashness nor timidity but in between the two. I think school curricula should reflect this principle. There is a mean between no workbooks and all workbooks, between fun and drudgery, and between flexibility and firmness.

Lastly, you can probably tell that I like lists. Well, lists can make your school go more smoothly, not just in the yearly planning stage, but in your weekly and daily planning. Once your children can read, make them a list of their work for the week or the day and turn them loose. They can do what is on the list and come to you for help only in difficulties or when they have finished the work that they are supposed to do by themselves and are ready to work with you. And after that, you can be otherwise occupied with . . . laundry, dinner, and all the other things the valiant woman of faith must do.

Curriculum Suggestions

I T IS THE ABILITY to think that is our goal in a classical curriculum; we want our children to acquire the art of learning. It is not the number of facts they are acquainted with that measures educational success, but what they are able to do with the facts: whether they are able to make distinctions, to follow an argument, to make reasonable deductions from the facts and, finally, to have a right judgment about the way things are.

Such a view of education has some practical consequences that are discussed at various stages in this curriculum. At this point it is appropriate to reflect on one of them. The question of what you should expect to do with a child, and what he can do on his own, is important.

The main goal of the early school years is to learn the basic skills of reading, writing and simple arithmetic. These are the first tools for any further learning. The subjects you use to acquire and practice these tools are, in a sense, secondary. This is so much the case that the mother of a large number of homeschooling children who is able to do only religion, reading, simple arithmetic and basic letter formation with her youngest grades should not worry that they are educationally neglected. The natural stimulation of a busy household will supply for the other subjects. Once a child can read, he is able to be an independent learner.

You should encourage him to take charge of his education where he can. This will foster the ability to learn that you are intending him to acquire. At the same time, classes require supervision and some discussion. Have your child do the reading, preparation and any exercises on his own, with an understanding that he will have some specific time with you to go over what he has prepared. Disciplines that are of particular difficulty for a given child or classes where the method requires the parent's presence should be done when you are going over his other, prepared work. This makes it possible to combine the virtues of different methods of teaching. There is one-on-one instruction with immediate feedback, but there is also self-direction.

This also makes it possible to teach a larger number of classes to more children. Start working with your youngest child first, and when he is finished with his schoolwork, move on to the next child. Do with each child only what he needs you to do with him. Work with two children together when possible. Multiple classes can be easily taken care of in this way, which is the way the one-room schoolhouse used to work.

Clearly, the first requirement in such a plan is to learn the skills necessary for any further learning. Concentrate on reading well and learning to write, in terms of both letter formation and powers of expression. Spend time acquiring facility in addition and subtraction. If these things are learned well, all the rest of one's schooltime will be much more profitable. For these reasons I do not emphasize science or history in kindergarten, first or second grade.

Even in third through sixth grades, studies will be ordered to the acquisition of a certain kind of formation, where observation, memory, and the beginning of definition are the heart of the curriculum. This formation is more important than the various subjects studied. These will provide material for the formation. Thus, if you begin to be overwhelmed with the chores and duties of a big household and you do not get done all that you would like to do or had planned to do educationally, do not worry about it. Make what you are able to do count by employing the methods appropriate to the stage of formation of your child.

Also, remember that your children learn from you by your conversation and example all day long, every day. Your faith, which informs your life, will inform theirs if they are with you. Your delight in God's creation will communicate to them the wonders God has given us and gratitude for them. It will inspire your children with an interest in learning.

Additionally, in a large family the children must help with the household chores, as a matter of survival. They learn to cook, do laundry and clean. This is great practical education and contributes in its own way to theoretical education, because the children learn about the common good from direct experience. It can also be used by you as a time for discussion; doing laundry or dishes together provides opportunities for conversation that might otherwise be scarce. In such a family the children see the good of the whole as their good; they see themselves as working with you for a common enterprise, as a comrade, rather than as part of a peer group to which adults do not belong. This attitude along with the fact that you get to learn new things (indeed, if you are like me, probably have to learn new things) are the two biggest benefits of homeschooling.

The classical curriculum is thus chiefly concerned with formation. The stages of formation are discussed within this curriculum at the beginning of each section. Though the stages are not rigidly tied to age or grade level, I have chosen to discuss grammar before third, dialectic before seventh and rhetoric before tenth grade. Look at those discussions when you are choosing your curriculum, and think about what stage is appropriate for your child. All of my curriculum suggestions are intended to be flexible. Ideas for fifth grade may work well for sixth or fourth, while art and music suggestions are often applicable in every grade. I offer these suggestions as things that have worked for us at about the grade levels listed.

All of the following text suggestions are just that: suggestions. Since every family and every student is different, there is not any one text that is the only text that will work in any given subject. The texts I mention here have worked well for me and in most cases for a number of other homeschoolers in my area. Nevertheless, what seems to me more important is the general advice and the goals to be achieved. If you know of something better that will achieve these goals, use it and tell me about it!

You will notice in examining these lists that certain areas are not mentioned at all, for example, physical education and penmanship. Still others are the presuppositions of formal learning.

Physical skills incorporating large motor development are very important for little children. Learning to skip, ride a tricycle, walk a balance beam and swing on a swing are examples of abilities that should be encouraged. I do not address these skills in my curriculum because I think that you do not need my advice in this area. Give children time and space and a little example, and they will develop these faculties on their own. Homeschooling, because it is such an efficient use of schooltime, leaves much more free time for such play.

As your children grow, participation in recreational programs will exercise physical skills. Soccer, Irish step dancing, baseball, track, swimming and gymnastics are all programs my own children have been involved in through the years.

I will not mention penmanship in what follows because my own approach does not change much through the years. If I address it here, I will have said what I have to say about it. In *The Writing Road to Reading*, by Romalda Spalding, there is a clear, easy manuscript taught. We use this and practice the letters as they are introduced and used in the text. When the time comes for cursive writing, which can vary radically from child to child, I have used the A Beka third grade cursive text. It is a pretty script, and the exercises are pleasant. Thereafter, at the beginning of each year, or if someone is getting sloppy, we review. I have just seen the Seton penmanship text, and it is very appealing, with Catholic references and attitudes. I plan to order some for next year to have around the house for practice when it is necessary.

Finally, there are certain activities presupposed by the suggestions that follow. Putting together puzzles, following the directions for Lego assemblies, exploring textures and smells, playing simple games with color matches and doing finger plays all involve pre-reading skills and should certainly be done with your children. I would like to point out that most children do these things, at least many of them, on their own, but the guidance of an adult or older sibling will direct a child to a specific skill more clearly.

All resources in this list are followed by a number that indicates which of the suppliers, listed at the end of the book, carries this item.

The Primary Stage

Kindergarten Curriculum

Sources for items followed by a number in parentheses may be found at the back of the book in the list of suppliers.

Religion—*The Childrens' Bible* (Golden Press) (21)

Read from *The Children's Bible* twice a week. On alternate days begin each class with the child's retelling of the previous story. Write it down in an artist's sketch book, and have the child illustrate his stories. At the end of the year he will have his own Bible.

The goals of this class are to become familiar with the Bible and to internalize the stories and doctrine of the early books of the Old Testament as well as to develop listening and "retelling" skills.

Mathematics—*Golden Step Ahead Workbooks* (5); number flashcards (5); *An Easy Start in Arithmetic,* by Ruth Beechick (45)

Twice a week work on familiarity with numbers. The idea here is to have the numbers mean something real. Using beans or Legos helps to make the concepts concrete. By the end of the year the child will probably be able to count to one hundred and recognize the numerals to twenty-five easily, and farther than that with some help. Simple addition and subtraction problems will be easy to do.

Reading—*Teach Your Child to Read in 100 Easy Lessons,* by Engelmann, Haddox and Brunet (21); for literature: *Honey for a Child's Heart,* by Gladys Hunt (21); *A Mother's List of Books,* by Theresa Fagan (21)

Have short reading lessons four times a week. There are other good phonetic texts available. The most important aspect of teaching reading is that it be done phonetically. I like this text because it teaches blending so well; you move beyond the c-a-t stage to "cat" easily and quickly.

Do not expect to finish this text in a year. Some children may move that quickly, but most of those I have known take longer. The purpose of this class is to learn to read on an "easy reader" level, and that level is reached before the end of the book. At this time of life what you read to your children is much more important, because it is much more formative, than what they read to themselves. Ideally there should be long, cozy, evening reading sessions with the whole family. If your kindergartner does not learn to read this year, or in the next three years, it will not ultimately make much difference in his life. But the stories of saints, the tales of noble actions performed by noble people, the fairy tales will make a lifelong difference.

Science—No text

Visits to the zoo, natural history museum, or beach and walks around the neighborhood are all occasions for science discussion. Science at this point could be better described as natural history, or getting to know the world around you. Raising animals, sprouting beans, helping in a garden are simple, natural ways of becoming familiar with the physical world.

Poetry—*A Child's Garden of Verses*, by Robert Louis Stevenson (6); *The Harp and Laurel Wreath: Poetry and Dictation for the Classical Curriculum*, edited by Laura Berquist (25)

Work for five minutes or so every day on a poem. When the poem is learned, make an occasion for the child to recite it to the family, or get a few families together for this purpose. This gives the child an opportunity to practice stage presence (a disposing factor in acquiring rhetoric) at an early age, before concern about what other people might think sets in. If you can keep it up, even your shy sixth grader will think that reciting poetry for the enjoyment of other people is part of life. It is also an incentive for getting the poem "down cold", and that will mean better retention. I have kept a record of each child's poems through the years, and the children who enjoy drawing have illustrated their poems. Illustrated or not, the record of poems learned is a treasure for the children to enjoy all their lives.

The poems we have memorized over the years are all included in the anthology *The Harp and Laurel Wreath: Poetry and Dictation for the Classical Curriculum*.

Art—*Mommy, It's a Renoir* (easy level) (21); drawing Bible pictures

Mommy, It's a Renoir is an art appreciation course that has numerous levels. This level contains pairs of pictures by the same artist. The child is asked to match identical picture pairs or similar picture pairs. My own little children have enjoyed this course. When they have mastered the intended goals of the class, we have gone on to do other things with the pictures. I have them make up a story about the picture, or I have them describe the picture, and then I try to pick out the right postcard from what they say. We look for other pictures by the same artist and talk about any similarities we can see. *For the Children's Sake*, by Susan Schaeffer MacCauley (21), has a very good section on art appreciation that is well worth reading. The immediate goal is to help the children be attentive to and begin to enjoy great works of art. But you also begin to develop their vocabulary, powers of expression and imagination by conversing with them about the pictures.

Drawing illustrations for the Bible book the children are writing in their religion studies will help them remember the stories as well as give them an opportunity to express their thoughts and feelings in a visual medium.

Music—Hymn singing, *36 Traditional Roman Catholic Hymns* (in easy arrangement for piano), compiled and arranged by Alan and Teresa Jemison (21)

Even little children can learn the hymns that are sung at church, or the ones that ought to be. This can be a family project, which will encourage participation in a church setting as well as make uncertain singers feel that their deficiencies are masked.

Sample Schedule for Kindergarten

Allow about forty-five minutes each day for school. This is ample time for formal subjects for such young children.

MON.	TUES.	WED.	THURS.	Fri.
Poetry	Poetry	Poetry	Poetry	(Free)
Reading	Reading	Reading	Reading	
Religion	Religion	Religion	Religion	
(Drawing)	Math	(Drawing)	Math	

Evenings—Literature, Music

There is now available a day-by-day breakdown of the courses listed for Kindergarten (36).

First Grade Curriculum

Sources for items followed by a number in parentheses may be found at the back of the book under the list of suppliers.

Religion—*St. Joseph's First Communion Catechism* (21); *Art 1 for Young Catholics,* from Seton Home Study (49); *Catholic Children's Treasure Box, No. 1–10* (53)

Read and discuss each chapter of the catechism. Have the child memorize the questions and answers, which will be easy for him to do because little children are like sponges. They soak in information and keep it. Also, memorization done now will pay off in a big way later because it develops a habit of retention. In addition to developing a retentive imagination, learning the answers in the catechism word for word is a good thing to do because the very words of the catechism are formative. Those words express "this" truth well and train the mind in a certain way of thinking. Use game formats to check and reinforce memorization (e.g., have the child supply the question for your answer, or give points and prizes for a certain number of correct answers).

Seton Home Study now has available an activity book keyed to the important feasts and seasons of the liturgical year. The instructions are clear and simple, and patterns are included with the text.

Catholic Children's Treasure Box is a series of little books with lovely stories of saints, poems, games and activities for Catholic children. They are reprints from many years ago, real treasures for those of us engaged in developing a Catholic culture within our homes.

Read saints' lives aloud, e.g., *Picture Book of Saints*, by Rev. Lawrence Lovasik (21). Have the child retell the story or draw a series of illustrations for the stories or make a book (with your help) of retold and illustrated stories.

Mathematics—*Arithmetic I* (A Beka) (1, 8) or *Math 1* (Saxon) (48)

These are both good books to use because they have a spiral approach to learning concepts. Once learned, a concept is practiced on a daily basis. The child never has a chance to forget how to do it.

Reading—*Teach Your Child to Read in 100 Easy Lessons*, by Engelmann, Haddox and Bruner (21); or *Alphaphonics,* by Sam Blumenfield (45); *Sound Beginnings*, by Julia Fogassy (40); Cardinal Readers (37); National Readers (37)

The basic point about teaching reading is to use phonics, which all of the above do. I have found *100 Easy Lessons* easy to use and satisfying because the child begins to read quickly. I can vouch for its effectiveness. However, I use *Sound Beginnings* after my children are able to read because the phonics principles are taught so clearly in it. The Cardinal and National Readers are good books. They provide new readers with a number of reading selections on their level.

Literature—Read literature aloud on a regular basis. *Honey for a Child's Heart*, by Gladys Hunt (21), has a good list of books, as does *A Mother's List of Books*, by Theresa Fagan. Back issues of *In Review,* by Bethlehem Books (7), has great lists and reviews of children's literature. *Catholic Authors,* 4-Sight edition (11), has lists of Catholic literature, much of it out of print, but worth knowing about for visits to used-book stores and thrift stores. Also, some of it is back in print or will be.

Concentrate on filling your child's imagination with stories of individuals who choose good in the face of difficulties. Beautiful language, while more difficult to listen to, develops both their vocabulary and their ear for language.

Science—No text

Continue with the method of the previous year. Talk about the world around you, and visit interesting natural history places. Perhaps you could make a bird feeder or acquire a cockatiel. An aquarium is fairly easy to maintain and provides a focus for natural history. Whatever you do, always be interested yourself. If you notice a spider web, point it out, and use the occasion for a little research on spiders. This class is not formal or scheduled, but it is important in this way: it is an opportunity for you to encourage a lifelong love for all of God's amazing creation. The natural history information and observational skills acquired now will help all through the school years, even when the subjects of philosophy and theology become the center of interest.

Poetry—*A Child's Garden Of Verses*, by Robert Louis Stevenson (6); or *Favorite Poems Old and New* (21); *The Harp and Laurel Wreath: Poetry and Dictation for the Classical Curriculum*, edited by Laura Berquist (25)

Every day spend three to five minutes memorizing a poem. When it is memorized, write it down in a separate notebook. Keep the notebook, and at the end of the year you will have a personalized record of all the poems learned.

Poems by Robert Louis Stevenson we have found to work well are "Windy Nights", "Bed in Summer", "Foreign Lands", "Where Go the Boats", "The Land of Counterpane", "My Shadow", "The Wind", "The Moon", "The Swing", "The Hayloft", "The Lamplighter", and "The Cow". These poems are all included in the anthology *The Harp and Laurel Wreath: Poetry and Dictation for the Classical Curriculum*. Poetry provides another opportunity to exercise the imagination and to train it. Recalling lines of poetry requires some discipline, even though poetry is easier to recall than prose. Memorizing poems develops, painlessly, a facile and obedient memory.

The book *The Harp and Laurel Wreath: Poetry and Dictation for the Classical Curriculum* contains not only the poems mentioned above but also a section titled Bible One-Liners. These short Scripture passages, reprinted below on pages 45–46, may be used for additional memorization and handwriting practice or dictation exercise for the advanced third grader.

Art—*Mommy, It's a Renoir* (intermediate level) (21)

This is a Montessori art appreciation program. It develops observational skills and appreciation for beautiful things and introduces children to great paintings. We usually use the postcards according to the text until the child has mastered the skills specifically intended by the program. Then we invent other uses for the pictures that will further those goals. Talking about the picture, distinguishing the forms from the colors, discussing the feelings evoked and the smells and sounds suggested will give a certain distinction to your child's observations. These exercises will also begin to develop an analytical power, thinking about why certain colors or figures are used, how they function in the picture as a whole. You don't need to discuss that explicitly, but by doing these exercises, this year and in subsequent years, you will as a matter of fact develop that power of analysis.

Aesop's Fables (6) can be used for art. Read a fable to the child, and have him retell it to you. Then write down what he says, and have him illustrate it. Later, when he is comfortable writing, you can write down sentences for him to copy, either of his composition or yours. This stage gives him valuable practice in hand-eye coordination. Finally, he can write his own summary. Keep these papers together, and your child will have his own illustrated version of *Aesop* at the end of the year.

This particular activity incorporates many skills that are important to this stage of development. It encourages retelling, which requires a concept of the whole, develops powers of expression, involves small motor coordination as well as hand-eye coordination and incorporates literature, art and composition. Additionally, because the fables are short, it does not take much time, and so far everyone has enjoyed it!

Music—The Music Masters series, part 1 (21)

Use The Music Masters series for music appreciation. It consists of a series of tapes or CDs that introduce the child to classical music, with information about the composers' lives. Conversing with the child after the tape is over allows you to talk both about the way the composer dealt with difficulties and about his gifts. It will also help fix that composer in the child's mind so that you can refer to him as you listen to his music. "This is by Mozart, do you remember him?" Clearly, it is more important to listen to the music than to know about the composer, and the aim of music appreciation is to become familiar with, and to enjoy, beautiful and important pieces of music. But learning about the composer can help achieve that end, and this is a good time to begin.

Sample Schedule for First Grade				
Allow about one and a half hours each day for school. This is ample time for formal subjects for young children.				
Mon.	Tues.	Wed.	Thurs.	Fri.
Math	Math	Math	Math	(Free)
Phonics	Phonics	Phonics	Phonics	
Religion	Religion	Religion	Religion	
Poetry	Art	Poetry	Poetry	
Evenings—Literature, music				
There is now available a day-by-day breakdown of the courses listed for first grade (36).				

BIBLE ONE-LINERS
(Used for memorization, penmanship and reference)

All references to Psalms are given with the Vulgate numbering.

Let us go to the house of the Lord.—Psalm 121:1

Thou dost show me the path that leads to life; in Thy presence there is fullness of joy, in Thy right hand are pleasures forevermore.
—Psalm 15:11

The Lord is my shepherd.—Psalm 22:1

Make me to know Thy ways, O Lord; teach me Thy paths.
—Psalm 24:4

One thing I have asked of the Lord, this will I seek, to dwell in the house of the Lord all the days of my life.—Psalm 26:4

How great are Thy works, O Lord!—Psalm 91:5

Thy word is a lamp to my feet and a light to my path.
—Psalm 118:105

Let Thy steadfast love, O Lord, be upon us, even as we hope in Thee.—Psalm 32:22

You will not fear the terror of night, nor the arrow that flies by day, nor the pestilence that stalks in the darkness, nor the destruction that wastes at noonday.—PSALM 90:5–6

And He shall rule from sea to sea, from the river unto the ends of the earth.—PSALM 71:8

Be still, and know that I am God.—PSALM 45:10

It is a holy and wholesome thought to pray for the dead, that they may be loosed from their sins.—2 MACCABEES 12:46

My soul finds rest in God alone; my salvation comes from Him. —PSALM 61:1

O God, come to my assistance; O Lord, make haste to help me. —PSALM 69:1

They who wait for the Lord shall renew their strength.—ISAIAH 40:31

I will satisfy the weary soul, and every languishing soul I will replenish.—JEREMIAH 31:25

My face shall go before thee, and I will give thee rest.—Exodus 33:14

May the God of hope fill you will all joy and peace as you trust in Him, so that you may overflow with hope by the power of the Holy Spirit.—ROMANS 15:13

I will sing of Thy strength; and I will extol Thy mercy in the morning.—PSALM 58:16

A tranquil mind gives life to the body.—PROVERBS 14:30

And the peace of God, which transcends all understanding, will guard your hearts and your minds in Christ Jesus.—PHILIPPIANS 4:7

All that the Lord has said will we do, and be obedient.—Exodus 24:7

A wise man will hear, and will increase in learning; a man of understanding shall attain unto wise counsels.—PROVERBS 1:5

Children, obey your parents in all things: for this is well-pleasing unto the Lord.—COLOSSIANS 3:20

It is good to give thanks to the Lord.—PSALM 91:1

Second Grade Curriculum

Sources for items followed by a number in parentheses may be found at the back of the book in the list of suppliers.

Religion—St. *Joseph's Baltimore Catechism No. 1* (21), lives of the saints (51)

Read and discuss the first fourteen chapters of the catechism. Memorize the questions and answers. I recommend doing a chapter in the catechism and working on the questions over a two-week period. The second week, when you are working on memorization only, can also involve a study of the lives of the saints.

The same reasons given earlier for memorizing still apply: it develops a habit of retention; it encourages attention to detail; and the very words of the catechism are formative. Those time-honored answers are formulas in terms of which one's very thought is formed.

The catechism has exercises at the end of every chapter, along with Scripture readings, which will aid the comprehension of the lessons in the chapter. Spend some time each day on the questions and answers, but the other activities can be spread out over the week. On Monday discuss the chapter. On Tuesday do the true/false and fill-in-the-blanks exercises. On Wednesday and Thursday review the questions to be memorized.

The next week review the material once, in addition to memorizing the questions and answers, but then spend some time with stories of saints.

Your child's First Communion will probably take place sometime during this year. The *First Communion Catechism* from last year has been a good preparation for this great event. Review that catechism, especially the parts dealing with Confession and Communion, as your child's First Confession and Communion draw near. Read the book *Patron Saint of First Communicants: The Story of Blessed Imelda Lambertini,* by Mary Fabyan Windeatt (53), with your child. Teach some special prayers for after Communion, perhaps "Soul of Christ, Sanctify Me" (a favorite prayer of St. Thomas Aquinas). The Ten Commandments will be studied in detail next year, but the examination of conscience in the *First Communion Catechism* involves a practical application of the Commandments in a way appropriate for little children.

Mathematics—*Arithmetic 2* (A Beka) (1, 8); *Math 2* (Saxon) (48); *Math-It,* by E. W. Brooks (45)

Arithmetic 2 will help the child learn to read, write, count, and use numbers up to one thousand. It presents the concept of place value to the hundred's place. It reviews counting in groups (twos, fives, tens) up to thirty and introduces counting by groups up to one hundred. Simple addition and subtraction are reviewed, and the child learns to carry and borrow. The multiplication tables are introduced by presentation of the fives and tens. Word problems are dealt with regularly, so that the child is able to "translate" from words to numerical operations. Telling time is reviewed from last year, and there is ample opportunity to practice reading a clock. There is some work done with money, both counting and writing amounts. And all of this is done in such a way that once the skill is learned, the child never has a chance to forget it, because there will be some problems of each kind in every lesson.

Math 2 presents the same concepts but emphasizes the hands-on approach.

Math-It provides practice in addition facts much like drill sheets, but it does not involve writing numbers. This is good for two reasons. Some children, especially boys, find writing difficult at this stage. With *Math-It* they don't have to write. Also mental math is a specific skill that should be exercised.

Math needs to be done every day to acquire facility with numbers.

Reading and Writing—*Sound Beginnings*, by Julia Fogassy (40); or *The Writing Road to Reading,* by Romalda Spalding (21); Step Up Books (Random House) (6); I Can Read Books (Harper Trophy) (8); *Primary Language Lessons*, by Emma Serl (32); *Little Angel Readers*, by Linda Bromeir (52); Cardinal Readers (37), National Readers (37)

The Writing Road is not the easiest text to use, and if your child is reading fluently, you may not think it is necessary. I do not know that it is, but I surely have enjoyed it. The phonics rules and decoding skills taught in the text are by far the clearest and most complete I have ever dealt with. There is a companion book by Katherine von Duyke called *The Month by Month Spelling Guide* (29) that makes the text more accessible and gives a sequential table that helps you know what to do when.

One of my children had begun to read by the time she was seven but was not confident and, because of that, did not enjoy reading. I used *The Writing Road* and taught her the phonograms, the seventy smallest units of sound in English, and her reading took off. It gave her the assurance that reading involved comprehensible rules that, when learned, would unlock the words. Prior to learning the phonograms, she had felt that the sound a particular combination of letters might make was governed purely by chance.

Not all of my children have felt the same way, but I think they have all benefited from *The Writing Road*. As a spelling text for the child who has difficulties with spelling, it is in my opinion un-equaled. It contains a list of the one thousand most-used words in the English language, divided into skill levels. The words are broken apart and marked in the way that a good natural speller would do. Thus you provide for the poorer speller the tools that the good speller uses without reflection. Even for the good speller, a list of the most common words in our language is helpful. *Sound Beginnings* is a beginning language program structured along the same lines as *The Writing Road to Reading*, but with scripted lesson plans. Thus, use of this text requires virtually no preparation and introduces both the student and the parent to the method of *The Writing Road to Reading*.

Once the child is able to read, he should be supplied with appropriate reading materials. *The Writing Road to Reading* has a fine reading list for the beginning reader and beyond, and the Step Up Books and I Can Read Books are also sources of material. Carolyn Haywood's *Penny* and *Eddie* series of books and Gertrude Chandler Warner's *Boxcar Children* (6) books have also been big hits in my house at this stage. The four *Little Angel Readers*, Cardinal Readers and National Readers can be used to provide reading practice.

Primary Language Lessons is a wonderful text for beginning writing skills. This emphasis is displayed in the copying and dictation work included in various lessons throughout the book. When I was younger, I had an idea that all copying was a mindless, boring activity. I now see that since children learn by imitation, this natural propensity should be capitalized on in every area, and judicious use of copy work is one way to do so. The child sees and internalizes the correctly written work when he copies it. The physical act of making the letters and putting in the correct punctuation fixes those models in his memory. The best thing about this series is the emphasis on learning about writing by close attention to well-written passages. There are additional suggestions for copying and dictation work in *The Harp and Laurel Wreath: Poetry and Dictation for the Classical Curriculum* (25).

Literature—*Honey for a Child's Heart*, by Gladys Hunt (21)

Reading to your child is still extremely important at this level of language development. You will be doing factual reading and discussing in history. In the evenings you might consider reading stories featuring families. *Mary Poppins,* by P. L. Travers; The Chronicles of Narnia, by C. S. Lewis; *The Railway Children,* by E. Nesbit; and *All-of-a-Kind Family,* by Sydney Taylor, are some examples of this type of book. These are fiction, but they are stories about recognizable characters in a family setting. They offer a contrasting way to learn truths about people.

Science—*Science with Air* (Usborne) (6); *Explorations with Earth Science* (Fearon Teacher Aids) (1); *Science with Plants* (Usborne) (1)

These texts are investigative in character and can be used in a way consonant with the science of the previous two years. The emphasis is on learning about the world around you by observation and conversation. There are simple experiments suggested in the texts that lend themselves to this approach. We usually spend time one day a week, or possibly every other week, on this class. But in the spring our family makes regular visits to the zoo, beach, botanical gardens and natural history museum.

History/Geography—Family history (your own); D'Aulaire's biographies (21); Childhood of Famous Americans Series (21); Usborne Books (6); states and capitals flashcards (21); *States and Regions* (Modern Curriculum Press) (21)

It seems to me that the right way to start the subject of history is to use an example that will be comprehensible to little children. Family history, especially the child's own early history, is understandable and intensely interesting to him. One can move from that to some analogous understanding of the history of our country's early leaders.

The D'Aulaire biographies are entertaining and informative. While you read the text to your child, he will be able work on listening skills, especially if you have him retell parts of the story. This encourages comprehension, oral expression, sequencing and interest. The D'Aulaire biographies include *Pocahontas, Benjamin Franklin, George Washington* and *Abraham Lincoln.*

The Childhood of Early Americans series is written on a second or third grade level. I think that these should be used when the child is reading fairly well on his own. If that is not yet, wait until next year. These are nice books for reading practice because they exercise the skill of reading on a subject that you want to cover anyway.

Many children enjoy the way the Usborne books are laid out. You might look some over to see if they fit your needs.

States and Regions is a reasonably laid out workbook. It introduces map-reading skills in a simple format. If you do not use it this year, you might use it next year.

Learning the states and capitals is part of the next stage of learning, the grammatical stage. Second and third graders can begin to acquire various lists by memory. The states and capitals constitute a list that is useful to know and do eventually lead to a better geographical knowledge of our country than many people have. I like flashcards for this exercise, but a simple list will do, or *Geo-Safari* (45), or a state board game.

I work for five minutes, four days a week, on the memorization, but the rest of the material is adequately covered in the course of the year by having class once a week.

Poetry—I recommend continuing the previous year's program.

Some poems that have worked well for us are "The Land of Storybooks", by Robert Louis Stevenson; "The Owl and the Pussycat", by Edward Lear; "The Christening", by A. A. Milne; "The Duel", by Eugene Field; "The Song of Mr. Toad", by Kenneth Grahame; "Stopping by Woods on a Snowy Evening", by Robert Frost; Psalm 100; Psalm 23 and the prayer "Soul of Christ, Sanctify Me". These poems are all included in the anthology *The Harp and the Laurel Wreath: Poetry and Dictation for the Classical Curriculum* (25).

The Scripture selections included in the book section would also be useful for memorization and dictation.

Art—*Mommy, It's a Renoir* (advanced level) (21); visits to art museums; crocheting; *What Shall I Do Today?* (Usborne) (6)

Though the material is slightly more difficult in this level of *Mommy, It's a Renoir,* the use of the material is basically the same as in previous years. One addition to my earlier suggestions is to add rough placement sketches by the child as a way of encouraging close observation. Have him look at the picture carefully and then turn it over. On a piece of blank paper have him sketch the picture with little concern for form but with attention to the placement of the forms in the picture. When he turns it over and looks at the picture again, he will notice things about the picture that he just never saw before.

Another way of expanding the exposure to beautiful works of art is by visiting a nearby museum. Such a visit is much more profitable with a little preparation. Obtain prints of some of the pictures that are in the museum. Use those prints for your art exercises, and spend enough time with them so that the child is really familiar with the paintings. Then go see the paintings in the museum. The encounter with the original will be delightful because it will involve recognition. It will be like meeting an old friend.

Simple crocheting is a skill that little children can master. They love to make long chains and will decorate the Christmas tree for you if you let them. Crocheting exercises the fine motor muscles and encourages coordination. *What Shall I Do Today?* provides ideas for fifty different art activities that can be easily done with young children.

Art activities can be done once a week, and the activities should be varied week by week.

Music—*Easy Recorder Tunes* (Usborne) (6); *Let's Learn Music #1* (Hayes) (23); The Music Masters series, part 2 (21); *32 More Traditional Catholic Hymns* (21)

If you learn to play the recorder, the music text will make more sense. Piano would do just as well, or any other instrument. If the child spends much time with an instrument, you could dispense with the text, because it would be superfluous. However, if you don't plan on music lessons right now, this text, with the recorder, will give your child the basic idea of the structure of the music he is listening to in the Music Masters series. He will begin to understand musical time, notation and recorder technique. He will also learn to play some simple tunes on the recorder.

I think that learning to play an instrument is a help to listening to music, and it is fun in itself. But I think that listening to good music and enjoying it are more important. Concentrate on that.

Sample Schedule for Second Grade

From this point on the amount of time spent each day on school subjects will vary so much from child to child that I no longer make suggestions for time allotments. Try for a mean between too much and too little time for your child. That is very general advice, but it is valid.

MON.	TUES.	WED.	THURS.	FRI.
Math	Math	Math	Math	Math
English	English	English	English	
Religion	Religion	Religion	Religion	
Music	Art	Science	History	

Evenings—Literature

There is now available a day-by-day breakdown of the courses listed for second grade (36).

The Grammatical Stage

THUS FAR in this proposed curriculum there has been a certain similarity of approach in most subjects. Variation in the classes has been supplied by the matter rather than by a difference in method, because the subjects have been seen as occasions to practice the skills appropriate to this level of formation. You practice reading and writing by doing it, which means reading and writing about something. But the primary aim is to learn to read and write, not to accumulate information. Of course religious doctrine is of the utmost importance in itself and is not just an occasion to practice skills. Nevertheless, it does not hurt to have the child practice oral reading while going over the catechism chapters with you.

In the next stage of educational formation, extending from third or fourth grade through seventh, the subjects again provide practice for the method.

Miss Sayers, in "The Lost Tools of Learning", calls this stage the "Poll-Parrot", "in which learning by heart is easy and, on the whole, pleasurable. . . . At this age, one readily memorizes the shapes and appearances of things; one likes to recite the number-plates of cars; one rejoices in the chanting of rhymes and the rumble and thunder of unintelligible polysyllables; one enjoys the mere accumulation of things."

This natural stage of development corresponds to the grammar of the Trivium, which I discussed in the introduction. In a classical education the Trivium was seen as the method of education. It came before the Quadrivium, which provided subjects. A classical education was designed to produce people who knew how to learn, who had acquired the "tools of learning".

Grammar pertains first and most specifically to language, and to some particular language. The faculties of observation and memorization, which are so lively at this time, make learning a language relatively easy and enjoyable. I prefer Latin for a variety of reasons. It is inflected, which means the nature of the speech is much more clearly seen in it. It is the key to the structure and vocabulary of the Romance languages; it underlies the technical vocabulary of the sciences and much of the literature of our culture. Further, learning to chant the paradigms is such fun at this age. "Amo, amas, amat" is very reminiscent of "eeny, meeny, miney, mo". Lastly, there are good texts available for third or fourth grade on up.

It is easy to see what grammar means with respect to language. It seems to me that there is an analogous meaning in relation to the other subjects. In each case, what is emphasized is the method of observation and memorization exercised on different disciplines. This approach both trains the mind and gathers together material for use in the next part of the Trivium, the dialectic. What is attempted is not a mere accumulation of facts, but a method of learning. Nonetheless, specific details will be learned.

At this stage, the classical curriculum will look similar to any other; the difference will be primarily in the acknowledgment that the method—the training of the mind by observation and the imagination by memorization—is more fundamental than the subjects on which it is exercised.

Third Grade Curriculum

Sources for items followed by a number in parentheses may be found at the back of the book in the list of suppliers.

Religion—*Child's Bible History,* by F. J. Knecht, D.D. (53); *Baltimore Catechism No. 1*(21); Ten Commandments book (by your child)

At this grammatical stage it is appropriate to learn about salvation history in outline. The narrative of creation, the fall and our redemption is presented simply and enjoyably in the Bible history stories. Complete understanding of the material is not what is aimed for; rather, the basic story should be known and remembered.

One suggestion for achieving this, which incorporates practice in other necessary skills, is the making of a Bible storybook. Reading the story either aloud or to himself and then writing a summary of the material familiarize the child with the history and encourage him to follow a logical sequence in telling or writing stories. A Bible storybook provides an area for writing where the child has something to say. It can become an illustrated text that you bind, incorporating both drawing and crafts.

If your child is a reluctant writer, break down the writing process into its constituent parts. Monday, read the story or have the child read it. Tuesday, have him retell the story to you while you write it down. Wednesday, have him copy the retelling, and on Thursday have him illustrate the story. This process results in a retelling of the stories of the Bible that is truly the child's own work, but the separation of the composition of the retelling and the physical act of writing makes it a much less burdensome procedure.

Last year the first section of the catechism was studied. This year the second section is considered. Since the Commandments are studied in some detail, another activity that is helpful is a Ten Commandments book. Highlight the positive side of the commandment, i.e., "Thou shall not kill" enjoins upon men a concern for and caretaking of the people around us. Have the child write the commandment at the top of a page and then draw a picture of what it means he should do. This is an exercise that employs fine motor skills and can be used to draw attention to color harmonies simply by talking about which colors go well together. It also helps the child remember the Commandments.

Alternate these activities. One week work on the catechism chapter, discussing it one day and doing the chapter exercises the next day. On the following two days, in addition to going over the questions and answers for memorization, you could work on the Commandment book. The next two weeks could be given to Bible history, while the questions and answers of the catechism are being memorized. This way there are three weeks for memorization of the chapter questions, and there is variety in the child's class.

Mathematics—*Arithmetic 3* (A Beka) (1, 8); or *Math 3* (Saxon) (48); *CalcuLadder* (The Providence Project) (21)

The grammar of mathematics includes the multiplication table, which, if learned now, will be learned with pleasure. Either of the texts, if followed, will lead the child to the acquisition of the skills appropriate to his age. They introduce division, practice identifying place value in five-digit numbers, teach about odd and even numbers, review addition and subtraction and introduce more difficult problems.

CalcuLadder is a drill program. It reinforces the child's knowledge of addition, subtraction, multiplication and division facts and encourages the child to do the problems quickly.

Reading, Writing and Language Arts—*The Writing Road To Reading,* by Romalda Spalding (21); *Primary Language Lessons,* by Emma Serl (32); *Honey for a Child's Heart,* by Gladys Hunt (21); *Catholic Authors,* 4-Sight Edition, by the Brothers of Mary (11); *A Mother's List of Books,* by Theresa Fagan (21); Greenleaf Press Books (22); poetry list, Cardinal Readers (37); National Readers (37); *The Harp and the Laurel Wreath: Poetry and Dictation for the Classical Curriculum,* edited by Laura Berquist (25)

Once children are reading well, what they can do to improve their reading is to read many good books. *The Writing Road to Reading* is not used at this point to teach reading, because that has been taught. It is an excellent text for reinforcing phonics rules and for spelling. There are other fine texts you might use to work on phonics and spelling; the text you use is not as important as the fact of doing it. These are subjects that improve with drill and can be learned well now. *The Month by Month Spelling Guide,* by Katherine von Duyke (29), is a useful companion text to *The Writing Road.*

As I mentioned earlier, *The Writing Road to Reading* has a literature list at the back of the book that is quite good. *Honey for a Child's Heart, Catholic Authors* and Greenleaf Press books are all other sources for reading material. It is still appropriate to spend some time reading more difficult books aloud to the child (or children; reading aloud is a great group activity). Listening to adult reading is a skill worth practicing. Fill the child's memory with stories of every kind.

Both the Cardinal and National Readers provide additional selections for reading on an appropriate level.

The primary vehicle for writing in this year is the Bible history, but *Primary Language Lessons* has additional exercises that teach simple punctuation, dictionary use and capitalization, as well as other appropriate skills. The rules learned here will be reinforced by application to the Bible stories.

Poems that we have used in third grade include "The Flag Goes By", by Henry Halcomb Bennett; "The Children's Hour", "The Village Blacksmith", "Christmas Bells", and "The Tide Rises, the Tide Falls", by Henry Wadsworth Longfellow; "Casey at the Bat", by Ernest Lawrence Thayer; and "Old Ironsides", by Oliver Wendell Holmes. The Preamble to the Constitution is another work to memorize. These poems and additional dictation selections are all included in the anthology *The Harp and the Laurel Wreath: Poetry and Dictation for the Classical Curriculum.*

Science—*Exploring God's World* with workbook (A Beka) (1, 8); Butterfly Garden activity kit (Insect Lore) (21)

This is an excellent, simple, science text with well-presented material. The workbook provides an opportunity to use reading skills to locate material as well as reinforce concepts. Memorizing the classes of animals and placing animals into their class is one of the activities of this text that fits the idea of the "grammar" of science.

The Butterfly Garden kit allows the child to watch the entire life cycle of a butterfly. It is interesting and develops the child's ability to observe objectively and accurately.

History/Geography—*How Our Nation Began*, by Don Sharkey, Sister Margaret and Fr. Furlong (42); Troll biographies (22); states and capitals flashcards (21)

The beginnings of our country will be studied through an acquaintance with prominent personalities of the time. This is an appropriate way to begin the study of history. Individual people are intelligible and accessible to small children and are therefore easier to remember than isolated events. Such a study also teaches that individuals can and do have an impact on society and that individual action is therefore important. It leads to a sense of responsibility to the whole framework of society, which is an attitude young Catholics should have.

If the child has not read all of the Childhood of Famous Americans series, now is a good time to do so.

A list of history dates should be memorized. This exercise employs the child's native abilities and is also an enormous help later on in establishing a historical perspective. There is a sample list at the end of this section.

The states and capitals should be reviewed if they were learned last year, and if not, they should be learned now.

Latin—*English from the Roots Up*, by Joegil Lundquist (21)

This is the first introduction to another language, the beginning of the study of Latin, with all the benefits I mentioned in "The Grammatical Stage". At this stage it is not necessary to use the text; use the cards, which can be purchased separately, and have your student simply learn the root words and their meanings. If you introduce three new cards each week and spend five minutes a day, four days a week, reviewing the words previously memorized, your student will easily and permanently learn all hundred root words over the course of the year.

Arts/Crafts—Craft kits (local craft store) or more crocheting; *Mommy, It's a Renoir* (steps four and five) (21)

The crafts provide a directed forum for both large and fine motor control exercises. My children have enjoyed hammered metal pictures, building a birdhouse, making pencil holders, orange-ball sachets, and so forth.

This level of *Mommy, It's a Renoir* involves learning the names of artists and famous pictures. It fits well with the idea of the "grammar" of the subject matter and provides more exposure to beautiful works of art. As I suggested earlier, once the immediate goals of the art program are met, there are other uses for the pictures that will also encourage familiarity with these works.

Music—*Let's Learn Music #2* (Hayes) (23); The Music Masters series, part 3 (21)

Let's Learn Music #2 continues the study of music begun last year. The recorder text from last year could be continued or used for review. If your student has finished this text, the local music store will have some simple recorder music available.

Continue the study of the great works of music that has been pursued the previous two years. Discuss the music and the composer's life with your child. Playing the pieces more than once helps fix the tunes in the imagination. It can be overdone, but some repetition is useful.

Sample Schedule for Third Grade				
MON.	TUES.	WED.	THURS.	FRI.
Math	Math	Math	Math	Math
English	English	English	English	
Religion	Religion	Religion	Religion	
Science	History	Geography	History	
Memory work	Memory work	Memory work	Memory work	
		Music		

Evenings—Literature

There is now available a day-by-day breakdown of the courses listed for third grade (36).

LIST OF HISTORY DATES

1620	*Mayflower* Lands Pilgrims At Plymouth, Mass.
1776	Declaration of Independence
1787	U.S. Constitution
1812	War of 1812
1849	California Gold Rush
1861	Civil War Begins
1865	Lee Surrenders at Appomattox
1914	World War I Begins in Europe
1918	End of World War I
1929	Stock Market Crash—Depression Begins
1941	Japan Attacks Pearl Harbor—U.S. Enters World War II
1945	Atomic Bomb Dropped on Hiroshima—End of World War II
1950	Korean War Begins
1957	Sputnik
1963	Vietnam War Escalates
1969	Neil Armstrong: First Man on the Moon

Fourth Grade Curriculum

Sources for items followed by a number in parentheses may be found at the back of the book in the list of suppliers.

Religion—Lives of the saints (correlated with history) (51); *St. Joseph's Baltimore Catechism No. 1* (21); *Bible History,* by Ignatius Schuster, D.D. (53); Latin prayers (see list)

During the first third of the year, concentrate on reading various lives of the saints. Have your child choose, each week, a saint from the list that accompanies this section. This is a list of saints who lived during the period of history the child will be studying this year. The child will read about the saint and prepare an oral report, which he should give to members of the family.

In addition to helping the child remember when the saint lived, the fact that the report is oral gives him a chance to inform others about something he knows, which is important. It also exercises his communication skills. Another positive aspect of this activity is that the children enjoy it.

In the second third of the year, the religion course will be concerned with Catholic doctrine. The child will use the third part of the *Baltimore Catechism*. His grasp of the material can be checked by having him do the exercises at the end of each chapter.

The questions and answers should be memorized. If you have more than one child in this class, or if you are willing to take a chance yourself, you can play games structured like spelling bees to provide motivation and variety. You can also have the child supply the question for your answer or give points and prizes for a certain number of correct answers. Always review previously learned material. It is better to move slowly through the text and learn the answers well than to go quickly and forget them as soon as the chapter is finished. However, this material will be covered again, so if something is difficult or just does not seem to stick, don't worry too much. It will come up again.

In the third segment of the year, Bible history will be studied. The subjects for writing this year will be in history and English. In Bible history the primary learning tool will be reading and conversing. Discuss the text with your child; have him summarize the chapter, and then go over chapter questions with him.

A portion of religion class should be devoted to Latin prayers, learning to write them as well as to say them. There is a list of prayers at the end of this section.

Mathematics—*Math 54* (Saxon) (48); *CalcuLadder,* by Edwin C. Meyers (The Providence Project) (21)

This text will introduce or review the basic fourth grade math skills. It has a cyclical approach, reviewing new material daily until it becomes second nature. *CalcuLadder* can be used to help the child do computations quickly.

Grammar and Composition—*Intermediate Language Lessons*, by Emma Serl (32); journal (by your child); *The Harp and Laurel Wreath: Poetry and Dictation for the Classical Curriculum*, edited by Laura Berquist (25)

Use *Intermediate Language Lessons*, following its internal order. Special attention should be paid to the writing sections of the text. It is intended to be used in fourth, fifth and sixth grades and has a section for each. This text provides practice in punctuation and capitalization, grammar and some variety in creative writing. The rules learned will be reinforced by application to the history summaries written at the end of each section of the history course.

The journal will be used as an extension of the text. When an exercise in the text is difficult and needs practice, or is particularly delightful, you can choose additional subjects for practice in the same kind of activity.

One of the exercises that my daughter found pleasant was turning poetry into prose. It seemed like a good thing to do since it required reading the poem closely, and because she thought it was fun, I would have her do one such exercise a month.

The journal may also be used to write descriptions of objects and special events, Latin prayers, dictation selections and the current poem. It will provide penmanship practice and help with memorization as well as increase writing skills. Selections for dictation are included in *The Harp and Laurel Wreath: Poetry and Dictation for the Classical Curriculum.*

Spelling—*The Writing Road to Reading,* by Romalda Spalding (21); *The Month by Month Spelling Guide,* by Katherine von Duyke (29)

If you have been using this text from the beginning, the phonics rules should be pretty familiar by now. The spelling list probably still contains words that are difficult. Use the spelling scale indicator available from the Spalding Education Foundation (50) to determine the proper spelling level for your child. Start at that point in the text and continue to use the words through the year. *The Month by Month Spelling Guide* gives a sequential table that helps you know what to do while using *The Writing Road to Reading.*

Also pay attention to accuracy in spelling in daily work. A list of correctly spelled words that have been misspelled in daily work might be kept in the child's journal.

Literature—(correlated with history) Landmark Books (21); *Books Children Love,* by Elizabeth Wilson (3); Greenleaf Press Books (22); *In Review* (Bethlehem Books) (7); *Let The Authors Speak,* by Carolyn Hatcher (21); *Catholic Authors,* 4-Sight edition, by the Brothers of Mary (11); *Honey For A Childs' Heart,* by Gladys Hunt (21); *A Mother's List of Books,* by Theresa Fagan (21)

Allow some time for reading literature each day, both silently and aloud. Discuss the stories with the children. *For the Children's Sake,* by Susan Schaeffer Macaulay, has good advice for how to discuss a text with your child.

I have included a list (at the end of this section) of suggested readings that fit with history for this year and are well written. Other texts can be found in the books I mention above.

Poetry—Poems from American authors (5, 21); *The Harp and Laurel Wreath: Poetry and Dictation for the Classical Curriculum,* edited by Laura Berquist (25)

Continue to encourage both memorization of enjoyable poems and recitation. When your child gives his oral report about the saint for the week, you could also have him recite his poem. If he is working on a more difficult poem, you could have him recite it as far as he is able, or you could just wait until the whole thing is learned. I have included a list of poems that you may consider at the end of this section. These poems are all included in the anthology *The Harp and Laurel Wreath: Poetry and Dictation for the Classical Curriculum.*

Science—*Understanding God's World* (A Beka) (1, 8) or How and Why Books (6)

Understanding God's World is a good text and easy for the teacher to use. Just follow the internal order of the book. It is Christian, and God's loving hand is seen in His creation in this book. However, it is difficult for some children and rather technical.

An alternative is to purchase How and Why Books on subjects like earth science, astronomy, sound, chemistry, machines and electricity. These books are informative and easy to read. They contain simple experiments that an older sibling could do with the student. Because they are accessible to the children, the material is likely to be retained.

History—*Evangelization of the New World*, by James R. Leek (21); *The Catholic Faith Comes to the Americas*, by Illeen Reninger (49); *Let the Authors Speak,* by Carolyn Hatcher (21); books about explorers and the colonization of the New World (4, 11, 20, 21, 22); *Turning Back the Pages of Time: A Guide to American History through Literature*, by Kathy Keller (21); *Our Pioneers and Patriots*, by Fr. Philip Furlong (53)

It is best to have some text to follow as an outline, and *Our Pioneers and Patriots* is a good Catholic text. It is in print and has an answer key. Protestant texts rarely have an objective view of the race for the New World.

Using the text you choose as an outline, read or have the child read the sections of the text dealing with the events and persons from the period of the early exploration of North America to the French and Indian War. Read each chapter, discuss it, and then have the child read supplementary books that cover the same material in more depth. When those books, as many or as few as you choose, are read, have the child write a report, not a book report, but a report about the material covered. I have included a list of books for this period at the end of this section. Other texts can be found in the books I mention above.

The Evangelization of the New World contains important material about this period in history. It is an objective account of the Spanish colonization in Central, South and North America. It has copies of original documents and additional information in the back of the text. The teacher's guide has good suggestions for discussion.

This way of doing history, where the textbook is an introduction to the information and not the primary vehicle, makes history come alive. Too often with a history text, the material seems dry and lifeless. The information is stored in the short-term memory and promptly forgotten after the chapter test. The people I am acquainted with who know and love history know the personalities and events as though they were personally acquainted with them. Writing about the outstanding people or events of each chapter will provide an opportunity to practice comprehension and composition skills.

This is a good time to start a timeline, to which you can add throughout the coming years. Or purchase a timeline that is already made but that can be referred to through the years. Timelines perform an important function because they tie together the studies of various disciplines chronologically.

Class time will vary from week to week depending on whether the chapter is being introduced, the material is being read or the summary being written. Keep the summaries throughout the year, and at the end of the year there will be a very satisfying, abbreviated history written by your child.

Geography—*Map Skills for Today*, Grade 4 (45); wooden U.S.A. puzzle (56); Fit-A-State (Lauri) (56); *Where In The World?* game (45); U.S. outline maps (45)

First review the states and capitals. Then work on filling in the states and capitals from memory in an outline map. Your child should learn major rivers, mountains and lakes and be able to place them correctly in the outline map.

Next use the map skills to learn map-reading skills. This should be accompanied by reading actual maps and playing games with the puzzle.

The game *Where in the World?* can be used to fill in if there is extra time in the school year. Games are useful learning tools because they are relatively painless. Two good lists to learn at this point are largest states by area and largest states by population. They are included at the end of this chapter.

Latin—*Latina Christiana I*, by Cheryl Lowe (34)

This continues the study begun last year of Latin and Greek roots commonly used in English. When using this program in fourth grade, concentrate on teaching the vocabulary and chants. In fifth grade you may use the same text, but do all the exercises. This allows the child to focus this year on memorization, which is appropriate to his developmental level, rather than translation, which is an analytic activity. As you teach this course, which only takes minutes a day, you will find your own vocabulary and understanding of language increasing. One of the tremendous side benefits of homeschooling is that you get to learn the things you didn't learn when you were in school.

Art—*Mommy, It's a Renoir* (Steps 6, 7 and 8) (21); *Drawing Textbook*, by Bruce MacIntyre (21)

I recommend using the *Drawing Textbook* in the first half of the year. The introduction by Mr. MacIntyre is a convincing defense of the need for literacy in visual expression. Not everyone is an artist, but anyone can learn to draw recognizable objects.

After your child has learned some of the principles of drawing, the later steps of *Mommy, It's a Renoir* will have added interest. Steps 6, 7 and 8 are about schools of art and the times when they flourished. When this information is mastered, other uses of the postcards are beneficial. One successful technique we have used is to have the child look at a particular picture, turn it over and then try to describe it so that it is visible to the listener. It is better if the listener has not just looked at the picture. Or the "listen-and-find" game, where one tries to pick out a picture from among many pictures by listening carefully to its description.

Music—*Let's Learn Music #3* (Hayes) (23); play recorder; listen to classical music; *Wee Sing America* (45)

Let's Learn Music #3 continues the study of music begun in second grade. Simple recorder music continues to be used for application of principles.

Continue the study of the great works of music that has been pursued in the previous years. If you have worked your way through The Music Masters series, now is the time to become familiar with particular pieces of music. Pick some of your favorites from the tapes, and play them often enough so that the child recognizes them. Then you can play recognition games, asking your child which piece of music this is and who wrote it. Recognition is a pleasure for everyone and is especially enjoyable in this grammatical period of education.

Wee Sing America teaches songs that have been important in the history of our country, so it is appropriate to use it as the history of our country is studied.

Sample Schedule for Fourth Grade				
MON.	TUES.	WED.	THURS.	FRI.
Math	Math	Math	Math	Math
English	English	English	English	
Religion	Religion	Religion	Religion	
Geography	Art	History	Science	
		Music		

Memorization practice in the various subjects every day.
There is now available a day-by-day breakdown of the courses listed for fourth grade (36).

Grade Four Resource Lists

LIST OF SAINTS

St. Kateri Tekakwitha

St. Rose of Lima

Bl. Junipero Serra

St. Isaac Jogues

St. Philip Neri

St. Alphonsus Liguori

St. John Baptist de la Salle

St. Elizabeth Ann Seton

St. John Neumann

St. John Vianney (the Curé d'Ars)

St. John Bosco

Pope St. Pius X

St. Thérèse of Lisieux

St. Angela Merici

St. Ignatius Loyola

St. Charles Borromeo

St. Francis Xavier

St. Peter Canisius

St. Francis de Sales

St. Vincent de Paul

St. Paul of the Cross

St. Bernadette

St. Dominic Savio

LATIN PRAYERS

Pater Noster (Our Father)

Pater noster, qui es in caelis:
sanctificétur nomen tuum;
advéniat regnum tuum;
fiat volúntas tua, sicut in caelo et in terra.
Panem nostrum cotidiánum da nobis hódie;
et dimítte nobis débita nostra,
sicut et nos dimíttimus debitóribus nostris;
et ne nos indúcas in tentatiónem;
sed líbera nos a malo.
Amen.

Ave Maria (Hail Mary)

Ave Maria, gratia plena, Dominus tecum,
benedicta tu in muliéribus, et benedictus fructus ventris tui, Jesus.
Sancta Maria, Mater Dei, ora pro nobis peccatóribus
nunc et in hora mortis nostrae.
Amen.

Gloria (Glory Be)
Gloria Patri, et Filio, et Spiritui Sancto,
sicut erat in princípio, et nunc et semper et in saecula saeculórum.
Amen.

Gratia (Grace before meals)
Benedic, Domine, nos, et haec tua dona,
quae de tua largitáte sumus sumptúri,
per Christum Dominum nostrum. Amen.
Animae omnium fidélium defunctórum
per misericórdiam Dei requiescant in pace. Amen.

(Note: Our Father's House (40) has a pronunciation tape of these and
other prayers.)

GEOGRAPHY LIST—LARGEST STATES

LARGEST STATES BY AREA

Alaska	590,000 square miles
Texas	270,000 square miles (half of Alaska)
California	160,000 square miles (a little more than half of Texas)
Montana	150,000 square miles

OTHERS OVER 100,000 SQUARE MILES:

New Mexico	120,000
Arizona	114,000
Nevada	110,000
Colorado	104,000

LARGEST STATES BY POPULATION (1990 CENSUS)

California	30 million	54 electoral votes
New York	18 million	33 electoral votes
Texas	17 million	32 electoral votes
Florida	13 million	25 electoral votes
Pennsylvania	12 million	23 electoral votes
Illinois	11 million	22 electoral votes
Ohio	11 million	21 electoral votes
Michigan	9 million	8 electoral votes

History Reading List—
The Age of Exploration

Used as supplements to the first half of *Pioneers and Patriots*, by Fr. Philip Furlong.

An "L" after the author's name indicates that the library or used-book sources will be your best bet for securing this title; "IP" indicates that the book is currently in print; "*" indicates an especially enjoyable book. If a book belongs to an identifiable series, I will indicate that by using one of the following abbreviations: VB—Vision Book (Catholic), AMB—American Background Book (Catholic), LKB—Landmark Book (Christian orientation), SB—Signature Book, NSB—North Star Book, CL—Clarion Book (Catholic).

The Vikings	Elizabeth Janeway	IP, LKB*
The Story of Rolf and the Viking Bow	Allen French	IP
The Black Fox of Lorne	Marguerite de Angeli	L*
Door to the North	Elizabeth Coatsworth	L*
Leif Ericson	William Steele	L*
He Went with Marco Polo	Louise Andrews Kent	L*
He Went with Vasco da Gama	Louise Andrews Kent	L*
Christopher Columbus	Nina Brown Baker	L, SB
The Voyage of Christopher Columbus	Armstrong Sperry	L, LKB
Columbus	Ingri and Edgar D'Aulaire	IP*
Columbus and the New World	August Derleth	L, VB*
Queen Elizabeth and the Spanish Armada	Frances Winwar	L, LKB
The Evangelization of the New World	Stephen Leek	IP*
New Found World	Katherine B. Shippen	L
Cortes of Mexico	Ronald Syme	L*
Balboa Discovers the Pacific	Jeannette Mirsky	L*
Ferdinand Magellan	Ronald Welch	L*
Ship's Boy with Magellan	Milton Lomosk	L*
Ferdinand Magellan	Seymour Pond	L, LKB

Henry Hudson, Captain of Ice-Bound Seas	Carl Carmer	L
Champlain of the St. Lawrence	Ronald Syme	L*
The Hudson Bay Company	Richard Morenus	L, LKB
The First Northwest Passage	Walter O'Meara	L, NSB
Peter Stuyvesant of Old New York	Anna and Russel Crouse	L, LKB
Jamestown	James E. Knight	IP
The Landing of the Pilgrims	James Daugherty	IP, LKB*
Cartier Sails the St. Lawrence	Esther Averill	L
I Sailed on the Mayflower	Pilkington	IP
Sailing the Seven Seas	Mary Chase	L, NSB
Clipper Ship Days	John Jennings	L, LKB
Captain Cook Explores the South Seas	Armstrong Sperry	L
Fear in the Forest	Cateau De Leeuw	L*
The French Are Coming	Wilma Hays	L, LKB
Rogers' Rangers: The French and Indian War	Bradford Smith	L
Ticonderoga: The Story of a Fort	Bruce Lancaster	L, NSB
St. Isaac and the Indians	Milton Lomask	IP, VB*
Cross among the Tomahawks	Milton Lomask	L, CL*
Sing in the Dark	Maude Thomas	L*
Indian Captive	Lois Lenski	L*
Captured by the Mohawks	Sterling North	L*
Battle for the Rock	Joseph Schull	L*
Madeleine Takes Command	Ethel Brill	IP
De Tonti of the Iron Hand	Ann Heagney	L, AMB*
The Explorations of Père Marquette	Jim Kjelgaard	L, LKM*
Father Marquette and the Great River	August Derleth	L, VB*
Crusaders of the Great River	Fr. William Doty	L*
The Cross in the West	Mark Boesch	L, VB*
Fr. Junipero Serra	Ivy Bolton	L*
Father Kino, Priest to the Pimas	Ann Clark	L, VB*
Padre Kino	Jack Steffan	L, AMB*

POETRY LIST

"Hiawatha's Childhood" from "The Song of Hiawatha"	Henry Wadsworth Longfellow
"Columbus"	Joaquin Miller
"America For Me"	Henry Van Dyke
"Sea Fever"	John Masefield
"Christmas Everywhere"	Phillip Brooks
"The Duel"	Eugene Field
"The Fool's Prayer"	Edward Sill
"The Bells"	Edgar Allan Poe
"Spring"	Alfred Lord Tennyson
"Requiem"	Robert Louis Stevenson
"Christopher Columbus"	Rosemary and Stephen Vincent Benet
"Hernando de Soto"	Rosemary and Stephen Vincent Benet
"Pocahontas"	Rosemary and Stephen Vincent Benet
"Captain Kidd"	Rosemary and Stephen Vincent Benet
"George Washington"	Rosemary and Stephen Vincent Benet

Fifth Grade Curriculum

Sources for items followed by a number in parentheses may be found at the back of the book in the list of suppliers.

Religion—*Faith and Life Catechism* for grade 5 *(Credo: I Believe)* (25); *St. Joseph's Baltimore Catechism No. 2* (21)

Read and discuss all thirty chapters in the catechism. This is an excellent treatment of the basic truths of our faith. The questions and answers in the text are from the Catechism of St. Pius X and are less distilled than the *Baltimore Catechism*. The doctrine presented is the same, but the articulation of that doctrine is more complex and therefore more difficult for little children. When I use this book, I substitute the *Baltimore Catechism* questions for those in the text.

Mathematics—*Math 65* (Saxon) (48)

Math 65 is a standard textbook for this grade level, so the appropriate concepts for this stage of learning will be covered. Once again the spiral approach to teaching makes this a first-rate text. The child never forgets a concept once learned because he practices it every day. Complete the text over the course of the year, with periodic quizzes and tests to check on progress.

Grammar and Composition—*Intermediate Language Lessons,* by Emma Serl (32) or *Learning Language Arts through Literature* (Purple Book) (16); or *Easy Grammar,* Level 1 (45); *The Great Editing Adventure,* vol. 1 (21); *The Harp and Laurel Wreath: Poetry and Dictation for the Classical Curriculum,* edited by Laura Berquist (25)

In our house the subject of writing concentration varies in the fifth grade. The child who really enjoyed last year's history writing program continues with it, but for those who are not as delighted with writing summaries, we use *Intermediate Language Lessons* as the primary writing source. This text emphasizes different kinds of writing with daily practice and exercises. There is practice in writing letters, invitations, original prose and poetry. There are also numerous opportunities for writing from dictation, which is a very beneficial practice. It requires concentration on spelling, punctuation and styles of writing. Additional selections for dictation can be found in *The Harp and Laurel Wreath: Poetry and Dictation for the Classical Curriculum*.

Grammar can be begun as a separate study this year. The Purple Book provides an introduction to such a study, as does *Easy Grammar*, level 1. Grammar is a subject that requires teacher interaction for mastery. It is possible to do the exercises without understanding, by simply following the examples. The teacher needs to be involved so that the pupil has to concentrate and think about not only the present concept but also the previously learned material. Grammar, composition, spelling, literature and poetry are all directed to giving the child a practical and theoretical knowledge of language that will enable him to read, write and think well. *The Great Editing Adventure*, vol. 1, provides practice in the mechanics of writing. It is easy to use, and the children enjoy it.

Spelling—*The Writing Road To Reading*, by Romalda Spalding (21); Spalding Education Foundation's Morrison-McCall Spelling Scale Indicator (50)

Though you have been using this text for some time and the phonetics rules are quite familiar, the spelling list probably still contains words that are difficult. If it does not, concentrate on spelling well in daily work, but do not have a separate text for spelling. Use the Morrison-McCall Spelling Scale Indicator to help determine whether your child will profit by continued work with this text.

In any case, pay particular attention to accurate spelling in daily work. A list of daily misspellings might be kept in a notebook.

Literature—(correlated with history) Landmark Books (21); *Books Children Love*, by Elizabeth Wilson (21); Greenleaf Press Books (22); *Catholic Authors*, 4-Sight edition, by the Brothers of Mary (11); *Let The Authors Speak*, by Carolyn Hatcher (21); *A Mother's List of Books*, by Theresa Fagan (21)

As you did last year, allow some time for reading literature each day. Discuss the stories with the children. Once again I would like to point out that *For the Children's Sake,* by Susan Schaeffer Macaulay (21), has good advice on how to discuss a text with your child.

Though discussing some of your child's reading with him is both rewarding and important (not to mention occasionally hilarious), not all texts lend themselves equally to discussion. Don't feel that every book your child reads has to be talked over. Further, each child should be able to do some reading with "no strings attached", just for fun, without any end in view other than enjoyment. The book list I have included has works on it that my own children have found delightful; all of these are marked with an asterisk.

I have included a list (at the end of this section) of suggested readings that fit with history for this year and are well written. Other texts can be found in the books I mention above.

Poetry—Poems from American authors (21); *The Harp and the Laurel Wreath: Poetry and Dictation for the Classical Curriculum*, edited by Laura Berquist (25)

Continue to encourage both memorization of enjoyable poems and recitation. This year you might include some longer speeches. It is more of a challenge to memorize prose than poetry and correspondingly strengthens the imagination and retentive powers.

At the end of this section I have included a list of poems and prose selections that you may consider. The poems in this list are all included in the anthology *The Harp and the Laurel Wreath: Poetry and Dictation for the Classical Curriculum.*

Science—*Concepts and Challenges in Science* (A), by Alan Winkler, Leonard Bernstein, Martin Schachter and Stanley Wolfe (published by Globe) (43, 54, 58)

Concepts and Challenges in Science contains an excellent presentation of the basic concepts of biology, physics, chemistry and earth science at this level. There are simple experiments that may be done as time permits. This text is not difficult and does not include large amounts of detail. But it does fit well with the aim of this curriculum, because it concentrates on basic formation and not on an accumulation of complex data. Have the child do one chapter each day to finish the book easily by the end of the year.

History—Books about the Revolutionary War period through the Civil War (22); *Pioneers and Patriots*, by Fr. Philip Furlong (53); *Let The Authors Speak,* by Carolyn Hatcher (21); *Turning Back the Pages of Time: A Guide To American History through Literature*, by Kathy Keller (21)

Using the text you choose as an outline, read—or have your child read—the sections of the text dealing with the events and persons from the period of the Revolutionary War through the Civil War. Read each chapter, discuss it, and then have the child read supplementary books that cover the same material in more depth. When those books, as many or as few as you choose, are read, have the child write a report, if this is the area you have chosen for writing practice. Otherwise, discuss the chapter in the light of the books covered. I have included a list of books for this period at the end of this section. Other texts can be found in the books I mention above.

As I mentioned in the fourth grade curriculum, this way of doing history, where the textbook simply introduces the information and is not the primary vehicle, makes history more interesting and memorable.

Dates are good to memorize in conjunction with such a study because they are hooks to hang the information on. Have your child keep track of important dates as they come up in the reading material. This can be a list for memory work.

Class time will vary from week to week depending on whether the chapter is being introduced or whether the material is being read or discussed.

Geography—Map study with an atlas (5)

We want our children to become proficient at locating cities and countries on a map. This requires attention to detail, so after reviewing the states and capitals, I recommend using an atlas and giving the student a small photocopied piece of map that contains an identifying feature (well-known city or mountain range). Cut a circle out of a piece of paper and place the paper on the map, with the cut-out positioned over the identifying feature. Then photocopy it. Instruct your child to find the map from which the piece is taken and answer questions about it. Ask him what continent the landmark is on, what country it is in, and what the latitude and longitude of the identifying feature are. (This is a homemade alternative to *Geo-Safari* or *Where in the World?* Its advantage is that it works with real maps, which the child is able to do but which most programs do not use. The disadvantage, obviously, is that it is more work for you.)

I have included a good list to learn at this point at the end of this section. It covers the continents and the island groups, giving their square mileage, highest points and estimated populations.

Latin—*Latina Christiana,* Book I, by Cheryl Lowe (34); or *Our Roman Roots*, by James Leek (40)

If you used *Latina Christiana* last year, concentrating on memorization, use it this year as a beginning study of translation. Do the exercises, following the internal order, and review all vocabulary and chants.

If you are beginning the study of Latin this year, *Latina Christiana* is a good place to start. For those who are ready to go on, having mastered *Latina Christiana*, *Our Roman Roots* would be a good next step.

Art—*Story of Painting* (Usborne) (30); *Drawing Textbook,* by Bruce MacIntyre (21)

I recommend using the *Drawing Textbook* again in the first half of the year. The child may review or pick up where he left off last year. Practice is necessary for literacy in visual expression. Though not everyone is an artist, anyone can learn, with practice, to draw recognizable objects.

With the background the child has acquired with *Mommy, It's a Renoir,* and after a review of some of the principles of drawing, *The Story of Painting* will have added interest. The text talks about the various artists and their histories. The schools of art and the times when they flourished are discussed.

Music—*Ready to Use Music Reading Activities Kit,* by Loretta Mitchell (21); play recorder; listen to classical music

> *Music Reading* continues the theoretical study of music. It is a program that teaches music using music. It has singing as well as instrumental playing. It is slow and methodical so that even a parent with no musical training can use it confidently. It does require a piano, keyboard or chromatic bells and rhythm sticks.
>
> Continue the study of the great works of music that has been pursued in the previous years. Work on familiarity with particular pieces of music. Pick some of your favorites, and play them often enough so that the child recognizes them. Then you can play recognition games, asking your child which piece of music this is and who wrote it. Recognition is a pleasure for everyone and is especially enjoyable in this grammatical period of education.

Sample Schedule for Fifth Grade				
MON.	TUES.	WED.	THUR.	FRI.
Math	Math	Math	Math	Math
English	English	English	English	Art
Religion	Religion	Religion	Religion	
Science	Science	Science	Science	
Music	Geography	History	History	
Latin	Latin	Latin	Latin	

Memorization practice in the various subjects every day.
There is now available a day-by-day breakdown of the courses listed for fifth grade (36).

Grade Five Resource Lists

HISTORY READING LIST—
THE BEGINNING OF THE UNITED STATES

Used as supplements to the second half of *Pioneers and Patriots,* by Fr. Philip Furlong.

An "L" after the author's name indicates that the library or used-book sources will be your best bet for securing this title; "IP" indicates that the book is currently in print; "*" indicates an especially enjoyable book. If a book belongs to an identifiable series, I will indicate that by using one of the following abbreviations: VB—Vision Book (Catholic), AMB—American Background Book (Catholic), LKB—Landmark Book (Christian orientation), SB—Signature Book, NSB—North Star Book, WWTB—We Were There Books.

William Penn, Quaker Hero	Hildegarde Dolson	L, LKB
Roger Williams, Defender of Freedom	Cecile Edwards	L
Builders of Catholic America	Albert Nevins, M.M.	IP
George Washington's World	Genevieve Foster	IP*
Arrow Book of Presidents	Sturges Cary	L
Book of the Presidents	American Heritage series	L
The Golden Book of America	Irwin Shapiro	L
Landmark History (two volumes)	Daniel J. Boorstin	IP*
The Witch of Blackbird Pond	Elizabeth George Speare	IP*
Sarah Morton's Day	Kate Waters	IP*
Ben Franklin of Old Philadelphia	Margaret Cousins	IP, LKB*
Ben and Me	Robert Lawson	IP*
Mr. Revere and I	Robert Lawson	IP*
The American Revolution	Bruce Bliven, Jr.	IP, LKB
John Carroll, Bishop and Patriot	Milton Lomask	L, VB*
Paul Revere and the Minute Men	Dorothy Canfield Fisher	L, LKB*
Drums	James Boyd	L
Silver for General Washington	Enid Meadowcroft	L*
Johnny Tremain	Esther Forbes	IP*

Cavalry Hero, Casimir Pulaski	Dorothy Adams	L, AM*
Birth of the Constitution	Edmund Lindop	IP
The Reb and the Redcoats	Constance Savery	L
Our Independence and the Constitution	Dorothy Canfield Fisher	L, LKB*
John Paul Jones, Fighting Sailor	Armstrong Sperry	L, LKB
A Boy Sailor with John Paul Jones	H. C. Thomas	L*
The Story of John Paul Jones	Iris Vinton	L
Old Ironsides	Harry Hansen	L, LKB
Marquis de Lafayette	Hodding Carter	L, LKB
Early American	Mildred Pace	L
A Spy in Old West Point	'Anne Emery	L
The West Point Story	Colonel Red Reeder and Nardi Reeder Campion	L, LKB
The Swamp Fox of the Revolution	Stewart H. Holbrook	L, LKB*
The Far Frontier	William Steele	L
Daniel Boone, Opening of the Wilderness	John Brown	L, LKB
General Brock and Niagara Falls	Samuel Adams	L, LKB
Traders and Trappers of the Far West	James Daugherty	L, LKB
Davy Crockett	Contance Rourke	L
The Louisiana Purchase	Robert Tallant	L, LKB
Lafayette, Friend of America	Alberta Graham	L
The Battle for New Orleans	F. Van Wyck Mason	L, NSB
The Pirate Lafitte and the Battle of New Orleans	Robert Tallant	L, LKB
Robert Fulton and the Steamboat	Ralph Hill	L, LKB
Wyatt Earp	Stewart H. Holbrook	L, LKB
Buffalo Bill's Great Wild West Show	Walter Havighurst	L, LKB
Up the Trail from Texas	J. Frank Dobie	L, LKB
Trail Blazer of the Seas	Jean Lee Latham	L*
Simon Brute and the Western Adventure	Elizabeth Bartelme	L, AMB*
Erie Canal	Samuel Adams	L, LKB
Kit Carson and the Wild Frontier	Ralph Moody	L, LKB*
War Chief of the Seminoles	May McNeer	L, LKB

We Were There at the Klondike Gold Rush	Benjamin Appel	L, WWTB
The Alaska Gold Rush	May McNeer	L, LKB
Dolly Madison	Jane Mayer	L, LKB
Abraham Lincoln's World	Genevieve Foster	L*
Robert E. Lee and the Road of Honor	Hodding Carter	L, LKB
By Secret Railway	Enid Meadowcroft	L*
Lincoln and Douglas: The Years of Decision	Regina Kelly	L, LKB
Gettysburg	MacKinlay Kantor	IP, LKB
Abe Lincoln: Log Cabin to White House	Sterling North	IP, LKB
We Were There at the Battle of Gettysburg	Alida Malkus	L, WWTB
Rifles for Watie	Harold Keith	IP*
Amos Fortune, Free Man	Elizabeth Yates	IP*
Across Five Aprils	Irene Hunt	IP*
The Story of Andrew Jackson	Enid Meadowcroft	L, SB
The Story of Clara Barton	Olive Price	L, SB
Stonewall Jackson	Jonathan Daniels	L, LKB
William Gaston, Fighter for Justice	Eva Betz	L, AMB*
Chaplain in Gray	H. J. Heagney	L, AMB*
Lee and Grant at Appomattox	MacKinlay Kantor	L, LKB
Man of the Monitor	Jean Lee Latham	L*
The Birth of Texas	William Johnson	L, NSB
Sam Houston: The Tallest Texan	William Johnson	L, LKB
Sam Houston	Booth Mooney	L
We Were There at the Oklahoma Land Run	Jim Kjelgaard	L, WWTB
The Buffalo Knife	William O. Steele	IP*
James Bowie	Shannon Garst	L
We Were There at the Driving of the Golden Spike	David Shepherd	L, WWTB
The Oregon Trail	Francis Parkman	IP*
We Were There on the Oregon Trail	William O. Steele	L, WWTB
Custer's Last Stand	Quentin Reynold	L, LKB

The Story of General Custer	Margaret Leighton	L, SB
The Story of Crazy Horse	Enid Meadowcroft	L, SB
The Story of Geronimo	Jim Kjelgaard	L, SB*
Heroines of the Early West	Nancy Ross	L, LKB
Caddie Woodlawn	Carol Ryrie Brink	IP*
The Little House books	Laura Ingalls Wilder	IP*
The Pioneers Go West	George Stewart	IP, LKB
Mr. Bell Invents the Telephone	Katherine Shippen	L, LKB
To California by Covered Wagon	George Stewart	L, LKB
Broken Hand Fitzpatrick	Shannon Garst	L
Young Man in a Hurry	Jean Lee Latham	L*
Sons of the Big Muddy	Wilbur Granberg	L
A First Steamboat on the		
Mississippi	Sterling North	L, NSB
The Story of Thomas Alva Edison	Margaret Cousins	L, LKB
Young Thomas Edison	Sterling North	L, SB
The Conquest of the North and		
South Poles	Russell Owen	L, LKB
Teddy Roosevelt and the		
Rough Riders	Henry Castor	L, LKB

Poems and Other Works
(suitable for memorization)

"George Washington"	Rosemary and Stephen Vincent Benet
"John Adams"	Rosemary and Stephen Vincent Benet
"Benjamin Franklin"	Rosemary and Stephen Vincent Benet
"Lewis and Clark"	Rosemary and Stephen Vincent Benet
"John Quincy Adams"	Rosemary and Stephen Vincent Benet
"John Paul Jones"	Rosemary and Stephen Vincent Benet
"The Star-Spangled Banner"	Francis Scott Key
"Paul Revere's Ride"	Henry Wadsworth Longfellow
"The War Inevitable,	
March, 1775"	Patrick Henry
"The Concord Hymn"	Ralph Waldo Emerson
"O Captain! My Captain!"	Walt Whitman
"Sheridan's Ride"	Thomas Buchanan Read

"The Destruction of Sennecharib"	Lord Byron
"Solitude"	Ella Wheeler Wilcox
"The Spider and the Fly"	Mary Howitt
"The Ride of Colin Graves"	J. B. O'Reilly
"How They Brought the Good News from Ghent to Aix"	Robert Browning
"Jesu dulcis memoria"	St. Bernard of Clairvaux (English translation, G. M. Hopkins)

OTHER WORKS

"Washington's Address to His Troops"
"Washington on His Appointment as Commander-in-Chief"

GEOGRAPHY LIST
CONTINENTS AND ISLAND GROUPS

Continent	Area (sq. miles)	Est. population (Dec. 1991)	Highest Point (feet)
CONTINENTS			
1. North America	9,400,000	431,565,000	Mt. McKinley, United States 20,320
2. South America	6,900,000	302,892,000	Cerro Aconcagua, Argentina 22,834
3. Europe	3,800,000	716,240,000	Mt. Elbrus, Russia 18,510
4. Asia	17,300,000	3,224,912,000	Mt. Everest, China, Nepal 29,028
5. Africa	11,700,000	664,913,000	Mt. Kilimanjaro, Tanzania 19,340
6. Australia	2,966,153	17,340,000	Mt. Kosciusko, N. South Wales 7,310
7. Antarctica	5,400,000		Vinson Massif 16,066
ISLAND GROUPS			
8. Oceania*	333,847	9,569,000	Mt. Wilhelm, Papua New Guinea 14,793
ENTIRE WORLD			
	57,800,000	5,367,431,000	

*includes Indian, Pacific and Atlantic Oceans

Sixth Grade Curriculum

Sources for items followed by a number in parentheses may be found at the back of the book in the list of suppliers.

Religion—New Testament (Mark and Luke); *Baltimore Catechism No. 2* (21); *History through the Saints,* by Wyatt and Candy Kmen (11)

In addition to the study of doctrine, there should be readings that inspire and stir the heart. Attentive reading of the Gospels will supply this need. It will also encourage familiarity with the New Testament, the heart of our written heritage of faith.

St. Mark's Gospel will be discussed with the child. Questions for each chapter are included at the end of this section. I recommend doing Mark's Gospel first and then St. Luke. Both for the sake of variety and because it is good in itself, have the child write a short synopsis of every chapter in the Gospel of St. Luke. Have him work on producing an account that is accurate, interesting, unified and coherent. With both Gospels include some oral reading of the text, and concentrate on smoothness and appropriateness of expression.

This *Catechism,* the *No. 2,* is the next level of the expression of the doctrine of the Church. It is the same material but formulated in a slightly more complex manner than in the previous text. Use the last third of the year for the first section of the *Catechism.* If there is an interest on the child's part for a more in-depth understanding of the chapters, use *The Baltimore Catechism Explained,* by Fr. Thomas L. Kincaid (53). *History through the Saints* adds specific information about the early Church to this study.

Mathematics—*Math 76* (Saxon) (48)

Mathematics is important for further learning because it is a kind of paradigm of knowledge and truth. It is also important in the practical needs of life. In general at this stage, we aim for facility in computation and the understanding of principles and proofs that is appropriate at this level of education. Use the text five days a week, following the internal order.

Grammar and Composition—*Voyages in English 6* (42) or *Easy Grammar*, Level 1 (45); *The Complete Book of Diagrams*, by Mary Daly (40); *The Great Editing Adventure*, vol. 2 (16); or *Editor in Chief*, book A (45); *The Harp and Laurel Wreath: Poetry and Dictation for the Classical Curriculum*, edited by Laura Berquist (25)

The Voyages in English text is a very good, thorough treatment of English grammar. The text contains both writing and grammar exercises, but the grammar itself will take the full year to go through carefully. Since there will be written assignments in both religion and history, it is not necessary to use the writing portion of the text. *Easy Grammar* is also a good text. It is easier to use than *Voyages 6* and has a workbook format. Whichever text you use, grammar is one subject that needs to be taught to be mastered. Go over the exercises with your student, asking him to give you reasons for his answers.

The Complete Book of Diagrams may be used as reinforcement for any grammar program. It contains wonderful, Catholic selections accurately diagramed, which may be used in a variety of ways. We study some of the sentences as examples first, then use the next group of sentences to fill in empty diagraming lines (which I provide from the already diagramed sentence in the book), and then try to diagram a number of the sentences without the empty lines. We finish up with an exercise where the child supplies and diagrams his own sentence.

The grammar of language is an important educational tool for the child over the next three years. Students can master this discipline. They see that it is possible to learn in such a way that the mind grasps the subject and is satisfied. Additionally, diagraming provides wonderful analytic practice. Attention must be paid to every part of the sentence, and a classification of each part is necessary. This is one of the skills that will lead into the next stage of the Trivium, the dialectic, where clearsighted analysis must be made of the parts of arguments.

The primary focus of composition this year is history, where the student will write a paper on each of the ancient civilizations he studies. These compositions give the student an opportunity to collate information from numerous sources, thus employing his powers of analysis, as well as memory and observation. In addition to these larger assignments, however, there should be smaller writing assignments given regularly. Break down the exercise into its steps and do one step at a time. For example, on Monday look at and discuss a work of art with your child. Tuesday have him describe the work while you sketch it (my children love to have me do this—they like my stick figures). As you draw, following his instructions, you will both realize what you remember clearly and what you do not. This process provides a subject for the writing assignment. Wednesday have the student write a simple first descriptive paragraph of the picture. Then go through the paragraph adding an adjective to each appropriate noun, making sure that there are adequate position words (e.g., the barking dog is to the right of the nervous woman) and arranging the sentences so that there is adequate variety in the way they begin (they should not all start with "there is a . . ."). Thursday have the child write a final copy. Generally speaking, the children I have worked with liked this procedure, and they learned to recognize a number of works of art.

The Great Editing Adventure and *Editor in Chief* both provide daily practice in the mechanics of writing. In each text the student is required to edit a selection, reviewing and learning grammar and punctuation as he searches for errors.

The Harp and Laurel Wreath: Poetry and Dictation for the Classical Curriculum contains numerous selections for dictation at this level. These selections may be used to provide additional practice in the mechanics of writing, as well as the opportunity to move from the spoken word to the written word, an activity that demands focused attention on the part of the student.

Spelling—*The Writing Road to Reading*, by Romalda Spalding (21); *The Month by Month Spelling Guide*, by Katherine von Duyke (29); and close attention to daily work

This is the last year we will use *The Writing Road to Reading*. The phonics rules should be well known by now, and the spelling lists familiar. *The Month by Month Spelling Guide* gives a sequential table that helps you know what to do while using *The Writing Road to Reading*. Primary attention in spelling will be to daily work, particularly in religion and history. Review the phonics rules as necessary, and use the latter parts of the spelling list.

Literature—(correlated with history) Landmark Books (21); *Books Children Love,* by Elizabeth Wilson (21); Greenleaf Press Books (22); *In Review* (7); *Catholic Author* lists (11); *Honey for a Child's Heart*, by Gladys Hunt (21); *Let The Authors Speak,* by Carolyn Hatcher (21); *A Mother's List of Books*, by Theresa Fagan (21)

It is crucial to fill the imagination of children with rich and varied images. Careful selection of poetry, literature and Scripture readings will do this and will contribute to a lifetime of thoughtful, serious, intelligent reading. I have included two lists at the end of this section that offer suggestions for literature and history selections. There is also a poetry list. Other texts can be found in the books I mention above.

As I mentioned earlier, discussing some of your child's reading with him is both rewarding and important. At the same time, each child should be able to do some reading just for fun, without any end in view other than enjoyment. This will encourage lifelong reading. Find out what kinds of books appeal to your child, and spend some time collecting more of that particular kind of book. Put them in an accessible place, and make sure there is some reading time each day. The history readings for this year are fewer than in other years, so I really encourage my children to read fictional works during this year. The book list I have included has works on it that both my children and I have found delightful.

Poetry—See list; *The Harp and Laurel Wreath: Poetry and Dictation for the Classical Curriculum*, edited by Laura Berquist (25)

Reading and memorizing beautiful and evocative English will be used to improve knowledge of rhetorical patterns as well as to contribute to a well-furnished imagination. Have your student work on a poem every day and when it has been memorized, copy it into a notebook. At the end of the year the student will have a personalized poetry anthology. The poems suggested in the Sixth Grade Resource Lists are all included in the anthology *The Harp and Laurel Wreath: Poetry and Dictation for the Classical Curriculum*.

Science—Tops *Magnetism* and *Electricity* units (21)

These units are largely a hands-on, self-teaching approach to the subjects. They encourage the child to explore and understand the principles of magnetism and electricity by the application of logical thinking skills to a restricted matter. They are relatively easy to use and allow opportunities for thoughtful analysis that is commensurate with the child's ability.

History—Books about ancient civilizations (22, 7); *The Old World and America*, by Fr. Philip Furlong (53); Answer Key to *The Old World and America* (28); *Let The Authors Speak*, by Carolyn Hatcher (21); *The ABC's of Christian Culture*, by Julia Fogassy (40)

The Old World and America is an excellent text. It is interesting and has good exercises and a Catholic perspective. This is the text I recommend using for the next three years, while studying ancient civilizations and the Middle Ages.

This course concentrates on the earliest cultures, the personalities and events in the early Egyptian, Assyrian, Babylonian and Hebrew civilizations. A short list of supplementary readings is included at the end of this section. Other texts can be found in the books I mention above.

Young children lack the experience to form judgments about political issues. In addition to being interesting in its own right, history provides for them a storehouse of data and human understanding. Learning about these peoples and nations provides the beginning of political prudence, right judgment and even philosophy. In the upcoming years particular attention will be paid to history for these reasons.

Have the child read the text and the supplementary works for each culture. As the reading for one civilization is completed, use the exercises at the end of the chapter either as reinforcement or as a test of how well the material covered is remembered and grasped. Then have the child write a paper incorporating the material about each subject from the various sources. This will encourage note-taking skills, the ability to organize information from reference materials and the application of proper word usage, punctuation and spelling to written reports.

Let the Authors Speak has numerous suggestions for additional reading material. These resources are indexed three ways: according to title, according to author and, best of all, according to time period.

The ABC's of Christian Culture may be used as a supplement to any history curriculum, or it can stand on its own. This program has outstanding history cards, color coded as to time period, with a portrait and name on the front of each card and a description of the person pictured, with dates, facts and a quote on the back. We love using these cards to test our "time-line sense". Additionally, the parent manual contains suggested writing assignments and wonderful map masters.

Geography—Map study with a historical atlas (5) or *World History Map Activities* (45)

Use the historical atlas in conjunction with your history studies, and have your child draw maps for each civilization as he studies it. Keep the maps in a binder with the papers he writes in history, and at the end of the year there will be an illustrated ancient history, which may be added to in subsequent years. Eventually your child will have a world history of his own production, an impressive achievement.

If you prefer a workbook, *World History Map Activities* is easy to use and has clear directions and many activities.

Latin—*Latina Christiana*, Book II, by Cheryl Lowe (34) or *Our Roman Roots*, by James Leek (40)

Latina Christiana, Book II, builds on the vocabulary and paradigm knowledge presented in the previous book. The children continue to practice the paradigms and do simple translations. This is an excellent text, but it moves quickly. To allow the children to make the information habitual, not just store it in the short-term memory, one might stretch out work on the book to last for two years and plan to review it in seventh grade.

Our Roman Roots would be an excellent text for those just starting their Latin study.

Art—*Kid's Calligraphy Funstation* (45); How to Draw . . . books (45); art books from the library, crafts

Calligraphy is an excellent skill for children to acquire. Practice in letter formation improves fine motor skills, so children who need work in this area benefit from exposure to calligraphy. Further, this skill draws children's attention to the importance of line and form in the visually beautiful.

The How to Draw . . . series of books, which includes *How to Draw Cats, How to Draw Buildings* and *How to Draw Animals*, takes the student step by step through the stages of drawing particular objects. The technique used builds upon the skills gained from *The Drawing Textbook*, which we have used in earlier years.

Music—Ballet music and videos, Gilbert and Sullivan music and videos, other favorites (39)

Children enjoy listening to familiar music in context. Ballets and operettas are more enjoyable when the music is known and the action of the story clear. I have included a few possibilities for this kind of music appreciation at the end of this section as well as some of our own favorites for listening enjoyment.

Sample Schedule for Sixth Grade				
MON.	TUES.	WED.	THURS.	FRI.
Math	Math	Math	Math	Math
English	English	English	English	Music
Religion	Religion	Religion	Religion	
Latin	Latin	Latin	Science	
History	Art	Geography	Latin	

There is now available a day-by-day breakdown of the courses listed for sixth grade (36).

Grade Six Resource Lists

Religion Study Guide— Questions for St. Mark's Gospel

Chapter 1

1. In the first fifteen verses, does it seem that the teaching of John and Jesus is the same? In what way is it the same, and in what way (if anything) is it different?
2. In verse 38, Jesus says He has come to preach. Where else in this chapter is there evidence that His teaching was more important to Him than His miracles?

Chapter 2

1. Answer the question in verse 9, and give a reason for your answer.
2. Answer the question in verse 7.
3. Find three names or descriptive terms that Jesus uses for Himself.

Chapter 3

1. In verse 27, what does the strong man represent? What does his house represent?
2. For what work did Jesus select the Twelve? What powers did He give them? How would these powers help them in their work?

Chapter 4

1. In verse 11, to whom do you think our Lord refers with the words "those outside"? Notice that the parable and its explanation are both preserved in Holy Scripture for all to read.

Chapter 5

1. Do you think the people in verses 14–17 were more afraid of Jesus than they had been of the unclean spirit? What might they be afraid of (verse 16)?
2. What does St. Mark say about why Jesus felt the touch of the woman in verses 27–30 as distinct from the general press of the crowd? Why did He ask the question He did?

3. After what earlier miracles were people charged to tell no one of it, as in verse 43? (Look in chapters 1 and 3.)

CHAPTER 6

1. What was the message of the Twelve when Jesus sent them out two by two? Was it a new message, or had it been previously announced by another?
2. In verse 34, Mark says Jesus began to teach the crowd, but He had come to that desert place for another reason. What was it?

CHAPTER 7

1. What does our Lord mean in verse 15 by the things that enter a man from the outside? What would His listeners first think of as "things that enter from outside" when discussing the laws of cleanliness?
2. In verse 27, who are the "children"?
3. How is the healing in verses 28–30 like that in 5:28–34? How is it unlike it?
4. How is the manner of healing in verses 31–36 different from that in 5:38–43? How is it alike?

CHAPTER 8

1. Can you tell when or where the bread is multiplied? (After____, but before ____.)
2. Think of what leaven does to bread; what leaven is like before and after it is put in bread. Leaven is useful, indeed necessary, in making bread. It also smells good. In these ways it is unlike the Pharisees and Herod. How might it be like these dangers?
3. In verses 26 and 30, who is told not to speak, and what is he told not to speak about? Do you think that this silence is to be temporary or permanent? Why do you think so?
4. In verse 35, does "gospel" refer to "a certain book of Holy Scripture" or "this good news"? How can you tell?

CHAPTER 9

1. Refer to question 2 for chapter 1, above. Then, in the Transfiguration account, find another piece of evidence that Jesus' teaching was more important than His miracles.

2. Jesus again tells someone not to tell others, but now He also says when he can tell. Whom does He tell, and when is the silence to end?

3. In the cure of the possessed boy, our Lord asks for something from the father. Can you see things in the father's response that must have pleased Jesus?

4. The disciples could not cast out this unclean spirit. What other evidence is there that this was a particularly powerful or difficult spirit to cast out?

5. In verse 31, the disciples are said to be "afraid". What can this mean?

CHAPTER 10

1. Before, it was the sick who sought to be touched by Jesus. Why do these people want Jesus to touch their children? Is touching a physical or spiritual act here?

2. Why are the ten angry at James and John? Explain how Jesus turns away their anger.

CHAPTER 11

1. Why did our Lord throw out the money changers?

2. What happened to the fig tree that had no fruit? Of what might this be a sign?

3. Our Lord says that we should forgive when we start to pray. What reason does He give?

CHAPTER 12

1. About whom was Jesus speaking in the parable of the vineyard (verse 12)? Why?

2. What is Jesus' answer to those who wish to catch Him in His words (verse 13)?

3. How did the Sadducees err in their question about whom the woman with the seven husbands would be married to in heaven?

4. In what way did the poor widow put in more money than all the others?

CHAPTER 13

1. Why will we be hated by all men (verse 13)?
2. What are the various things our Lord warns us about in this chapter?

CHAPTER 14

1. Why was what the woman with the ointment did acceptable? Why did those who grumbled do so?
2. Who betrays Jesus, and what does he receive for this act? What does our Lord say about him?
3. Who goes with Jesus to Gethsemane? What does He do there? What do they do?
4. Did Peter betray Christ? Is he like Judas in this? How does he differ from Judas?
5. What did Jesus say that the high priest objected to? How did those around our Lord act once judgment was pronounced?

CHAPTER 15

1. Why had the chief priests delivered up Jesus? Does Pilate know this? Why does he have Jesus crucified?
2. Why does the centurion who is present at the Crucifixion say, "Indeed this man was the Son of God"?

CHAPTER 16

1. Where is Peter singled out from the other disciples? Why do you think that might be?
2. Did those who heard Jesus was alive believe it? What did Jesus say to them when He appeared?
3. What did Jesus tell the disciples to do?

LITERATURE LIST

Most of these are in print, and they are all good. See *Honey for a Child's Heart*, by Gladys Hunt (21), and *A Mother's List of Books*, by Theresa Fagan (21), for more titles.

Born Free	Joy Adamson
The Wolves of Willoughby Chase	Joan Aiken
Black Hearts in Battersea	Joan Aiken
Nightbirds on Nantucket	Joan Aiken
The Secret Cave	Claire Huchet Bishop
Caddie Woodlawn	Carol Ryrie Brink
Daniel Boone	James Daugherty
The Door in the Wall	Marguerite de Angeli
The Twenty-One Balloons	William Pène Dubois
The Matchlock Gun	W. D. Edwards
The Melendy Family	Elizabeth Enright
Thimble Summer	Elizabeth Enright
The Moffats	Eleanor Estes
The Book of Valour	Faith and Freedom 7 Reading Book
Understood Betsy	Dorothy Canfield Fisher
Blue Willow	Doris Gates
My Side of the Mountain	Jean George
Brighty of the Grand Canyon	Marguerite Henry
Rip Van Winkle	Washington Irving
Smokey	Will James
Captains Courageous	Rudyard Kipling
Big Red	Jim Kjelgaard
Snow Treasure	Marie McSwigan
The Railway Children	E. Nesbit
The House of Arden	E. Nesbit
The Phoenix and the Carpet	E. Nesbit
Five Children and It	E. Nesbit
The Treasure Seekers	E. Nesbit
The New Treasure Seekers	E. Nesbit
Mrs. Frisby and the Rats of NIMH	Robert C. O'Brian
The Island of the Blue Dolphins	Scott O'Dell
Swallows and Amazons	Arthur Ransome

Red Hugh: Prince of Donegal	Robert T. Reilly
The Singing Tree	Kate Seredy
The Good Master	Kate Seredy
Miracles on Maple Hill	Virginia Sorenson
The Mitchells: Five for Victory	Hilda van Stockum
Canadian Summer	Hilda van Stockum
Friendly Gables	Hilda van Stockum
All-of-a-Kind Family	Sydney Taylor
The Crystal Snowstorm	Meriol Trevor
Follow the Phoenix	Meriol Trevor
Flint's Island	Leonard Wibberley
Rebecca of Sunnybrook Farm	Kate Douglas Wiggin
The Children Who Stayed Alone	Bonnie Worline

HISTORY READING LIST— ANCIENT CIVILIZATIONS

Used as supplements to *The Old World and America*, by Fr. Philip Furlong (part 1).

An "L" after the author's name indicates that the library or used-book sources will be your best bet for securing this title; "IP" indicates that the book is currently in print; "*" indicates an especially enjoyable book. If a book belongs to an identifiable series, I will indicate that by using one of the following abbreviations: VB—Vision Book (Catholic), AMB—American Background Book (Catholic), LKB—Landmark Book (Christian orientation), SB—Signature Book, NSB—North Star Book.

Usborne Books:
—*World History Dates*
—*Warriors and Seafarers*
—*Book of Long Ago—Pharaohs and Pyramids*

The 22 Letters	Clive King	L*
Pyramid	David Macaulay	L*
The Story of the Amulet	E. Nesbit	IP*
The Pharaohs of Ancient Egypt	Elizabeth Payne	IP, LKB*
The World of the Pharaohs	Hans Baumann	L

Piankhy, the Great	E. Harper Johnson	L
Egyptian Adventures	Olivia Coolidge	L*
The Book of History	Olive Beaupre Miller and	
	Harry Neal Baum	L*
Mara, Daughter of the Nile	Eloise Jarvis McGraw	IP
The Golden Goblet	Eloise Jarvis McGraw	IP
The Hittite Warrior	Joanne S. Williamson	IP

See Greenleaf Press for More Titles (22).

POETRY LIST

"The Charge of the Light Brigade"	Alfred Lord Tennyson
"Opportunity"	Edward Sill
"Father William"	Robert Southey
"The Lake Isle of Innisfree"	William Butler Yeats
"The Old Woman of the Roads"	Padraic Colum
"Be Strong"	Maltbie D. Babcock
"The Night Has a Thousand Eyes"	Francis W. Bourdillon
"The Violet"	Jane Taylor
"The Builders"	Henry Wadsworth Longfellow
"Jabberwocky"	Lewis Carroll
"The Children's Hour"	Henry Wadsworth Longfellow

MUSIC LIST

TCHAIKOVSKY
—*The Nutcracker* (music and video)
—*Sleeping Beauty* (music and video)

MOZART
—The Magic Flute
—The Clarinet Quintet

VAUGHN WILLIAMS
—English Folksongs
—Dives and Lazarus
—Five Mystical Songs

COPLAND
—American Folksongs
—Appalachian Spring

GILBERT AND SULLIVAN
—*The Pirates of Penzance* (music and video)
—*The Mikado* (music and video)

The Dialectical Stage

THE NEXT STAGE of the Trivium begins sometime around seventh grade. There is a certain overlap of levels, and one continues to gather materials for the dialectical stage even after it has begun. Nevertheless, there is a change in emphasis from the grammar of subjects, employing observation and memory, to the dialectic of subjects, which uses the discursive reason.

This difference is seen in the importance *analysis* has in the curriculum. In language grammar the children will continue to diagram sentences, which is an analytic exercise. They will also learn about the nature of language by using a text that compares Latin and English grammar.

In history and religion they will begin to concentrate on seeing the reasons for actions and positions. First they must see clearly what is being said, and then why. There will be reasonable arguments given for opposing positions and then a resolution proposed based on ethical and dogmatic principles. This will be done both in writing and in conversation.

Literature will concern itself with the same method. Careful reading of a text and the presentation of the position will be the focus of the courses. Because men learn by imitation, the careful study of others' arguments will provide examples of what the student will learn to do. The study of poetry will center on dramatic performances, particularly plays, wherein an argument is stated in dramatic form.

Mathematics moves to the more advanced forms, algebra and geometry. In these studies the nature of the subject matter, where the mind moves from premise to premise, is seen clearly. In my curriculum I try not to make this particular change abruptly or too soon. I have found a slower, more thorough approach is better.

Science and geography provide other material for the practice of the method of dialectic. Geography is often incorporated in historical discussions, contributing to the understanding of why someone acted as he did.

Religion is moving toward dogmatic theology, with the kind of treatment of Scripture that was begun last year as a beginning step.

All of these subjects are intended to provide an opportunity for analysis, for learning how to understand and produce an argument. It is a way of studying logic, not as one will study it in Aristotle's *Prior* and *Posterior Analytics,* but in a way that prepares the student for that study.

In "The Lost Tools of Learning", Miss Sayers says of this stage, "All events are food for such an appetite. An umpire's decision; the degree to which one may transgress the spirit of a regulation without being trapped by the letter: on such questions as these, children are born casuists, and their natural propensity only needs to be developed and trained—and, especially, be brought into intelligible relationship with events in the grown-up world."

Seventh Grade Curriculum

Sources for items followed by a number in parentheses may be found at the back of the book in the list of suppliers.

Religion—Lives of the saints; New Testament (The Acts of the Apostles); *The Story of the Church*, by Fr. George Johnson, Fr. Jerome Hannan and Sr. M. Dominica (53); *The Bronze Bow*, by Elizabeth George Speare (45); *Fabiola*, by Cardinal Wiseman (42)

In the first six weeks, read various lives of the saints. Concentrate on the saints of the early Church. Choose a saint each week from the list provided at the end of this section. Have your child read about the saint and prepare an oral report. The saints on the list are contemporaneous with the period being studied in history in the latter part of the year.

The next eighteen weeks will be devoted to a detailed study of the Acts of the Apostles. Read and discuss the text every week. I have included a list of discussion questions at the end of this section. *The Bronze Bow* and *Fabiola* will help give a sense of the period in which Acts takes place.

During the last twelve weeks, study early Church history from the beginning of the Church through A.D. 300. This will bring secular history and Church history together as one whole.

Mathematics—*Math 87* (Saxon) (48)

This text is a bridge between basic arithmetic and algebra. Have the child do a lesson in the text every day, and monitor his progress by use of the tests that come with the homeschool packet. The student will develop a certain facility in computation and understanding of principles and proofs.

Grammar and Composition—*Voyages in English* 7 (42); or *Basic Language Principles through Latin Background*, by Ruth M. Wilson (21); or *Easy Grammar Plus* (45); *The Complete Book of Diagrams*, by Mary

Daly (40); *Editor in Chief*, Books B and C (45); *The Harp and Laurel Wreath: Poetry and Dictation for the Classical Curriculum*, edited by Laura Berquist (25)

As I have said before, grammar is important both as a tool for understanding language itself and for mastering other languages. It is also important because this is an area that a seventh grader can comprehend. It is proportioned to the capacity of the student in a way that most subjects are not at this age. A child must study and have a disciplined mind in order to accomplish this, but it can be done. Achieving this at this time of life, in an area where it can truly be done, shows the child what intellectual mastery is and what a satisfaction it is.

Editor in Chief is another series in which children are asked to edit punctuation and grammar. This series includes critical thinking skills as well, which makes it well suited to the student in the dialectical stage. These selections may be used for dictation exercises as well as practice in mechanics. *The Harp and Laurel Wreath: Poetry and Dictation for the Classical Curriculum* also contains selections for dictation at this level.

Reference Skills—*Library Skills*, Books I and II (45)

Library Skills is a practical supplement that teaches the proper use of reference materials by giving children an opportunity to use them. It provides worksheets of items about which the student needs to look up information. Figuring out where to find the necessary information is the key to success.

Spelling and Vocabulary—*Wordly Wise* 4 (19)

Follow the internal order of the text, doing one lesson each week. Use the vocabulary words for a spelling list, and give tests once a week. This text has a useful vocabulary, and the information about word origins and relationships fits with the study of the nature of language.

Literature (correlated with history)—*Books Children Love*, by Elizabeth Wilson (21); Greenleaf Press Books (22); *In Review* (7); *Catholic*

Authors, 4-Sight edition, by the Brothers of Mary (11); *Honey for a Child's Heart,* by Gladys Hunt (21); *Let the Authors Speak,* by Carolyn Hatcher (45); *A Mother's List of Books,* by Theresa Fagan (21)

In this year literature and history are virtually identical. The history list provides ample reading material, and other texts can be found in the books I mention above. The books studied will help the student understand the beginnings of Western civilization. This understanding is important for political prudence and right judgment. History is interesting in itself, but it also provides vicarious experience about events and people.

Poetry—Shakespeare (6); *Tales from Shakespeare,* by Charles and Mary Lamb (21); *Shakespeare in the Classroom,* by Albert Cullum (21); *The Harp and Laurel Wreath: Poetry and Dictation for the Classical Curriculum,* edited by Laura Berquist (25)

Memorizing beautiful and evocative passages from Shakespeare will improve the child's knowledge of rhetorical patterns, encourage imitation and give the children familiarity with one of the greatest English authors. Use *Shakespeare in the Classroom* as a guide, or simply do some editing of Shakespeare yourself, and whole plays or portions of plays may be attempted. The children enjoy dramatization and using beautiful words. These activities will give them an opportunity to do so and lead them to a lifelong love of Shakespeare.

   One way to introduce Shakespeare is to pick a selection from the list at the end of this section. Have the child read the play in *Tales from Shakespeare,* then memorize the passages chosen and then read the play in Shakespeare. If the child is then able to see the play performed, he will have a good basis for real enjoyment of the production. The selections from Shakespeare recommended in the Seventh Grade Resource Lists are included in the anthology *The Harp and Laurel Wreath: Poetry and Dictation for the Classical Curriculum.*

Science—*Concepts And Challenges in Science* (B), by Alan Winkler, Leonard Bernstein, Martin Schachter and Stanley Wolfe (published by Globe) (43, 54, 58); Fabre books (57)

Four times a week have the student read the text and do the exercises in each chapter. Unit tests will provide a check of comprehension. This text, like the previous volume, concentrates on a basic understanding of biology and physics, chemistry and earth science. There is not a great deal of detail, but there are clear explanations of the principles.

Most of the Fabre books are out of print. I will mention some titles to look for because they are wonderful examples of natural history, the kind of thing that will lead to love for and understanding of nature. They fit very well with this stage of the Trivium because they explore why the animals act the way they do. *Our Humble Helpers*; *The Life of the Spider*; *Field, Forest and Farm: Things Interesting to Young Nature Lovers*; *The Story Book of Birds and Beasts*; and *The Insect World of J. Henri Fabre* are some of Fabre's works. These are all currently out of print.

History—Books about Ancient Greece and Rome (21, 22); *The Old World and America*, by Fr. Philip Furlong (53); *Let the Authors Speak*, by Carolyn Hatcher (21); *The ABC's of Christian Culture*, by Julia Fogassy (40)

As I mentioned before, *The Old World and America* is an excellent text. This is the text I recommend using for sixth, seventh and eighth grades because it is interesting and has good exercises and a Catholic perspective.

It is worthwhile to have the student answer the questions of the exercises completely, citing the portion of the text where the answer was found. This gives the child a chance to practice locating material in a text, which leads to attentive reading. Make sure that the answers are logical and that the reasons given for the answers make sense.

This course concentrates on the beginning of Western civilization, the personalities and events in the Greek and Roman civilizations. A list of supplementary readings is included at the end of this section. I have also included a list of significant dates the student may memorize. The child who enjoys writing narrative summaries may continue his "book of history".

Though I have included many readings on my list, not all are equally important. I have starred those that are particularly good and recommend that you start with those and read the rest as time permits. There are other texts about the same time period that can be found in *Let the Authors Speak*. *The ABC's of Christian Culture* can be used to supplement any history curriculum. The history cards, writing suggestions and map masters are especially helpful.

Geography—*World History Map Activities* (45); *World Discovery Deluxe* (56); drawing maps of the ancient world to go with the history text

World History Map Activities is a complete geography program that teaches the physical features in connection with history. This is achieved through map activities using a research and instruction sheet and a map that is to be filled in.

Much the same goal may be achieved by a homemade alternative. Have your student trace the outline of the part of the world to be studied, perhaps the country that is the subject of your history course. Make seven copies of the traced outline map. That is one week's lesson. Next week give the original traced outline map back to the student, and tell him to fill it in with the important physical and political features. Then for six consecutive weeks give him one of the copied outline maps and let him try to fill it in from memory. Each week he fills in what he can and then looks at the completed map to see what is missing. Finally, have him fill in the last copied outline map as his "test". You can cover four different areas a year with this method, and you will find that the memory improves through the year.

Something else to consider is *World Discovery Deluxe*, a very satisfactory computer geography program that seems to keep the children's interest and teaches them geographical information.

Latin—*Basic Language Principles through Latin Background*, by Ruth M. Wilson (21); or *Latina Christiana II*, by Cheryl Lowe (34); or *Our Roman Roots*, by James Leek (21)

Basic Language Principles is an outstanding book. It solidifies the child's grasp of English grammar and provides an excellent beginning in Latin. It moves slowly and carefully, with plenty of opportunity for practice. Use this, and your students will never forget the first and second declensions and the first conjugation. And most children really like it—not because of a flamboyant format (it doesn't have that) but because of intellectual satisfaction.

There are fifty lessons, so you need to start out with more than one lesson a week. That way when you get to the more challenging lessons, you will be able to do one lesson each week and still finish the text in a year.

There is now an answer key available, so even if you are not a Latin whiz you can use this text comfortably.

If you started *Latina Christiana II* last year but the student did not master it, you might have him review and continue this text. Or, if you are a first-time Latin teacher, try *Our Roman Roots*. It is delightful and easy to use.

Art—*How to Draw and Paint People*, by Angela Gair (30); What Makes a . . . series (30); or any of the previous years' suggestions

How to Draw and Paint People has been one of the best texts we have used for teaching more advanced drawing technique. It proceeds step by step, breaking down the process of drawing into manageable pieces.

After studying how to draw figures, look into the What Makes a . . . series. Discuss the various artists (Raphael, Rembrandt and Degas are included in the series) in the light of the drawing technique that has been studied.

Music—*Minimum Repertoire of Plain Chant* (40); *Music Maestro* (45); The Best of . . . series (from Amazon.com); *Understanding Music* (4)

Minimum Repertoire of Plain Chant contains the Ordinary of the Mass in Latin, as well as some of the best-known and best-loved Latin hymns of the Church. Everyone should know, and preferably be able to sing, the *Salve Regina*. There is also an audio tape of the material available.

The seventh grader is able to analyze, and he enjoys doing it. The game *Music Maestro* helps the student become familiar with the parts of the orchestra, so that he is able to identify the individual instruments in pieces he hears. The Best of . . . series contains an hour of the best music from various composers. After playing *Music Maestro*, listen to one of the CDs and try to identify the instruments being played. It's fun!

Understanding Music is published by Usborne. It discusses the various styles or types of music. Read through the sections with your student, and, as you finish each section, listen to one of the Sketches series that exemplifies music of that type. Eventually, try listening to some unfamiliar pieces of music and try to classify them.

Sample Schedule for Seventh Grade				
MON.	TUES.	WED.	THURS.	FRI.
Math	Math	Math	Math	Math
English	English	English	English	
Science	Science	Science	Science	
Religion	Religion	Religion	Religion	
History	History	History	History	
Latin	Latin	Latin	Latin	
	Music		Art	

There is now available a day-by-day breakdown of the courses listed for seventh grade (36).

Grade Seven Resource Lists

Religion Study Guide—
Questions for The Acts of the Apostles

Chapter 1

1. What is the full title of Acts?
2. The book begins right after an important event, or series of events. What is it? or What are they?
3. Jesus gave the apostles a final instruction. What did He say? And what happened next?
4. To what city do the apostles go after the Ascension?
5. How was Matthias chosen to be an apostle? Whose place did he take?
6. Why does Peter conduct the election?

Chapter 2

1. Which came first, Pentecost or the Ascension?
2. Describe the events of the coming of the Holy Spirit. They were together in one place and . . .(1, 2, 3, 4)
3. People heard about this amazing event and gathered together. What surprised them?
4. Who first said, "And it shall come to pass in the last days (saith the Lord), I will pour out my Spirit upon all flesh . . ."? What was he talking about?
5. Who first said, "Thou [God] wilt not leave my soul in hell, nor suffer thy Holy One to see corruption. . . ."?
6. To whom did he refer?
7. Why did Peter tell the people that Joel and David were talking about Christ?
8. What did Peter tell the Jews they should do?
9. How many were converted that day?
10. What signs of charity and divine favor attended the first Christian community?

CHAPTER 3

1. Speaking in tongues preceded Peter's great sermon in chapter 2. Here, another miracle precedes Peter's second great sermon. What is it?
2. How does Peter heal a man? What does Peter say about how the man was healed?
3. In this sermon what does Peter exhort the people to do?

CHAPTER 4

1. How many people had now come to believe in our Lord?
2. Who apprehends Peter and John? What does Peter say that makes them angry?
3. What did the council tell the apostles to do? Did Peter and John agree to this?
4. When Peter and John went back to their own company, what happened?

CHAPTER 5

1. What was the sin of Ananias and Sapphira?
2. Why were the apostles apprehended the second time?
3. Did they stay in prison?
4. Why did Peter disobey the order of the council not to preach the Name of Jesus?
5. Who urged moderation on the council, and what was he?
6. What punishment did the apostles receive?

CHAPTER 6

1. For what service were Stephen and six others selected?
2. With what ceremony were they selected?
3. In what ways was Stephen outstanding in the Christian community?
4. Of what did the false witnesses accuse him?
5. What indicates that Stephen's speech in response was inspired by the Holy Spirit?

CHAPTER 7

1. Stephen told the council, "As your fathers did, so do you." What did their fathers do?

2. And what did the Jewish leaders of his day do?
3. What was Stephen's last act?
4. Why do you think the Roman government was not involved in this first persecution of the Church?

CHAPTER 8

1. What happened immediately after the martyrdom of Stephen?
2. Who preached the good news of Christ to the Samaritans?
3. How did they receive it?
4. What did Peter and John add to the baptisms in Samaria?
5. What was Simon's sin?
6. Why did Philip leave Samaria?
7. What was God's plan for him on the road to Gaza?

CHAPTER 9

1. Saul had a purpose in going to Damascus. What was it?
2. The Lord had a purpose for Saul. What does He tell Ananias that Saul has been chosen to do?
3. What did Saul do after he regained his sight?
4. Where did Saul begin to preach?
5. Why did he leave? How?
6. Why were the disciples afraid of Saul in Jerusalem?
7. What miracle did Peter work at Lydda?
8. Who was Tabitha?
9. What did Peter do for her?

CHAPTER 10

1. What was Cornelius' job?
2. In what two acts did he show his piety?
3. What did the voice tell Peter after his vision of the animals?
4. Peter interpreted this to mean that he could do something further (not connected with eating) that the Jews have not been permitted to do. What?
5. What did those who came with Peter see that showed them that the Holy Spirit had indeed come upon the gentiles there?
6. What does "those of the circumcision" mean?

CHAPTER 11

1. What saying of Jesus does Peter recall that he can now understand as supporting his baptism of gentiles?
2. Where next was the gospel preached to non-Jews? Who preached there?
3. What prophecy was made there?

CHAPTER 12

1. How did Herod persecute the Church at this time?
2. What did the angel who came to the prison do for Peter?
3. What did he tell Peter to do himself?
4. Why was Herod struck dead?

CHAPTER 13

1. What were the Christians in the Church at Antioch doing when the Holy Spirit spoke, telling them to set apart Paul and Barnabas?
2. What did Saul do to the sorcerer attached to the pro-consul on Cyprus?
3. What effect did this have on the pro-consul?
4. In both Cyprus and Pisidia Antioch, where was the first place Saul and Barnabas went to preach?
5. In Paul's speech at Pisidia Antioch, how did he say the inhabitants of Jerusalem fulfilled the prophecies?
6. How did Paul say God has fulfilled the promise made to their fathers?
7. What did Paul say he would do when the Jews rejected the word he preached?

CHAPTER 14

1. What did the people in Lystra think of Paul and Barnabas when Paul cured the man lame from his birth?
2. In each of the cities in this chapter, why did they have to leave?

CHAPTER 15

1. What question did Paul and Barnabas go to Jerusalem to discuss?
2. Who said, "Why then do you now try to test God by putting on the neck of the disciples a yoke which neither our fathers nor we have been able to bear?"

3. Which of the following restrictions did the council decide were still necessary?
    a. circumcision
    b. abstaining from blood
    c. not marrying foreigners
    d. abstaining from pork
    e. abstaining from things offered to idols
    f. ritual hand washing
    g. abstaining from anything strangled
    h. avoiding immorality

CHAPTER 16

1. Why did Paul circumcise Timothy?
2. In what two ways did the churches improve?
3. How did Paul decide what cities to travel to?
4. Who insisted that Paul stay in her house in Macedonia?
5. Why did the masters of the possessed girl bring Paul and Silas before the magistrates?
6. What did they accuse Paul and Silas of?
7. How were they freed from their imprisonment?
8. Why did the guard want to kill himself?
9. What did Paul want to be done before he would leave the prison?

CHAPTER 17

1. Paul and his companions went to Thessalonica. What did they do there? And for how long?
2. What happened and why?
3. Next Paul went to Beroea. How did the Jews there receive him?
4. What happened at Beroea? Where did Paul go next?
5. Paul preached to the Athenians. What idea did he use to begin telling them about Jesus? Why did he use this instead of the Law and the Prophets of the Old Testament?

CHAPTER 18

1. Was Paul successful with the Jews at Corinth?
2. What did Jesus tell Paul he should do?
3. Why did the Jews bring Paul before Gallio? What did Gallio say?
4. What did Apollos do for the Church?

CHAPTER 19

1. Had the members of the Church in Ephesus been baptized?
2. Paul found that, after three months, certain of those in the synagogue were hardened, speaking evil of the way of the Lord. What did he do?
3. Could anyone cure using the way of the Lord?
4. Why was the man Demetrius upset about the way of the Lord? What did he do?
5. How did the town clerk quiet the tumult?

CHAPTER 20

1. Can you see, in verse 4, a sign of the catholicity of the Catholic Church?
2. What miracle did Paul do at Troas?
3. What are the important points of Paul's discourse?

CHAPTER 21

1. Did Paul know what awaited him at Jerusalem?
2. What advice did those in Jerusalem give him?
3. Did this appease those who were angry with Paul?
4. What did those men intend to do to Paul? Why didn't they do it?

CHAPTER 22

1. Paul spoke to the multitude, and they listened until what point? Why did this make them so angry?
2. The centurion was going to scourge and torture Paul. Why didn't he do it?

CHAPTER 23

1. What device did Paul use to deflect interest from himself?
2. How did Paul escape from the plot of the Jews?
3. Where was Paul sent?
4. Did the governor hear Paul's case immediately?

CHAPTER 24

1. Who came to accuse Paul? Of what did they accuse him?
2. What was his defense?

3. What did Felix do?
4. Why do you think Felix was terrified by the things Paul preached?

Chapter 25

1. Festus asked Paul if he would go to Jerusalem to be judged. Paul objected. What are his grounds?
2. What did Paul do then?
3. Who came and wished to hear Paul?

Chapter 26

1. What kind of Jew was Paul?
2. What did King Agrippa think of Paul's account?

Chapter 27

1. Did Paul go alone to Rome?
2. Did Paul think it advisable to sail from Crete? Was he right? How did he know?
3. How many people were in the ship? How many were saved?

Chapter 28

1. Why did the Melitians think Paul was a god?
2. Paul went to Rome and called together the local leaders of the Jews. He explained why he was there. He told them also of Jesus. Did they believe?
3. What did Paul say of them?

List of Saints and Early Christian Writers

St. Agnes
St. Lucy
St. Lawrence
St. Cyprian of Carthage
St. Justin
St. Irenaeus
(Origen)

St. John Chrysostom
St. Ambrose
St. Jerome
St. Augustine of Hippo
St. Leo the Great
St. Athanasius
(Tertullian)

POETRY LIST—SHAKESPEARE

The Tempest   Act V, i, 34–58
  "This rough magic I here abjure. . . ."
Hamlet   Act I, iii, 55–81
  "This above all: To thine own self be true."
Hamlet   Act I, iii, 55–81
  "Yet here, Laertes! Abroad, abroad, for shame. . . ."
Julius Caesar   Act III, ii, 76–109
  "Friends, Romans, countrymen. . . ."
Henry V   Act IV, iii, 17–67
  "This day is called the feast of Crispian. . . ."
Henry V   Act IV, i, 229–83
  "Upon the King! Let us our lives, our souls,
  Our debts, our careful wives,
  Our children, and our sins lay on the King!"

LIST OF HISTORY DATES

B.C.   c. 1200   Trojan War.
       c. 1050   King David.
        c. 753   Romulus and Remus found Rome.
        c. 630   Lycurgus gives laws to Sparta.
           586   Nebuchadnezzar's army sacks Jerusalem.
           515   Temple is rededicated.
           509   Roman Republic begins with expulsion of Tarquin kings.
           490   Darius is defeated at the Battle of Marathon.
           479   Spartan defense of Thermopylae; Xerxes is defeated at Salamis (sea) and Plataea (land).
           438   The Parthenon is completed under Pericles' leadership.
           404   Peloponnesian War ends with Sparta defeating Athens.
           401   Xenophon's *Anabasis*—"March of the Ten Thousand".
           399   Execution of Socrates.
           390   Gauls sack Rome.
           336   Alexander becomes King of Macedonia.
        c. 300   Euclid's *Elements* (Geometry) is written.
           202   Scipio defeats Hannibal.

160 Rise of the Maccabees.
133 Tiberius Gracchus is killed in Senate.
60 Jerusalem is captured by Pompey.
44 Julius Caesar becomes dictator of Rome.
31 Octavius defeats Antony and Cleopatra at Actium.
27 Augustus Caesar (formerly Octavius) becomes first citizen.

A.D.
29 Crucifixion of our Lord (reformed calendar).
123 Hadrian's wall is completed in Britain.
313 Constantine issues Edict of Milan.
395 Roman Empire is divided.
430 Augustine, bishop of Hippo, dies.
476 End of the Roman Empire in the West.

History Reading List

An "L" after the author's name indicates that the library or used-book sources will be your best bet for securing this title; "IP" indicates that the book is currently in print; "*" indicates an especially enjoyable book. If a book belongs to an identifiable series, I will indicate that by using one of the following abbreviations: VB—Vision Book (Catholic), AMB—American Background Book (Catholic), LKB—Landmark Book (Christian orientation), SB—Signature Book, NSB—North Star Book.

Ancient Greek History

Used as supplements to *The Old World and America,* by Fr. Philip Furlong (part 2) (pp. 25–61 in the 1984 edition published by TAN Books).

Greek Myths	Ingrid and Edgar D'Aulaire	IP*
The Greek Army	Peter Connolly	IP
The Greeks	(Usborne)	IP
Empires and Barbarians	(Usborne)	IP
Lives from Plutarch: The Modern American Edition of Twelve	Edited by John McFarland	L*
Children's Homer	Padraic Colum	IP*
The Histories	Herodotus	IP*

—translated by Aubrey de Selincourt, Penguin Classics Edition, 1996

Read the following parts:
    Marathon: bk. 6, pp. 355–64
    Thermopylae: bk. 7, pp. 430–50
    Salamis: bk. 8, pp. 451–81
    Plataea: pp. 491–98, 500–503, 507–26

Temple on a Hill	Ann Rockwell	L*
Men of Athens	Olivia Coolidge	L*
Theras and His Town	Caroline Snedeker	L*
The White Isle	Caroline Snedeker	L
The Spartan	Caroline Snedeker	L
The Exploits of Xenophon	Geoffrey Household	IP*
The Adventures Of Odysseus	Andrew Lang	L
The Trojan War	Olivia Coolidge	IP*
Golden Days of Greece	Olivia Coolidge	IP*
Greek Myths	Olivia Coolidge	IP
A Wonder Book	Nathaniel Hawthorne	IP*
The Tale of Troy	Roger Lancelyn Green	IP*
The Golden Fleece	Padraic Colum	IP*
Tales of the Greek Heroes	Roger Lancelyn Green	IP*
Dolphin Rider	Bernard Evslin	L
The Golden God	Doris Gates	IP
The Greek Gods	Bernard Evslin, Dorothy Evslin and Ned Hoopes	IP
Heroes and Monsters of Greek Myth	Bernard Evslin, Dorothy Evslin and Ned Hoopes	IP
The Story of the Greeks	H. A. Guerber	L
Children of the Dawn	Elsie Finnimore Buckley	L*
The Heroes	Charles Kingsley	L
The Adventures of Ulysses	Gerald Gottlieb	IP, LKB
Fifteen Decisive Battles of the World (Marathon)	Edward Creasy	IP*
The Walls of Windy Troy	Marjorie Braymen	L
How We Learned the Earth Was Round	Patricia Lauber	IP
Black Ships before Troy	Rosemary Sutcliff	IP*
Greek and Roman Plays	Albert Cullum	IP*
Archimedes and the Door of Science	Jeanne Bendick	IP*

Ancient Roman History

Used to supplement *The Old World and America,* by Fr. Philip Furlong (chapters 3–4) (pp. 63–118 in the 1984 edition published by TAN Books).

City	David Macaulay	IP*
"Horatius" from *The Lays of Ancient Rome*	Thomas Lord Macaulay	L*
The Roman Army	Peter Connolly	L
The Romans	(Usborne)	IP
Empires and Barbarians	(Usborne)	IP
Eagle of the Ninth	Rosemary Sutcliff	IP*
The Silver Branch	Rosemary Sutcliff	IP*
The Lantern Bearers	Rosemary Sutcliff	IP*
A Triumph for Flavius	Caroline Snedeker	L*
Lives from Plutarch: The Modern American Edition of Twelve	Edited by John McFarland	L*
The Truce of the Games	Rosemary Rutcliff	L
Augustus Caesar's World	Genevieve Foster	IP
Roman People	Olivia Coolidge	L*
Caesar's Gallic Wars	Olivia Coolidge	IP*
Lives of Famous Romans	Olivia Coolidge	IP*
The Aeneid for Boys and Girls	A. J. Church	L*
Men of Rome	Olivia Coolidge	L*
Julius Caesar	John Gunther	L, LKB
St. Helena and the True Cross	Louis de Wohl	L, VB*
Blood Feud	Rosemary Sutcliff	L
Christ the King, Lord of History (chapter 6)	Ann Carroll	IP*
Famous Battles by Land and Sea (chapter 3)	Edited by Thomas Bailey Aldrich	L
Living in Roman Times	Jane Chisolm	L
Roman Engineers	L. A. and J. A. Hamey	IP*
The Roman Army	John Wilkes	IP
The Young Carthaginian	G. A. Henty	L
Life in Ancient Rome	Pierre Miquel	L
The Romans and Their Empire	Trevor Cairns	IP

Augustus Caesar	Monroe Stearns	IP*
Julius Caesar	Manuel Komruff	L
Legions of the Eagle	Henry Treece	L*
Rome and Romans	(Usborne)	IP*
Ancient Rome (Eye Witness Books)	Simon James	IP
Two Thousand Years Ago	A. J. Church	L*
The Ides of April	Mary Ray	IP

The Bronze Bow   Elizabeth George Speare

Eighth Grade Curriculum

Sources for items followed by a number in parentheses may be found at the back of the book in the list of suppliers.

Religion—Faith and Life 8th grade text *(Our Life in the Church)* with activity book (25); *Baltimore Catechism No. 2* (21); *The Case for Christianity,* by C. S. Lewis (21)

The Faith and Life catechism studies the doctrine of the Church on the sacraments in general and on Confirmation in particular. I recommend reading it with the corresponding chapters in the *Baltimore Catechism No. 2,* both because the questions and answers in the *Baltimore Catechism* are more succinct and because its treatment of the subjects is more formal. The statement of the doctrine is clearer in the *Baltimore Catechism.* In this way the two texts work well together; the Faith and Life text fleshes out or explains what is in the *Baltimore Catechism.* An even more thorough explanation of the doctrine is contained in *The Baltimore Catechism Explained,* by Fr. Thomas L. Kincaid (53).

The catechisms can be covered in less than a year, and the last six weeks given to a study of *The Case for Christianity.* I have included a study guide at the end of this section that will help the student see the argument in the text. This is a work that repays close attention on the part of the student. It is not too difficult for the eighth grader, and he will enjoy seeing the argument Lewis gives for the Christian faith.

Mathematics—*Algebra* $\frac{1}{2}$ (Saxon) (48)

Algebra is a discipline that fits well with this stage of the Trivium. It employs argument, i.e., rational movement from one premise to the next, in a way that the student can follow fairly easily. This text is a good introduction to algebra and will prepare the student for the next level. As in all the other Saxon books, there is a constant review of material so that a concept never has a chance to be forgotten.

Grammar and Composition—*Voyages in English* 8 (42), or *Easy Grammar Plus* (45); *The Harp and Laurel Wreath: Poetry and Dictation for the Classical Curriculum*, edited by Laura Berquist (25); papers in history

Both grammar and writing exercises should be done regularly. When the student is working on a paper in history, then writing exercises may be laid aside. At the beginning of the year, choose the exercises that seem best to you, then concentrate on those. There are suggestions for writing assignments included in the lists at the end of this section. Dictation exercises may be continued using suggestions included in the anthology *The Harp and Laurel Wreath: Poetry and Dictation for the Classical Curriculum*. Whatever the source of the student's writing, work diligently on rewriting. Have the child pay attention to reasoned positions. Does what he says follow from the opening premise? Does he actually answer the question? If he writes a narrative account, a retelling of what happened, is it chronological? Do the paragraphs hold together, with one central idea for each? The student at this stage is capable of really thinking about these kinds of questions and revising his papers in the light of such considerations.

This is the last time that grammar will be studied intensively all year, so it should be a year of review and concentration on trouble spots. The most important, because most fundamental, thing the student should be able to do is break down a sentence into its parts. What is the simple subject, simple predicate, and object? That is the first step in analysis.

Spelling and Vocabulary—*Wordly Wise* 5 (19)

This text is the next in the series we used last year and should be used the same way. Follow the internal order of the text, doing one lesson each week. Use the vocabulary words for a spelling list, and give tests once a week. This text has a useful vocabulary, and the information about word origins and relationships fits with the study of the nature of language.

Literature (correlated with history)—*Books Children Love*, by Elizabeth Wilson (21); Greenleaf Press Books (22); *In Review* (7); *Catholic Authors*, 4-Sight edition, and *Catholic Authors*, Crown edition, both by the Brothers of Mary (11); *Honey for a Child's Heart*, by Gladys Hunt (21); *Let the Authors Speak*, by Carolyn Hatcher (45); *A Mother's List of Books*, by Theresa Fagan (21)

Though there will be numerous history readings this year, I also include a literature list and mention other sources for lists. The child is able to read significantly more difficult material by this age and should be encouraged to do so. It would be best if the parent also reads the book and discusses it with the child. However, even if you do not read the book, you should discuss it with your child. Have him tell you the story and what ethical implications it has. Have your child characterize the people in the story. Discuss the author's point of view and whether it is also your point of view. This is the best way for your child to develop the critical skills he needs to read well.

The books that you choose to read and discuss with your child should not be the only books he reads. Each child should also be reading for the sheer enjoyment of it. Pick some of the books on the literature list for your discussions this year, but have the others in an accessible place and make time each day for reading. This is not wasted time but an important formative activity.

The book list I have included has many of my own favorites on it, but there are an abundance of other good books you might choose.

Poetry—Shakespeare (6), see list; *The Harp and Laurel Wreath: Poetry and Dictation for the Classical Curriculum*, edited by Laura Berquist (25)

Memorizing some of the sonnets and other passages from Shakespeare will continue to improve the child's knowledge of rhetorical patterns and encourage imitation.

I have included some other suggestions as well in the list at the end of this section. All of the selections recommended are included in the anthology *The Harp and Laurel Wreath: Poetry and Dictation for the Classical Curriculum*.

Science—*Concepts and Challenges in Science* (C), by Alan Winkler, Leonard Bernstein, Martin Schachter and Stanley Wolfe (published by Globe) (43, 54, 58)

Four times a week read the text and do the exercises in each chapter. Unit tests provide a check of comprehension. This text, like the previous volumes, concentrates on a fundamental understanding of biology and physics, chemistry and earth science. There is not a great deal of detail, but there are clear explanations of the principles.

History—Books about medieval times (21, 22); *The Old World and America,* by Fr. Philip Furlong (53); *Christ the King, Lord of History,* by Anne Carroll (53); *Let The Authors Speak,* by Carolyn Hatcher (45); *Catholic History through Biography* (Roman Catholic Books) (46); *ABC's of Christian Culture*, by Julia Fogassy (40)

As I mentioned before, *The Old World and America* is an excellent text. This is the text I recommend using for sixth, seventh and eighth grades because it is interesting and has good exercises and a Catholic perspective. *Christ the King, Lord of History* is useful as an additional resource. It has an intensely Catholic perspective and information that is hard to find elsewhere.

It is worthwhile to have the student answer the questions of the exercises in *The Old World and America* completely, citing the portion of the text where the answer was found. This gives the child a chance to practice locating material in a text, which leads to attentive reading. Make sure that the answers are logical and that the reasons given for the answers make sense.

This course concentrates on the Middle Ages, the personalities and events in medieval times. A list of supplementary readings is included at the end of this section, and other texts about the same time period can be found in *Let the Authors Speak. The ABC's of Christian Culture* has many helpful resources as well. I have also included a list of significant dates the student may memorize. The child who enjoys writing narrative summaries may continue his "book of history".

Geography—*The Ultimate Geography and Timeline Guide*, by Maggie Hogan and Cindy Wiggens (21); or drawing maps of the ancient world to go with the history text; *Explore Europe* (5); *World Discovery Deluxe* (56); geography list

Either *The Ultimate Geography and Timeline Guide* or the homemade alternative mentioned in the seventh grade geography curriculum may be used again to achieve mastery of this class. Pay special attention to the European maps because that will help with an understanding of the history program.

The game *Explore Europe* is fun and encourages a familiarity with European cities.

I have included a geography list to memorize at the end of this section. It includes European capitals, countries and bodies of water.

Latin—*Ecce Romani,* books 1 and 2 (3); or *Latin I,* by Fr. Robert Henle (21)

The *Ecce Romani* books carry on from the base you have built over the last few years. They move slowly, with plenty of opportunity for practice. There are many support materials: tests and key, workbook and key, text translation. The drawback to this text is that the keys are available only to licensed teachers. I found a cooperative Christian school to order my materials for me.

You could use the Fr. Henle text. If you wish to achieve a certain level of competence in Latin and then go on to a modern language or concentrate on other subjects, that is probably the thing to do. If, however, you wish to stay with Latin for all of high school, in preparation for college Latin, you should wait to do Fr. Henle's text so that you don't find yourself in the last year without a text.

Art—*Art through Faith* (49), or any of the previous years' suggestions

Art through Faith includes lovely prints by and backgrounds of various artists, including Giotto, Van Eyck, Michelangelo, da Vinci and Renoir. The text has helpful background information on the artists and gives some direction in the interpretation of the pictures.

Music—*Music of the Great Composers*, by Patrick Kavanaugh (30, 6); *Jubilate Deo* (28)

Music of the Great Composers is a thorough text that covers many aspects of music. It gives a more in-depth history of music, composers and musical instruments than have the previous years' texts. Use it in conjunction with the suggestions in *Jubilate Deo* for the best recordings of the greatest musical works.

Typing—*Typing Tutor* (5)

If your child does not yet type, it is a good idea for him to learn now. I realize that this is not a part of a classical curriculum, but it is easier to read typed papers than handwritten ones!

There are many alternatives to *Typing Tutor*, both other educational computer programs and books that can be used with a typewriter. The basic point is to learn to type.

Sample Schedule for Eighth Grade				
MON.	TUE.	WED.	THURS.	FRI.
Math	Math	Math	Math	Math
English	English	English	English	
Latin	Latin	Latin	Latin	
Religion	Art	Religion	Religion	
Science	Science	Science	Science	
History	Geography	History	Music	

History reading and writing to be done in the evening or on Friday. There is now available a day-by-day breakdown of the courses listed for eighth grade (36).

Grade Eight Resource Lists

RELIGION STUDY GUIDE—*The Case for Christianity*

PART I, CHAPTER 1

C. S. Lewis makes two points in the first section. What are they? Which common way of behaving supports the first point, and which the second?

PART I, CHAPTER 2

In this section Lewis begins by giving three arguments to prove something about the Moral Law. What is he trying to establish?

Then he gives two reasons for thinking that the Law of Human Nature (or Moral Law) is a real truth (like math), not a convention (like traffic laws). What are the two reasons?

Do you understand the final point he makes about distinguishing between differences of morality and differences of belief about facts?

PART I, CHAPTER 3

What makes the "Law of Human Nature" different from the laws of nature?

What examples show that the Moral Law (what a man ought to do) is different from what is convenient or profitable? Give two examples.

Summarize Lewis' summary, that is, list the points he has made about the Moral Law.
1. Men ought to be _____.
2. The Moral Law is not a _____.
3. The Moral Law is not a _____.
4. The Moral Law is not a _____.
5. Therefore, _____.

PART I, CHAPTER 4

Copy the sentence in the first paragraph that best states what has been established by Lewis' reasoning so far.

What, roughly, are the two views of how the universe came to be? Can science answer the question, "Why is there a universe?"

If there is a power behind the things that are, that creates them and directs them, where would we look for evidence of it?

What three names does Lewis give for the in-between view he mentions in the note?

PART I, CHAPTER 5

When do you make progress by going back?

What are the two "bits of evidence" we have, without the Bible, about the Somebody behind the Moral Law?

Why is the second bit of evidence better?

How have we made ourselves the enemies of the Somebody who made the Moral Law?

PART 2, CHAPTER 1

How is a Christian more tolerant of other religions than an atheist?

Why is it that an atheist, who does not believe that the universe or anything in it was designed by Someone on purpose, cannot trust his own thinking to be true?

The first division of humanity is into those who believe in God and those who do not. Of those who believe in God, the next division is according to the sort of God they believe in. What two sorts are there?

Why is Christianity a fighting religion?

How does the injustice of the world prove that there must be a God?

PART 2, CHAPTER 2

What is the Christian explanation of "a universe that contains much that is obviously bad and meaningless, but containing creatures who know it is bad and meaningless"?

If we distinguish between a Good Power and a Bad Power in the universe, what third thing do we need in order to judge which is which?

Since Christianity is not Dualism, how does it explain the existence of a dark power?

PART 2, CHAPTER 3

What did God give us that made it possible for the world to have evil in it?

What was the sin of Satan and the sin he taught to us?

What three things (before Jesus' coming) did God do to counteract the evil Satan did?

What three claims of Christ were "talking as if he was God"?

PART 2, CHAPTER 4

What did Jesus come mainly to do?

If it is necessary to have a complete understanding of Christ's sacrifice, what is necessary to be believed?

What is the "catch" in repentance?

PART 2, CHAPTER 5

What three things spread Christ's life to us?
What does "believing things on authority" mean?
If we receive the Christ-life by these three things, why are we obliged to do anything else?
The Christian doesn't think God will love us because we're good, but that . . .

LITERATURE LIST

Pride and Prejudice	Jane Austen
Death Comes for the Archbishop	Willa Cather
Father Brown series	G. K. Chesterton
Two Years before the Mast	R. H. Dana
Sherlock Holmes series	Sir Arthur Conan Doyle
The White Company	Sir Arthur Conan Doyle
The Kitchen Madonna	Rumer Godden
In This House of Brede	Rumer Godden
Riders of the Purple Sage	Zane Gray
All Creatures Great and Small	James Herriot
Prisoner of Zenda	Anthony Hope
Tom Brown's School Days	Thomas Hughes
Tom Brown at Oxford	Thomas Hughes
The Chronicles of Narnia	C. S. Lewis
Out of the Silent Planet	C. S. Lewis
Perelandra	C. S. Lewis
That Hideous Strength	C. S. Lewis
Ivanhoe	Sir Walter Scott
The Hobbit	J. R. R. Tolkien
The Lord of the Rings	J. R. R. Tolkien
Around the World in Eighty Days	Jules Verne
Journey to the Center of the Earth	Jules Verne
Twenty Thousand Leagues under the Sea	Jules Verne
They Loved to Laugh	Kathryn Worth

POETRY LIST

"Horatius"	Thomas Lord Macaulay
"On First Looking into Chapman's Homer"	John Keats
"The Splendor Falls on Castle Walls"	Alfred Lord Tennyson
"The Lady of Shallot"	Alfred Lord Tennyson
"Lochinvar"	Sir Walter Scott
The Idylls of the King (excerpts)	Alfred Lord Tennyson

SHAKESPEARE

Macbeth   Act V, v, 19–27
  "Tomorrow, and tomorrow, and tomorrow
    creeps in this petty pace from day to day. . . ."
The Merchant of Venice   Act IV, i, 180–201
  "The quality of mercy is not strain'd. . . ."
The Merchant of Venice   Act V, i, 53–88
  "How sweet the moonlight sleeps upon this bank!"
Sonnets XVIII, XIX, XXX, XXXVI, CXVI, CXXXVIII

SUGGESTIONS FOR WRITING ASSIGNMENTS

Have the student retell the best part of the book he is reading as if he were telling it to a friend. He is then writing about something he knows and likes, so the content of the exercise is not difficult. Discuss what he will say before he begins, so that he knows what is expected. Then he can focus on spelling, the mechanics of writing and the inclusion of relevant details.

Later have the student tell the same part of the story from a different point of view. For example, if he told about the fight between David and Goliath from the Israelite point of view, now have him tell the same story from the point of view of one of the Philistines.

Have your student write directions for making something. The directions should be clear enough that someone reading and following them could complete the project successfully.

Have your student rewrite a familiar passage in a different tense. If the selection is written in the present, have the student rewrite it in the future. This requires close attention to the details of writing, without the additional task of inventing content. It also focuses attention on the need for consistent verb tenses, which is often a problem for young authors.

Pick a poem of manageable complexity, and have your student convert it to prose. As his writing improves, he can try longer and more difficult poems. *The Complete Book of Diagrams* (40) contains a few parsed selections from Shakespeare. Study these, and have your student do the same. Have him try a few passages on his own. If he can parse the sentences, he can figure out the meaning of the selection. Then he can render it in intelligible prose.

Have your student pick a speech from *The World's Great Speeches* (21) to read and outline. Then have him rewrite the speech from the outline, without looking at the original text. He should pay attention to mechanics, content and the order of the content.

Pick a book familiar to a number of people in your family. Have several of the children, or even the parents, write a characterization of one of the principals in the story. Do not name the person outright; let the other members of the family guess who is being discussed.

Pick a picture, perhaps one from the *Influential Artists* text. Discuss it with your student until he has a clear image in his memory. Then have him write such a detailed description of the picture that someone else, reading it, could draw a sketch of the picture. After seven or so of these descriptions have been done, lay out the descriptions and the pictures on a table and see if an unsuspecting third party can match them up.

History Reading List— Medieval History

Used as supplements to *The Old World and America*, by Fr. Philip Furlong (chapters 5–9).

An "L" after the author's name indicates that the library or used-book sources will be your best bet for securing this title; "IP" indicates that the book is currently in print; "*" indicates an especially enjoyable book. If a book belongs to an identifiable series, I will indicate that by using one of the following abbreviations: VB—Vision Book (Catholic), AMB—American Background Book (Catholic), LKB—Landmark Book (Christian orientation), SB—Signature Book, NSB—North Star Book, CL—Clarion Book (Catholic), WWTB—We Were There Book.

Augustine Comes to Kent	Barbara Willard	IP, CL*
Fingal's Quest	Madeleine Polland	IP, CL*
The King's Thane	Charles Brady	L, CL*
Beorn the Proud	Madeleine Pollard	IP, CL*
Son of Charlemagne	Barbara Willard	IP, CL*
Mission to Cathay	Madeleine Polland	IP, CL*

If All the Swords in England	Barbara Willard	L, CL*
The Two Trumpeters of Vienna	Hertha Pauli	L, CL*
A Trumpet Sounds	Henry Garnett	L, CL*
The Blue Gonfalon	Margaret Hubbard	L, CL*
Where Valour Lies	Adele and Cateau De Leeuw	L, CL*
William the Conqueror	Thomas B. Costain	L, LKB*
Man with a Sword	Henry Treece	L*
Swords from the North	Henry Treece	L*
Song of Roland	(unknown)	
Castle	David Macaulay	IP*
Idylls of the King	Alfred Lord Tennyson	IP*
Ivanhoe	Sir Walter Scott	IP*
The Door in the Wall	Marguerite de Angeli	IP*
Cathedral	David Macaulay	IP*
Boy Knight of Reims	Eloise Lownsbery	L
Joy in Stone	Sabra Holbrook	L
St. Dominic and the Rosary	Catherine Beebe	L, VB*
Francis and Clare, Saints of Assisi	Helen Homan	IP, VB*
St. Thomas Aquinas and the Preaching Beggars	Brendan Larnen, O.P, and Milton Lomask	L, VB*
The Crusaders	A. J. Church	L
The Crusades	Anthony West	L, LKB
We Were There with Richard the Lionhearted	Robert Webb	L, WWTB
St. Louis and the Last Crusade	Margaret Hubbard	L, VB*
King Arthur and His Knights	Thomas Malory	IP*
Castles	(Ladybird book)	L
The Story of a Castle	John Goodall	IP
Sir Gawain and the Green Knight	J. R. R. Tolkien	IP*
Otto of the Silver Hand	Howard Pyle	IP*
Looking into the Middle Ages	Huck Scarry	L
Spice Ho! A Story of Discovery	Agnes Hewes	L
The Travels of Marco Polo (various editions)	Marco Polo	IP
Ghengis Khan and the Mongol Horde	Harold Lamb	L, LKB
The Bayeaux Tapestry	Norman Denny and Josephine Filmer-Sankey	IP*

The Age of Chivalry	National Geographic	IP
The War of the Roses	Elizabeth Hallam	IP
The Plantagenet Chronicles	Elizabeth Hallam	IP
Four Gothic Kings	Elizabeth Hallam	IP
Fifteen Decisive Battles of the World	Edward Creasy	IP*
Life of St. Joan	Louis de Wohl	L, VB*
In the Days of King Hal	Marion Taggert	L*
The Fall of Constantinople	Bernadine Kielty	L, LKB
The Trumpeter of Krakow	Eric Kelly	IP*
Master Skylark	John Bennet	IP*
The Life of Thomas More	William Roper	IP*
A Proud Tale of Minerva and Scarlet	E. L. Konigsburg	IP*
The Golden Book of the Renaissance	(Golden Press)	L
Adam of the Road	Elizabeth Gray	IP*
St. George and the Dragon	Margaret Hodges	IP*
Beowulf	(Ian Serraillier, trans.)	IP*
Canterbury Tales	Chaucer (Barbara Cohen, trans.)	IP*
Jackaroo	Cynthia Voigt	IP
The Black Arrow	Robert Louis Stevenson	IP*
The Adventures of Robin Hood	Roger Lancelyn Green	IP*
The Merry Adventures of Robin Hood	Howard Pyle	IP*
King Arthur and His Knights of the Round Table	Roger Lancelyn Green	IP*
The Story of the Grail and the Passing of Arthur	Howard Pyle	IP*
I, Juan de Pareja	Elizabeth Borten de Trevino	IP*
Don Quixote and Sancho Panza	Margaret Hodges	IP*

The Vikings   Elizabeth Janeway
The Story of Rolf and the Viking Bow   Allen French

History Dates List

A.D.

529   St. Benedict establishes monastery at Monte Cassino, Italy.

529   Emperor Justinian issues *Codex Justinianus.*

550   King Arthur reigns in England.

598   Pope Gregory I (the Great) sends Augustine to England.

622   Muhammad makes hejira to Medina.

732   Charles the Hammer stops the Moslem advance at Tours.

800   Charlemagne is crowned Holy Roman Emperor by
      Pope Leo III.

886   Alfred the Great drives the Danes from Wessex.

1066   Duke William of Normandy conquers Saxon England.

1099   First Crusade takes Jerusalem.

1146   Louis VII and Conrad III "take the cross"—Second Crusade.

1187   Saladin recaptures Jerusalem.

1192   Richard the Lion-Heart and Saladin make truce to end the
      Third Crusade.

1204   Fourth Crusade sacks Constantinople.

1208   St. Francis founds the Franciscan friars.

1215   Magna Carta signed by King John.

1270   St. Louis (King Louis IX) dies on crusade.

1272   St. Thomas Aquinas stops work on the *Summa Theologiae.*

1295   Marco Polo returns to Venice from China and the court of
      Kublai Khan.

1321   Dante dies.

1346   Battle of Crecy—victory of Edward III and his longbows.

1348   The Black Death devastates Europe.

1415   Henry V of England wins battle of Agincourt in Normandy.

1429   Joan of Arc relieves Orleans.

1453   Fall of Constantinople.

1453   End of the Hundred Years' War between England and France.

1492   Columbus discovers the New World.

Geography List—
European Capitals and Their Rivers

Capital City	*Country*	*River or Sea*	*Empties into*
Rome	Italy	Tiber	Tyrrhenian Sea
Paris	France	Seine	English Channel
London	Great Britain	Thames	North Sea
Vienna	Austria	Danube	Black Sea
Warsaw	Poland	Vistula	Baltic Sea
Berlin	Germany	Spree	Elbe
Athens	Greece	Aegean Sea	Mediterranean Sea
Istanbul*	Turkey	Bosporus Strait	Sea of Marmara
Lisbon	Portugal	Tagus	Atlantic Ocean
Madrid	Spain	Manzanares	Tagus
Moscow	Russia	Oka	Volga

*Constantinople

Ninth Grade Curriculum

Note: The author advises the reader to refer to the chapter on "The High School Years" (p. 185) before proceeding with the ninth grade curriculum.

Sources for items followed by a number in parentheses may be found at the back of the book in the list of suppliers.

Religion—*Chief Truths of the Faith* and *Catholic Morality*, by Fr. John Laux (53). There is a syllabus available for this course (36).

Chief Truths of the Faith is a beginning theology text, providing the initial steps of a theological formation. It contains a good overview of the doctrines of the Catholic Church in an easy to understand format. The questions after each chapter are helpful because they lead the student through the argument in such a way that he can see it clearly and then reproduce it. The suggestions for writing assignments are particularly good because they help the student do just what he should be doing at this stage of development: presenting a cogent, well-reasoned argument.

Having the students prepare for and take several tests or quizzes on this material is helpful for them. A series of five quizzes (and the answers to those quizzes), which I developed for my children, is included in my ninth-grade religion syllabus. You could do this on your own, however, using questions and answers right from the text. A quiz helps reinforce the concepts learned because it encourages review of the material. This, in turn, provides a situation in which the whole and its parts can be more clearly seen.

Catholic Morality is the second in the series of four religion texts by Fr. Laux. It presents the arguments young people should understand with regard to moral choice and also discusses the moral and theological virtues. As in *Chief Truths*, there are excellent suggestions for writing assignments, and, again, I recommend giving a number of exams.

For those who are looking for additional or more difficult material, I recommend reading through relevant portions of *Fundamentals of Catholic Dogma*, by Ludwig Ott (51), and the *Catechism of the Catholic Church* (25). Part one of the *Catechism* addresses the basic doctrines enunciated in the Creed, so it expounds the information presented in *Chief Truths*. Part three of the *Catechism* addresses in greater detail the questions of choice and virtue that *Catholic Morality* introduces.

Mathematics—*Algebra I*, by John Saxon, Jr. (2d ed.) (48); or *The Key to Algebra*, from Key Curriculum (45); or *Algebra I*, from Keyboard Enterprises (27)

The internal order of the Saxon text should be followed throughout the year. Mathematics is one subject that needs to be done five days a week, all year long. The text can be finished and mastered if it is worked through in this systematic way. The constant practice in applying the concepts learned reinforces them so that they stay in the mind. Long breaks from math problems or skipping lessons or doing only part of each lesson will usually result in a deficiency in understanding. On the other hand, even the student with a certain weakness in this area can master it by working regularly, consistently, and thoroughly.

If your student does one lesson a day, four days a week, with a test on most Fridays during the year, he can finish the text easily in thirty-two weeks. If one lesson takes too long to do in the allotted daily time, cut the lessons in half for a while and only do tests occasionally. Or decide to use the text for both this year and part of next year, so that the student proceeds at a pace suitable for him. What is necessary is that a reasonable amount of math be done each day, not that a lesson be finished each day.

Algebra I is a text I have used successfully with a number of students of varying abilities. As with all the Saxon books, once a concept is learned, it is reviewed in the subsequent lessons so that the student does not have a chance to forget it. There is a solutions manual available to help those of us who will be called upon for explanations but whose algebra skills have gotten a little rusty. The second edition of the text is better than the first because it contains more geometry, thus helping prepare the student for the PSAT and SAT tests.

However, if you think that your student is likely to have some trouble with algebra, and you do not want just to slow down the pace, you might like a text that breaks down the concepts into smaller parts and looks somewhat less intimidating. Key Curriculum has a series of workbooks called *Key to Algebra* (45) that has those qualities. *Key to Algebra* goes all the way to quadratic equations, so it covers the required material for *Algebra I*.

There is one other program that I think is worth mentioning here. Keyboard Enterprises (27) has an algebra class on video that many high school students have used successfully. The explanations given on the tape are clear and cogent.

Grammar and Composition—*Warriner's English Grammar and Composition, Third Course* (21); *The Complete Book of Diagrams*, by Mary Daly (40). There is a syllabus available for this course (36).

Spelling and Vocabulary—Either *Warriner's Third Course*; or *Spelling Power*, by Beverly Adams-Gordon (45); or *The Writing Road to Reading*, by Romalda Spalding (21), with *Month by Month Spelling Guide*, by Katherine von Duyke (29). *English from the Roots Up*, by Lundquist (21), can be very helpful for vocabulary.

Follow the internal order of the *Warriner's* text during the course of the year. This order is reasonable and easy to follow. If you are going to use the vocabulary and spelling sections at the end of the book, they should be worked on throughout the year.

Warriner's Third Course is a good text. The grammar sections provide an ample review for the student who has been studying grammar regularly, and the student who has not had grammar instruction can learn quite well from this text. If your student has been doing grammar regularly, either English or Latin, have him do the review exercises in the grammar sections first to determine whether to spend time on those sections. If you decide to do all the exercises, the review exercises can be regarded as tests. The *Complete Book of Diagrams* provides interesting selections for additional diagraming practice.

The composition instruction in *Warriner's* is clear and simple. It can be very helpful. However, determine your own topics for use in the composition exercises. I suggest that you use religion papers for some of these compositions. Also, the writing sections give helpful guidance in composing summaries, reports and stories for history and English classes.

When these writing exercises are being done, have your student work diligently on rewriting. He will learn more about good writing skills from a few well done papers than from many papers done poorly. One well done paper, with a carefully constructed, clear argument will do more to teach a student how to write, how to learn, how to communicate and how to think than any number of sloppy efforts.

You might decide to have your student review the vocabulary in *English from the Roots Up* if he has done it before or to include it in your weekly curriculum if he has not. In the latter case, add three words each week, memorizing the meanings and working through the vocabulary words included with each root word. This text makes the students aware of the correlation between the Latin and Greek roots and our own language. It is great preparation for the PSAT and SAT.

If a student has particular difficulty with spelling, I recommend using *Spelling Power* or *The Writing Road to Reading* rather than the *Warriner's* list. *Spelling Power* is easy to use; students can give the tests to each other. The lists are arranged in such a way that the student is studying words at his level of difficulty, and the suggestions for learning those words are helpful.

Students who are naturally good spellers should not use any of these texts. They should just pay attention to spelling well in their daily work. Similarly, the student who already has a well-developed vocabulary should concentrate his energy in other areas.

American History—*Christ and the Americas*, by Anne Carroll (53), with answer key (28); or *The March of Democracy*, by John Truslow Adams (57); *The World's Great Speeches*, edited by Lewis Copeland and Lawrence W. Lamm (21); *Let the Authors Speak*, by Carolyn Hatcher (21); *The ABC's of Christian Culture*, by Julia Fogassy (40).

There is a syllabus available for this course using *Christ and the Americas* (36).

The March of Democracy is an interesting and readable series of books about American history from the Revolution to World War II. Though out of print, it is pretty widely available in used-book stores; it must have been popular at one time.

If you use this series, have the student read and summarize about fifty pages a week, and then, over the course of the year, assign three substantial papers of about fifteen hundred words. The resource section provides a list of possible topics for ninth grade, and I recommend that each paper take a different approach to the chosen topic. Such approaches include first-person descriptions of the time read about, as though you were living in it (Washington's description of the war, for example), the pros and cons of a particular question (Was the North correct in insisting that the South could not secede?), the imagined conversation between two important characters from history (Jay and Madison discussing limited government) and narrative essays.

Incorporate the part of the *Warriner's English Grammar and Composition, Third Course* that discusses writing summaries and reports.

An alternative to *The March of Democracy* is Anne Carroll's book *Christ and the Americas*, which provides a framework for the study of American history. The use of biographies, resource books and historical fiction to supplement this text will help bring the topics to life for the student. At the end of the ninth grade section, there is a history list, arranged according to topic and time period, that can be used in such a project.

In this approach to history, you would incorporate your literature course as well. You might, in this case, include the writing of a story in addition to the narratives previously described. Use the part of the *Warriner's Third Course* that deals with writing stories.

During the year, whichever method of teaching history you decide to follow, use *Great Speeches* for practice in dialectic. Have the student read a speech from a period in history that is of interest to him. Have him outline it, lay the outline aside and a few days later use that outline to reproduce the speech to the best of his ability. Have him jumble the order of the outline, lay it aside and then later try to reduce the confusion to the best possible order. Comparing his finished work with the original, a student will discover faults and amend them. Shorter speeches are better for beginners, and familiarity with the issues raised in the speech is an asset for such a project.

A useful tool in any history course is a time line. Time lines pull together information from different areas and frames of reference. They give the students an integrated understanding of periods of history. I remember how surprised my children were to discover that Mozart was alive during the Revolutionary War and that the Little Flower's short life encompassed the years immediately following the Civil War, which was also the time period Laura Ingalls Wilder wrote about in *The Little House in the Big Woods*. At the end of this section you will find instructions for putting together the kind of time line my family has found most helpful.

The books included on my lists are those books my children and I have read or have enough knowledge of to recommend confidently. (I have not read all the Francis Parkman books, but I know enough of the author to have confidence in his work.) There are, however, many other such books; *Let the Authors Speak* is an excellent source of information and guidance about books to use in your history program.

The ABC's of Christian Culture is another helpful resource for your history program. It contains wonderful maps for each time period studied, suggestions for information resources and an outstanding set of cards about important historical figures from the Old Testament through modern times. The author also includes some writing suggestions for each time period and some quizzes. I have used this resource mostly in the junior high years, but it is intended for use throughout the school years. If you have a number of students, this is an economical program because it can be used at most levels.

An additional resource that is worth an investment is an older (1907–1913) *Catholic Encyclopedia*. It is amazing how many topics are covered and in what depth. Most important, the point of view is accurate, a wonderful antidote to the materialistic, secular culture in which we live.

Earth Science—*Geology: Rocks and Minerals* (Milliken Press) (45); *Geology* (Golden Guide) (2); *The Solar System* (Milliken Press) (45); *The Sky Observer's Guide* (Golden Guide) (2); *Oceanography* (Milliken Press) (45); *Oceans for Every Child*, by Janice VanCleave (Wiley Nature Editions) (6); *Weather* (Milliken Press) (45); *Weather* (Golden Guide) (2); or *Earth Science for Christian Schools*, by George Mulfinger, Jr., and Donald E. Snyder (49). A syllabus is available for this course, using the Milliken texts (36).

For experiments or other hands-on materials:

Geology—Acorn Naturalists (2) markets an inexpensive rock and mineral collection that could be used in conjunction with *Rocks and Minerals: The Golden Guide to Field Identification* (21). (This is different from the earlier mentioned Golden Guide *Geology*.)

Oceanography—*Oceans for Every Child,* by Janice VanCleave (6)

Meteorology—Home Training Tools (24) has kits for constructing a weather station and other weather-related activities.

Astronomy—*Astronomy for All Ages: Discovering the Universe through Activities for Children and Adults*, by Philip Harrington and Edward Pascuzzi (20)

Earth Science traditionally treats four topics: geology, astronomy, oceanography and meteorology. These topics are intended to be covered in such a way as to summarize what the students have done in each area during grade school and to add some depth to their understanding. The following suggestions are meant to do just that, but in a non-traditional way.

Have each student keep a nature journal for the course of the year. In this journal (an artist's blank sketchbook) he will write about the concepts being studied and sketch pictures to help him visualize the material. Use the Milliken transparencies as reinforcement and the tests included in the Milliken book as a guide to the concepts that should be covered. The Golden Guide *Geology*, or some similar resource, can be used as the primary source of information. Additionally, in each of the four areas of study, one kind of hands-on project may be done.

Thus, for example, in the part of the course dealing with geology, examine the first of the worksheets and tests in the Milliken book *Geology: Rocks and Minerals*. Using this as a guide, have your student look up information on the layers of the earth, the characteristics of each layer, the means of discovery of this information and what erosion is and where it takes place. We use the Golden Guide *Geology* for this information, but the students are encouraged to look at other sources as well. The following day, have the student enter this information in his nature journal, sketching and labeling appropriate pictures and writing a paragraph or two. Next have the student examine the first transparency and compare it with his pictures. He may modify his sketches if he wishes. Have him answer the study questions on the transparency either orally or in writing. Give a cumulative test at the end of the quarter.

During the study of rocks and minerals, the hands-on project we enjoy is using a field guide and a number of identified rock and mineral specimens for practice in typing rocks. On page 67 of *Rocks and Minerals: The Golden Guide to Field Identification*, the text suggests: "Use this book as a study guide. Compare the descriptions and illustrations with known specimens. . . . Only after much study and examination of known minerals is it possible to go into the field and make positive identification of minerals." So we study known specimens and keep that information in the back of the nature journal.

For each of the other areas of earth science, follow a similar procedure. Sources for hands-on activities in each area are listed separately above.

If you prefer the textbook approach, *Earth Science for Christian Schools* is the best textbook I have seen on this subject. It does contain some anti-Catholic sentiments, however, so you will need to preview the material before handing it to your student. Be prepared to discuss the Galileo question. An older edition of *The Catholic Encyclopedia* will have the information needed, and *Lay Witness*, the newsletter of Catholics United for the Faith (14), published an account of the matter in volume 14, number 7, the April 1993 issue, which is a very helpful discussion of the matter. *Catholic*

Dossier magazine's July/August 1995 issue is devoted to this question (18).

In recent years, as I have been homeschooling high school students, I have noticed that, like their younger brothers and sisters, high schoolers both retain information better and get a better formation (habit of thought) if they do more than simply read a textbook. Textbooks are good sources of information, and they are convenient and economical. But, with rare exceptions, unless the material learned through a textbook is reinforced by other activities, the students tend not to retain the concepts presented or to profit from the particular disciplines' formation. My suggestions for the earth science course follow from this understanding.

Whichever approach you use in science, remember that ninth grade is a good time to work on analytic skills. Pose problems in the areas your student is studying (for example: What do the different cloud formations indicate? What physical processes produce those differences in formation? In what kind of land feature would one be most likely to find igneous rock?).

Art—*Metropolitan Museum of Art Catalogue* (35); *Drawing from Nature*, by Jim Arnosky (45); *Landscapes in Pencil*, by Gene Franks (6); *Land and Landscapes: Views of American History*, by Tony Lewis (38)

If you have been homeschooling in the grade-school years, your child has probably spent time looking at great works of art. He will have learned to be attentive to and to appreciate beautiful paintings and sculpture. He will have developed his artistic vocabulary, power of expression and imagination in these fields.

Talking about such works gives a kind of clarity to the student's observations. Ask questions that help him to distinguish the subject, the action and the forms used in the composition of the picture as a whole. Talk about the colors employed and the textures used, discussing the feelings evoked by each and noting as well the smells and sounds suggested in the picture. This kind of conversation can also play a role in the development of his analytic power. Reflections on why certain colors and figures are used and how they function in the picture as a whole are analytic in nature and are therefore appropriate to the ninth-grade student. There is a *quasi* argument in a painting: the artist wishes you to see something he sees in the way that he sees it. Talk about how he accomplishes that.

In addition to talking about the picture in the terms suggested above, have your student make sketches of the works of art he is studying. Have him look at the picture and then turn it over and try to sketch it. When he looks at it again he will see all sorts of things he did not see before. Have him write a description of the picture as a whole or of the colors used or of the composition of the figures in the picture. You might have him draw it from the description, thus encouraging fuller and more accurate descriptions.

Pay some attention to schools of art; this year study the similarities within each of the groups mentioned on the list of American painters in the resource section for ninth grade. Then contrast the groups of artists. Notice that the divisions among schools are based on style of painting, but they are also more or less chronological divisions. *Land and Landscapes: Views of American History* may help in this exercise.

Students should also attain some degree of drawing literacy. Not everyone is going to be a great artist, and not everyone is a talented composer of pictures. But everyone can learn the basic drawing techniques that enable one to transfer what he sees to a piece of paper. Two texts we have used that help in this endeavor are *Drawing from Nature* and *Landscapes in Pencil*.

Music—*Music of the Great Composers*, by Patrick Kavanaugh (Zondervan Press) (30, 6)

With regard to music, an approach similar to that suggested for art is desirable. Look at the chronological list provided in the ninth-grade resource lists and the book *Music of the Great Composers*, by Patrick Kavanaugh. Locate some of the particular compositions Mr. Kavanaugh mentions that fit with the time period you are studying in history. On a regular basis, at least once a week, spend time just listening to the music.

Never underrate the activity of simply looking and listening intelligently. Direct observation, uncluttered by someone else's interpretation, gives the student immediate and fresh access to the work itself. Books that interpret works of art or music should be used only after the student has had an opportunity for unmediated exposure to the works himself. If such books are used too soon, they stifle further observation on the part of the learner. One understands more by working on appreciating the art work or music oneself than by having someone else explain too soon all that the painting or composition contains and how it achieves its effects.

Music of the Great Composers is a wonderful introduction to classical music, giving a quick synopsis of the various forms of musical compositions and excellent suggestions for accessible pieces.

Enjoyable reinforcement activities can be done with your ninth grader throughout the year. In the ninth-grade resource section there are two charts. One chart contains descriptions of different kinds of music, and the other has the same categories but blank spaces for the student to fill in with the names of particular pieces as he listens to them.

After introducing and exploring the types of music, play a piece and ask what kind of music it is—orchestral, choral, operatic, chamber music or song. Once the student has listened repeatedly to a number of pieces of music, he will enjoy seeing whether he can recognize and put a name to them. After a longer time spent listening to several pieces by each of the composers studied, introduce a new piece of music by one of the composers. Ask your student if he recognizes the style of the piece. Is it Baroque, Classical, Romantic or Modern? Can he tell who the composer probably is?

Literature and Poetry—See the lists in the grade nine resource section.

Whether your student is using *March of Democracy* or *Christ and the Americas* for history this year, he will be reading large quantities of material in his history course. He will be writing in history as well as in religion. Further, in terms of units and courses required for graduation, ninth-grade literature is unnecessary. For these reasons I recommend foregoing a full-fledged literature course in the ninth grade.

Whether or not literature is going to be a formal course in ninth grade, the student ought to read good literature during the year. In the resource section for this grade is a list of books that I have used successfully in the study of literature at this level. Some of the works included in this list are also found in the History and Literature List for ninth grade. However, I singled out as literature texts those I have read and discussed with a number of high-school students. These books are both readable and discussable for students of this age. Also included in the resource section are general questions that may be used with any literary work.

Discussion is important, particularly in this first year of high school, when there is a transition from the dialectical phase of the Trivium to the rhetorical. The suggested readings involve difficult material considered in the light of both the argument of the author and the means he employs to make that argument. There are subtle considerations to be made, more subtle than the student has been used to making. For example, most students will need help in identifying the irony that leads to a conclusion that, on the face of it, is opposed to the reasoning process. The context will be more important than it has been previously in understanding the author's way of proceeding. This kind of consideration needs adult guidance, at least initially.

Also, spend some time on the study of poetry. I have included suggestions for poetry readings in the list at the end of this section. Compare different poems, and talk about their differences. Is there a mood created in the poem? What is it, and how does the author produce it? Have the student write out in prose what the poem says in verse. Encourage him to memorize and recite a poem or two, paying attention to eye contact, tempo, enunciation, posture and expression.

At this stage it is more important for the student to think carefully about the poem than to see every literary device it contains. One actually learns more by working on understanding the poem than by having someone else explain too soon all that it contains and how it achieves its effects. Familiarity with particular poems will lead to an understanding of the art form, which in turn leads to enjoyment.

Additionally, it is important that the ninth grader be reading for pleasure, without any end in view other than enjoyment. Many of the books listed are very entertaining. Put a pile of books that you think your student would enjoy in an accessible place, and tell him that this is a resource for his leisure hours. Then make sure that he has some leisure hours.

Latin—*Latin I*, by Fr. Robert Henle, with answer key (21); and *Latin Grammar* (21). There is a syllabus available for this course (36).

Like literature, Latin is optional for the ninth grader in terms of units and courses required for graduation. However, if you have been doing Latin up to this point, do not abandon it now. Recognize the amount of difficult material in the curriculum this year, and plan your Latin course accordingly. You might do only half of the Fr. Henle *Latin I* in the ninth grade. Proceed slowly and thoroughly, and really learn the language. In the sophomore year, finish up *Latin I*. With this very solid foundation, either do *Latin II* in the junior and senior year or do *Latin II* in the junior year and *Latin III* in the senior year.

Sample Weekly Schedule for Ninth Grade

Name	Week 1	Date

MONDAY

Math	Lesson 1.
English	Spelling: pp. 619–24, exercises 1, 2, 3, 4.
	Grammar: pp. 3–6, exercises 1, 2, 3.
Latin	Read the introduction and first lesson with me; pp. 3–8.
Religion	Read the introduction and "The Hound of Heaven".
Science	Make a title page and illustration for your nature journal. Look over your books for geology.
History	Read fifty pages in March of Democracy this week.

TUESDAY

Math	Lesson 2.
English	Spelling: pp. 624–26, exercises 5, 6, 7.
	Grammar: pp. 6–10, exercises 4, 5.
Latin	Do exercises 1, 2, 3.
Religion	Write a short paper on no. 1, p. xviii. Use the outline provided. Read and incorporate "Suggestions for Study".
Art	Discuss the picture. Then make a list of observations

about the subject and action of the picture, colors employed, textures used, feelings evoked and smells and sounds suggested in the picture. Write a short description, and make a sketch in your notebook as a record of the work studied.

Science	Find out about the earth's interior. What are the layers called, and what are their characteristics? Write a paragraph in your journal describing the interior, and draw a sketch.
History	Read.

WEDNESDAY

Math	Lesson 3.
English	Spelling: pp. 626–28, exercises 8, 9, 10.
	Grammar: pp. 10–15, exercises 6, 7, 8, and review exercise A
Latin	Read nos. 2–3, pp. 9–13. Do exercises 4, 5.
Religion	Go over paper with me.
Science	Research the Mohorovic discontinuity, plate tectonics and lithospheric plates. Write about them in your journal, and illustrate as you are able.
Geography	Read.
History	Read.

THURSDAY

Math	Lesson 4.
English	Spelling: pp. 628–31, exercises 11, 12, and review exercise A.
	Grammar: pp. 15–20, exercises 9, 10, 11, 12, 13.
Latin	Read no. 4, pp. 13–16. Do exercises 6, 7, 8, 9.
Religion	Read chaps. 1 and 2 in section 1.
Science	Compare your illustrations to the transparencies in your book. Do the worksheet on the earth's interior.
History	Read.

<u>FRIDAY</u>

Math	Lesson 5.
Literature	Pick book and poem, and enter the date on your list.
Music	Read chap. 1 in *Music of the Great Composers*.

Grade Nine Resource Lists

HISTORY AND LITERATURE

The starred entries are my suggestions for a "core course" in history. These are not necessarily the best titles of those I mention or even the best for teaching each period of history. They *are* titles I know can be used successfully with ninth graders.

Though my curriculum proposes American history in ninth grade, I have included a certain number of titles written by European authors and set in Europe. This allows the student to see what was going on elsewhere in the world contemporaneously with significant American events. These European titles will be useful in eleventh grade as well, when European history is studied.

HISTORICAL SURVEYS

The Landmark History of the American People	Daniel J. Boorstin
Home of the Brave	John A. Carroll

EXPLORATION AND COLONIZATION 1400–1700

SPANISH COLONIZATION

Columbus and Cortez*	John Eidsmoe
The Eyes of Discovery	John Bakeless
Evangelization of the New World	James Leek
Odyssey of Courage	Maia Wojciechowska
Spanish Missions	

FRENCH COLONIZATION

Shadows on the Rock*	Willa Cather
Cartier Sails the St. Lawrence	Esther Averill
Samuel de Champlain	W. S. Jacobs
The Explorations of Père Marquette	Jim Kjelgaard
Journey and Discovery of Several Countries	Père Marquette

La Salle and the Discovery of the Great West   Francis Parkman
The Jesuits in North America   Francis Parkman
Pioneers of France in the New World   Francis Parkman
Père Marquette: Priest, Pioneer, Adventurer   Agnes Repplier

ENGLISH COLONIZATION

*Mourt's Relation**   Mourt
The Pilgrim Story   William F. Atwood
Betty Alden   Jane G. Austen
Americans: The Colonial Experience   Daniel J. Boorstin
A History of Plimmoth Plantation   William Bradford
Constance: A Story of Early Plymouth   Patricia Clapp
Muskets along the Chickahominy   Gertrude Finney
The Scarlet Letter   Nathaniel Hawthorne
This Dear Bought Land   Jean Lee Latham
Captain Bacon's Rebellion   Helen Lobdell
Captured by the Mohawks   Sterling North
Quaker Cavalier   J. Reason
The Witch of Blackbird Pond   Elizabeth Speare

EUROPE AT THE SAME PERIOD

I, Juan de Pareja   E. B. de Trevino

AMERICAN REVOLUTION 1700–1800

*Thomas Jefferson: Man on a Mountain**   Natalie Bober
*Miracle at Philadelphia**   Catherine Drinker Bowen
*Autobiography of Benjamin Franklin**   Benjamin Franklin
*Catholic Makers of America**   Stephen M. Krason
*The American Revolutionaries**   Milton Meltzer
The Narrative of Col. Ethan Allen's Captivity Ethan Allen
John Adams and the American Revolution   Catherine Bowen
Drums   James Boyd
George Washington   Richard Brookhiser
On American Taxation   Edmund Burke
On Conciliation with the American Colonies   Edmund Burke
Patrick Henry, Firebrand of the Revolution   Nardi Campion

Tree of Freedom	Rebecca Caudill
Minutemen of the Sea	Tom Cluff
The Virginia Comedians	John Esten Cooke
The Spy: A Tale of Neutral Ground	James F. Cooper
The Red Rover	James F. Cooper
The Deerslayer	James F. Cooper
The Pathfinder	James F. Cooper
The Last of the Mohicans	James F. Cooper
Decision at Philadelphia	Christopher Collier
Sketches of Eighteenth Century America	Michel–Guillaume St. Jean de Crevecoeur
Letters from an American Farmer	Michel–Guillaume St. Jean de Crevecoeur
Poor Richard	James Daugherty
Leader by Destiny	Jeanette Eaton
Drums along the Mohawk	Walter Edmond
Citizen Tom Paine	Howard Fast
April Morning	Howard Fast
Redcoat in Boston	Ann Finlayson
America's Paul Revere	Esther Forbes
Paul Revere and the World He Lived In	Esther Forbes
Johnny Tremain	Esther Forbes
Poor Richard's Almanack	Benjamin Franklin
Tom Paine, Freedom's Apostle	Leo Gurko
Knickerbocker History of New York	Washington Irving
Notes on the State of Virginia	Thomas Jefferson
Journal (1704–1705)	Sarah Kimble Knight
Carry on, Mr. Bowditch	Jean Lee Latham
Thomas Jefferson	Gene Lisitzky
Guns for the Saratoga	Stephen W. Meader
Master Simon's Garden	Cornelia Meigs
The Bill of Rights	Milton Meltzer
The Crisis	Thomas Paine
Common Sense	Thomas Paine
Abigail Adams and Her Times	Laura E. Richards
Arundel	Kenneth Roberts
Oliver Wiswell	Kenneth Roberts
Northwest Passage	Kenneth Roberts

The Partisan	William G. Simms
The Scent	William G. Simms
Woodcraft	William G. Simms
Calico Captive	Elizabeth G. Speare
The Green Mountain Boys	Daniel P. Thompson
The First Salute: A View of the American Revolution	Barbara Tuchman
John Treegate's Musket	Leonard Wibberly
Peter Treegate's War	Leonard Wibberly
Sea Captain from Salem	Leonard Wibberly
Treegate's Raiders	Leonard Wibberly
Sally Wister's Journal	Sally Wister

SPEECHES FOUND IN *The World's Great Speeches*

*John Hancock's Speech about the Boston Massacre
*Patrick Henry's Speech before the Virginia Convention of Delegates
*Samuel Adams' Speech at the State House in Philadelphia
*Benjamin Franklin's Speech on the Faults of the Constitution
*James Madison's Speech before the Convention of Virginia
*John Marshall's Speech before the Convention of Virginia
*Alexander Hamilton's Speech before the Constitutional Convention of New York
*George Washington's Inaugural Address
*Thomas Jefferson's First Inaugural Address

LITERATURE OF EUROPE AT THE SAME TIME PERIOD

Wuthering Heights	Emily Brontë
Adam Bede	George Eliot
The Vicar of Wakefield	Oliver Goldsmith
Treasure Island	Robert L. Stevenson
A Tale of Two Cities	Charles Dickens
The Rights of Man, The Reign of Terror	Susan Banfield
Reflections on the Revolution in France	Edmund Burke
The Song at the Scaffold	Gertrude von le Fort
The Scarlet Pimpernel	Baroness Orczy

WESTWARD EXPANSION 1780–1860

*Death Comes for the Archbishop**	Willa Cather
*Bold Journey: West with Lewis and Clark**	Lewis and Clark
*The Oregon Trail**	Francis Parkman
Log of a Cowboy	Andy Adams
The Lieutenant's Lady	Bess Streeter Aldrich
A Lantern in Her Hand	Bess Streeter Aldrich
Journals of Lewis and Clark	ed. J. Bakeless
Simon Brute and the Western Adventure	Elizabeth Bartelme
A Gathering of Days	Joan Blos
The Cross in the West	Mark Boesch
Travels through North and South Carolina	William Bartram
Madeleine Takes Command	Ethel C. Brill
The Fur Lodge	Beverly Butler
The Far-Off Land	Rebecca Caudill
All This Wild Land	Ann Nolan Clark
Sequoya	Catherine Cate Coblentz
Empire on the Platte	Richard Crabb
Life of David Crockett	David Crockett
The Cross in the Wilderness	Kay Cronin
Marcus and Narcissa Whitman	James Daugherty
Of Courage Undaunted	James Daugherty
Fear in the Forest	Cateau De Leeuw
Incident at Hawk's Hill	Allan Eckert
The Hoosier School Master	Edward Eggleston
The Buffalo Trace	Virginia Eifert
Forth to the Wilderness	Dale van Every
Greenhorn on the Frontier	Ann Finlayson
By the Great Horn Spoon	Sid Fleishman
Buffalo Bill	Shannon Garst
Man without a Country	Edward Everett Hale
Song of the Pines	Walter and Marion Havighurst
The Luck of Roaring Camp	Francis Bret Harte
The Story of John S. Audubon	Joan Howard
Better Known as Johnny Appleseed	Mabel Leigh Hunt
The Turquoise Rosary	L. V. Jacks

Torrie	Annabel and Edgar Johnson
Sod House Winter: They Came from Sweden	Clare Ingram Judson
Bargain Bride	Evelyn Sibley Lampman
The Voyage of the Javelin	Stephen W. Meader
Swift Rivers	Cornelia Meigs
Little Britches: Father and I Were Farmers	Ralph Moody
The Adventures of the Broken Hand	Frank Moriss
The Parkman Reader	ed. Samuel Eliot Morison
On to Oregon	Honore Morrow
The First Steamboat on the Mississippi	Sterling North
The Island of the Blue Dolphins	Scott O'Dell
A Long Way to Frisco	Alfred Powers
Mother Seton and the Sisters of Charity	Alma Power-Waters
Captain Caution	Kenneth Roberts
The Gold Race	Alexander Scharbach
The Sodbuster Venture	Charlene Joy Talbot
Frontier Living	Edwin Tunis
Adventures of Tom Sawyer	Mark Twain
Leopard's Prey	Leonard Wibberly
Red Pawns	Leonard Wibberly
The Last Battle	Leonard Wibberly

SHORT STORIES

"The Luck of Roaring Camp"	Bret Harte
"The Ransom of Red Chief"	O. Henry
"The Gift of the Magi"	O. Henry
"The Retrieved Reformation"	O. Henry
"Little Bo-Peep"	O. Henry
"Neighbor Rosicky"	Willa Cather
"The Great Stone Face"	Nathaniel Hawthorne
"Rip Van Winkle"	Washington Irving
"The Legend of Sleepy Hollow"	Washington Irving

LITERATURE OF EUROPE AT THE SAME TIME PERIOD

Pride and Prejudice *	Jane Austen
Sense and Sensibility	Jane Austen
Persuasion	Jane Austen

Emma	Jane Austen
Jane Eyre	Charlotte Brontë
David Copperfield	Charles Dickens
Oliver Twist	Charles Dickens
Bleak House	Charles Dickens
Pickwick Papers	Charles Dickens
Silas Marner	George Eliot
Damian the Leper	John Farrow
Tom Brown's School Days	Thomas Hughes
Les Misérables	Victor Hugo
Mr. Midshipman Easy	Frederick Marryat
The Man of Molokai	A. Roos
The Song of Bernadette	Franz Werfel
Swiss Family Robinson	J. Wyss

CIVIL WAR 1860–1870

*The Red Badge of Courage**	Stephen Crane
*Lincoln: A Photobiography**	Russell Freedman
*Across Five Aprils**	Irene Hunt
*Voices from the Civil War**	Milton Meltzer
*The Killer Angels**	Michael Shaura
Little Women	Louisa May Alcott
Charlie Skedaddle	Patricia Beatty
Civil War Book	Bruce Catton
This Hallowed Ground	Bruce Catton
Stillness at Appomattox	Bruce Catton
The Day Fort Sumpter Was Fired On	Jim Haskins
Echoes of the Civil War: The Blue	Stephen Forman
Echoes of the Civil War: The Gray	Stephen Forman
America's Robert E. Lee	Henry Steele Commager and Lynd Ward
Abraham Lincoln	James Daugherty
Abraham Lincoln's World	Genevieve Foster
Narrative of the Life of Frederick Douglass	Frederick Douglass
My Cousin Abe	Aileen Fisher
Lee of Virginia	Douglas Southall Freeman

Dr. George Washington Carver: Scientist	S. Graham and G. Lipscomb
George Washington Carver: An American Biography	Rackham Holt
Andersonville	MacKinlay Kantor
Lee and Grant at Appomattox	MacKinlay Kantor
Virginia's General: Robert E. Lee and the Civil War	Albert Marrin
Rifles for Watie	Harold Keith
The Lincoln-Douglas Debates	A. Lincoln and S. Douglas
Phantom of the Blockade	Stephen W. Meader
The Long Road to Gettysburg	Jim Murphy
Abe Lincoln Grows Up	Carl Sandburg
The Perilous Road	William O. Steele
Uncle Tom's Cabin	Harriet Beecher Stowe
Underground Man	Milton Meltzer
The Underground Railroad: Life on the Road to Freedom	Ellen Hansen

LITERATURE OF EUROPE AT THE SAME PERIOD

Under a Changing Moon	Margot Benary-Isbert

SHORT STORIES

"The Devil and Daniel Webster"	Stephen V. Benet

SPEECHES FOUND IN *The World's Great Speeches*

Daniel Webster's Speech to the Senate
*Rufus Choate's Speech at Fanueil Hall
*John Caldwell Calhoun's Speech to the Senate
*Henry Clay's Speech to the Senate
*Charles Sumner's Speech to the Senate
*John Brown's Speech to the Court
*Stephen Arnold Douglas' Speech in Debate with Lincoln
*Jefferson Davis' Speech upon the Decision to Secede
*Abraham Lincoln's Speeches

RECOVERY 1870–1900

Up from Slavery*	Booker T. Washington
The Virginian*	Owen Wister
Free Land	Rose Wilder Lane
Reconstruction: Binding the Wounds	Cheryl Edwards
Little Britches	Ralph Moody
The Home Ranch	Ralph Moody

EUROPE AND EUROPEAN COLONIES AT THE SAME TIME PERIOD

The Adventures of Sherlock Holmes	Sir Arthur Conan Doyle
Kim	Rudyard Kipling
Captains Courageous	Rudyard Kipling
The Story of a Soul	St. Thérèse Martin
Apologia pro Vita Sua	John Henry Cardinal Newman

SPEECHES FOUND IN *The World's Great Speeches*

Grover Cleveland's First Inaugural Address
Booker T. Washington's Speech to Harvard Alumni
Albert J. Beveridge's Speech to the Union League Club
Theodore Roosevelt's Speech in Chicago in 1899

TURN OF THE CENTURY, WORLD WAR I AND ITS AFTERMATH 1900–1927

Stalin: Russia's Man of Steel	Albert Marrin
All Quiet on the Western Front	Erich Maria Remarque
The Proud Tower	Barbara Tuchman
The European Powers 1900–45	Martin Gilbert
World War One	Hanson Baldwin
First World War	John D. Clare
America at War: World War I	Peter Bosco
The Real War	B. H. Liddell Hart
The Western Front	John Terraine
Revolt in the Desert	Thomas E. Lawrence
Woodrow Wilson and World War One 1917–1921	Robert Ferrell

In Flanders Fields	Leon Wolff
The Zimmermann Telegraph	Barbara Tuchman
Never Give In: The Extraordinary Character of Winston Churchill	Stephen Mansfield
1918: The Last Act	Barrie Pitt
Decisive Battles of the U.S.A.	J. F. C. Fuller
Strategy	Basil H. Liddell Hart
Between Two Fires	David C. Large

WORLD WAR II 1927–1945

*The Spirit of St. Louis**	Charles Lindbergh
*Roll of Thunder, Hear My Cry**	Mildred Taylor
*No Promises in the Wind**	Irene Hunt
*House of Sixty Fathers**	Meindert De Jong
*When Hitler Stole Pink Rabbit**	Judith Kerr
*The Trapp Family Singers**	Maria von Trapp
*The Hiding Place**	Corrie Ten Boom
*Anne Frank: The Diary of a Young Girl**	Anne Frank
*Escape from Warsaw**	Ian Serraillier
*Journey to America**	Sonia Levitin
Grapes of Wrath	John Steinbeck
Hitler	Albert Marrin
The Story of Britain: Early Times to World War II	R. J. Unstead
World War II: The European Theater	Phyllis Raybin Emert
World War II: The Pacific Theater	Phyllis Raybin Emert
The United States in World War Two	A. Russell Buchanan
The Origins of World War II	Peter Allen
When Jays Fly to Barbino	Margaret Balderson
The Ark	Margot Benary-Isbert
Rowan Farm	Margot Benary-Isbert
Castle on the Border	Margot Benary-Isbert
From Casablanca to Berlin	Bruce Bliven, Jr.
Story of D-Day	Bruce Bliven, Jr.
The Inn of the Sixth Happiness	Alan Burgess
Winston Churchill and the Story of the Two World Wars	Olivia Coolidge

The Moon Tenders	August Derleth
Rescue: The Story of How Gentiles Saved	
Jews in the Holocaust	Milton Meltzer
All Things Wise and Wonderful	James Herriot
The Lord God Made Them All	James Herriot
North to Freedom	Anne Holm
Victory in the Pacific	Albert Marrin
The Sea Snake	Stephen W. Meader
The Black Joke	Farley Mowat
The Hero of Auschwitz	(Prow Books, Franciscan Marytown Press)
History of the Second World War	Basil H. Liddell Hart
Crusade in Europe	Dwight D. Eisenhower
A Soldier's Story	Omar N. Bradley
The Longest Day	Cornelius Ryan
A Bridge Too Far	Cornelius Ryan
The Second World War	Winston Churchill
Goodbye Darkness	William Manchester
The Desert Generals	Correlli Barnett
Stilwell and the American Experience in	
China, 1911–45	Barbara Tuchman
The Final Secret of Pearl Harbor: The	
Washington Background of the Pearl Harbor	
Attack	Robert A. Theobald
The Story of the Second World War:	
The Axis Strikes	Col. Red Reeder
The Story of the Second World War:	
The Allies Conquer	Col. Red Reeder
The Chestry Oak	Kate Seredy
The Borrowed House	Hilda van Stockum
The Winged Watchman	Hilda van Stockum
The Zion Covenant	Bodie Thoene
The Zion Chronicles	Bodie Thoene
The Flying Tigers	John Toland
A Man for Others	Patricia Treece
Silence over Dunkerque	John R. Tunis
His Enemy, His Friend	John R. Tunis

The British Empire: An American View of Its History from 1776–1945	R. J. Unstead
The Life of Winston Churchill	Leonard Wibberly
The Rose Round	Meriol Trevor

SPEECHES FOUND IN *The World's Great Speeches*

Stephen S. Wise's Speech to the Lincoln Centennial Association
*Woodrow Wilson's Speech to the Senate
Woodrow Wilson's Speech to a Joint Session of Congress
*F.D.R.'s First Inaugural Address
Bishop Fulton Sheen's Speech "The Cross and the Double Cross"
*Winston Churchill's Speeches
Pius XII's Appeal for Peace

THE COLD WAR 1945–1989

The Korean War	Carter Smith
The Vietnam War: How the United States Became Involved	Mitch Yamasaki
The Elephant and the Tiger: America in Vietnam	Albert Marrin

TIME LINE FOR HISTORY

To make a notebook time line, take an artist's sketchbook, which has blank pages, and draw a line across the top of each of twenty-five pages. If the line on each page stands for two hundred years and is so numbered, twenty-five pages will cover the years from 3000 B.C. to A.D. 2000. If you have fifty pages, the line on each page could stand for one hundred years.

Do not start right out with the time line, however. Use the first page for the seven days of creation and the second page for the fall. Then on the third page note the flood. The fourth page should state "From the flood to 3000 B.C." On the next page, the fifth, begin writing the line at the top of the page. It goes from 3000 to 2800 B.C. in increments of twenty years:

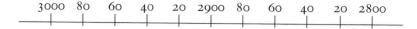

The next page goes on from there. As I said, twenty-five pages from the beginning of the time line will be the year A.D. 2000.

When the students read about an important person or event, they put the information on their time line. The year is noted on the line itself, either by a number or a figure, and the information corresponding to the number or figure is written down on the page under the line.

Here is an example from my daughter's notebook:

(1) St. Hermenegild was the son of King Leovigild. He was originally an Arian but converted after marrying Ingonedes, who was a Catholic. His father was furious, and after trying fruitlessly for a long time to turn Hermenegild back to Arianism, King Leovigild finally had Hermenegild killed.

(2) St. Isidore was the Bishop of Seville. He was a part of the council that chose Spain's new king when needed. He was a great fighter against heresy and a wise councilor. He died April 4, 636.

(3) In the seventh century the Visigoths extended their rule over the entire Spanish peninsula.

HISTORY QUESTIONS

1. Why was the Revolutionary War fought? Consider the course of the negotiations between the colonists and England. How did the Stamp Act, the Tea Tax and other ordinances from England affect the decision of the colonists? How does this compare to the revolution in France?

2. The U.S. is said to have a tradition of limited government. Show from the Constitution what some of those limits are. Is this idea of government found in the Declaration of Independence? Can government aim at making men good and happy and still be limited?

3. Why does the U.S. have both state and national governments? How did this arrangement arise at the Constitutional Convention?

It is generally agreed that the states have lost power over time. Do you think that this is true? If so, discuss two cases where the change took place.

4. What was the Civil War fought about? Consider the status of slavery in the Constitution, its relation to the Declaration of Independence, the Northwest Ordinance, the Compromises of 1820 and 1850, the Dred Scott decision, Lincoln's career and the outcome of the war, including the thirteenth and fifteenth amendments.

5. Write about an important figure in American history. Consider both his character—virtues and vices—and his effects for good or ill on society at large.

6. The U.S. experienced massive immigration from 1900 to 1920. Discuss the immigrants' reasons for coming, the problems they met and the question of "Americanization" of the newcomers. What special advantages did Catholics have, and what difficulties did they meet?

7. What is an income tax? Why did the Constitution have to be amended to allow one? What are the reasons for and against such a mode of taxation? How did the rates change over the period from 1911 to 1945? How do they compare to present rates?

8. What was the grand strategy of the Allies in World War II? Select and discuss several key decisions American leaders had to make, and evaluate their decisions. Examples might be: use of the A-bomb, timing and location of D-Day, invasion of Italy, the "Germany first" decision, island hopping in the Pacific, strategic bombing of Germany. Use Catholic principles about war and the tactics of war in such an evaluation.

9. After the stock market crash of 1929, the country experienced an economic crisis called the "Great Depression". Describe the seriousness and depth of the depression and the response of the so-called "New Deal". Discuss the policy, including its constitutionality. (See especially Article I, section 8, in the Constitution and *Federalist*, 41.)

AMERICAN ARTISTS

AMERICAN NEOCLASSICISM

John Singleton Copley (1738–1815)
Charles Willson Peale (1741–1827)
Raphael Peale (1774–1825)
Rembrandt Peale (1778–1860)
Gilbert Stuart (1755–1828)
Thomas Sully (1783–1872)
John Trumbell (1756–1843)
Benjamin West (1738–1820)

HUDSON RIVER VALLEY SCHOOL

Albert Bierstadt (1830–1902)
Frederic Edwin Church (1826–1900)
Thomas Cole (1801–1848)
Jasper Francis Cropsey (1823–1900)
Asher B. Durand (1796–1886)
Martin Johnson Heade (1819–1904)
George Inness (1825–1894)
John Frederick Kensett (1816–1872)
Thomas Moran (1837–1926)
Samuel F. Morse (1791–1872)

AMERICAN REALISM

John James Audubon (1785–1851)
George Catlin (1796–1872)
Thomas Eakins (1844–1916)
William Michael Harnett (1848–1892)
Winslow Homer (1836–1910)
John Frederic Peto (1854–1907)
Frederic Remington (1861–1909)
Charles Russell (1864–1926)

GENRE PAINTING

George Caleb Bingham (1811–1879)
Eastman Johnson (1824–1906)

AMERICAN IMPRESSIONISM

Mary Cassatt (1845–1926)
William Merritt Chase (1849–1916)
Frederick Childe Hassam (1859–1935)
John Singer Sargent (1856–1925)
James McNeill Whistler (1834–1903)

IMPORTANT COMPOSERS
ARRANGED CHRONOLOGICALLY

BORN DURING THE COLONIAL PERIOD, 1400–1700

Johann Pachelbel (1653–1706)
Arcangelo Corelli (1653–1713)
Fr. Antonio Vivaldi (1678–1714)
Johann Sebastian Bach (1685–1750)
George Frideric Handel (1685–1759)

BORN DURING THE REVOLUTIONARY WAR PERIOD, 1700–1800

Joseph Haydn (1732–1809)
Wolfgang Amadeus Mozart (1756–1791)
Ludwig van Beethoven (1770–1827)
Niccolo Paganini (1782–1840)
Gioacchino Rossini (1792–1868)
Franz Schubert (1797–1828)

BORN DURING THE PERIOD OF WESTWARD EXPANSION, 1780–1860

Hector Berlioz (1803–1869)
Felix Mendelssohn (1809–1847)
Frederic Chopin (1810–1849)
Robert Schumann (1810–1856)
Franz Liszt (1811–1886)
Richard Wagner (1813–1883)
Giuseppe Verdi (1813–1901)

Jacques Offenbach (1819–1880)
Johann Strauss (1825–1899)
Stephen Foster (1826–1864)
Alexander Borodin (1833–1887)
Johannes Brahms (1833–1897)
Modest Mussorgsky (1839–1881)
Peter I. Tchaikovsky (1840–1893)
Antonin Dvořák (1841–1904)
Arthur Sullivan (1842–1900)
Edvard Grieg (1843–1907)
Nicholas Rimsky-Korsakov (1844–1908)
Gabriel Fauré (1845–1924)
John Philip Sousa (1854–1932)
Giacomo Puccini (1858–1924)

BORN DURING THE PERIOD OF THE CIVIL WAR, 1860–1870

Claude Debussy (1862–1918)

BORN DURING THE PERIOD OF RECOVERY, 1870–1900

Ralph Vaughn Williams (1872–1958)
Sergei Rachmaninoff (1873–1943)
Maurice Ravel (1875–1937)
Ottorino Respighi (1879–1936)
Igor Stravinsky (1882–1971)
Sergei Prokofiev (1891–1953)

BORN DURING THE PERIOD OF THE WORLD WARS

Aaron Copland (1900–1990)
Benjamin Britten (1913–1976)

MUSICAL PERIODS

Baroque (1650–1750)

GENERAL STYLE: "cathedral" music; grand.

MUSIC/MELODIES: polyphonic; ornamental notes; vocal lines as if written for instruments.

RHYTHM: complicated rhythms resulting in a thick texture of sound.

DYNAMICS: loud or soft, no crescendo or decrescendo; can create an echo-like effect.

INSTRUMENTS: recorder, viola de gamba, clavichord, harpsichord.

MAIN CATEGORIES: chorus and orchestra

PERFORMANCE: more often in churches than in concert halls.

Classical (1750–1830)

GENERAL STYLE: "powdered wig" music; more stately than Baroque; restrained, graceful, balanced, elegant, even predictable.

MUSIC/MELODIES: one uniform phrase follows the other; compositional simplicity produces lighter music; tunes made to whistle; instrumental lines sound vocal or singable.

INSTRUMENTS: piano emerges as a soloist and accompanist for voices and other instruments.

MAIN CATEGORIES: symphony (new); string quartet.

PERFORMANCE: in cultured parlors.

Romantic (1830–1900)

GENERAL STYLE: "big is beautiful"; passionate, intense, melodramatic; more national in flavor as marked differences appear between composers from different countries.

MUSIC/MELODIES: long and expansive, with complex harmonies.

RHYTHM: full range; much use of rubato with its abrupt tempo changes.

DYNAMICS: full range.

INSTRUMENTS: prominent woodwinds; brass solos; much-enlarged string section.

MAIN CATEGORIES: orchestras growing; opera.

Twentieth Century

GENERAL STYLE: "dissonance"; harmonies no longer resolve into major chords; polytonality and atonality compete with tonality.

MUSIC MELODIES: (1900–1950) strong reaction against excesses of Romanticism leads to music that strives to be intellectually interesting; (1950–2000) "experimentalism"—anything goes.

ELEMENTS OF MUSICAL FORM

Melody, harmony, rhythm, key, form (such as ABA, ABACADA; theme with variations; sonata).

DEFINITIONS

symphony: specific type of musical composition written for orchestra.

sonata: (a) blueprint of first movement of classical sonata, (b) title given to a four-movement composition in specific format.

polytonality: simultaneous use of many musical keys.

atonality: music composed in no key at all.

CHART COMPILED BY ELLEN MARTIN

	BAROQUE	CLASSICAL	ROMANTIC	20th CENT
INSTRUMENTAL				
Orchestra A large group of musicians who perform music together				
Concerto Solo instrument and orchestra				
Chamber Music Small ensembles				
Solo One instrument unaccompanied				
VOCAL				
Choral Usually with an orchestra; sacred and secular				
Opera With orchestra; like a play with acts; arias (principal songs) and recitative (everything else)				
Song (Lieder) Usually accompanied by piano				

CHART COMPILED BY ELLEN MARTIN

Literature List

The Virginian	Owen Wister
Jane Eyre	Charlotte Brontë
Wuthering Heights	Emily Brontë
Tom Sawyer	Mark Twain
Red Badge of Courage	Stephen Crane
The Deerslayer	James F. Cooper
Oliver Twist	Charles Dickens
Silas Marner	George Eliot
Lorna Doone	Richard Blackmore

Alternatives

The Scarlet Letter	Nathaniel Hawthorne
The House of the Seven Gables	Nathaniel Hawthorne
Huckleberry Finn	Mark Twain
Great Expectations	Charles Dickens
A Tale of Two Cities	Charles Dickens
David Copperfield	Charles Dickens
Kidnapped	Robert L. Stevenson
Treasure Island	Robert L. Stevenson
The Count of Monte Cristo	Alexander Dumas
Mutiny on the Bounty	Charles Nordoff and James Norman Hall
Les Misérables	Victor Hugo
Death Comes for the Archbishop	Willa Cather
Shadows on the Rock	Willa Cather
"The Prophecy of Socrates"	Plato
"The Death of Socrates"	Plato
Selections from *The Autobiography of Benjamin Franklin*	

Short Stories

"The Luck of Roaring Camp"	Bret Harte
"The Ranson of Red Chief"	O. Henry
"The Gift of the Magi"	O. Henry
"The Retrieved Reformation"	O. Henry

"Little Bo-Peep"	O. Henry
"The Devil and Daniel Webster"	Stephen V. Benet
"Rip Van Winkle"	Washington Irving
"The Legend of Sleepy Hollow"	Washington Irving
"The Most Dangerous Game"	Richard Connell
"The Secret Life of Walter Mitty"	James Thurber
"Dr. Jekyll and Mr. Hyde"	Robert L. Stevenson
"Neighbor Rosicky"	Willa Cather
"The Great Stone Face"	Nathaniel Hawthorne

POETRY LIST AND OTHER WORKS TO MEMORIZE

"The Daffodils"	William Wordsworth
The Second Inaugural Address	Abraham Lincoln
"The Flute"	Wilfrid Gibson
"Lepanto"	G. K. Chesterton
"A Thing of Beauty"	John Keats
"The Day Is Done"	Henry Wadsworth Longfellow
Sonnets from the Portuguese	E. B. Browning
"When I Was One and Twenty"	A. E. Housman
"Love"	George Herbert
"The Pulley"	George Herbert
"Evangeline"	Henry Wadsworth Longfellow

GENERAL QUESTIONS FOR WORKS OF LITERATURE

All of the following questions are applicable to any literary work. Have your student start any such discussion with a retelling of the story, particularly if you have not read it. Then go on to cover these questions, unless they have already been answered. Some of the questions will have been answered implicitly in the retelling of the story, but the answers need to be made explicit.

What is the setting of the story? How do the changes in scene relate to the action of the plot? Do certain kinds of action go on only in certain kinds of places?

Who are the major characters in this work? How do they relate to one another? What are the conflicts in the story? What changes take place in the major characters over the course of story? Are these changes for the better or not? What are the incidents that precipitate the changes that take place?

Who are the minor characters? What is their function in the work?

What are the important values in this work? Does good triumph over evil? With whom are you intended to identify in the story? How can you tell? What does this tell you about the values of the author? Does this work embody Catholic attitudes? Is this an optimistic or pessimistic work? In what sense?

Additionally, the following questions regarding the excellence of the work can be used in the discussion of any book:

Are the characters well drawn, that is, do they seem real? Is their personality consistent with their behavior? Would such a person do this kind of thing?

Do the events follow one another believably? Would this actually happen after that? Is coincidence employed to further the plot, or does the plot make use of a natural sequence of events?

Is there a true view of reality present in the work? That is, is the evil presented as evil and the good as good? Or do you find yourself sympathizing with a character who is objectively bad? In that case evil has been presented as good, or the sinner has been presented as lovable. When the values of the work are true, do they flow from the actions and conversation of the characters, or does the author have to tell you what to think in his narration because you would not be able to tell from the story itself?

Does the work as a whole seem to come from a realistic perception of the way things actually work? Is the view of life that the author portrays reasonable and balanced? Or is there too much emphasis on one aspect or another, for example, dwelling on the evilness of men without a view of the good that men can do as well? Is the work either overly optimistic or too pessimistic?

Is the book entertaining? Even a serious book, if it is well written, will entertain. It will hold the attention of the reader and in some measure delight him, perhaps by the vividness of the descriptions, by recognition of the characters or by the explanation of some difficult point.

AMERICAN POETS AND POEMS

Those poets marked with an asterisk have poems included in the anthology *The Harp and Laurel Wreath: Poetry and Dictation for the Classical Curriculum* (25).

BORN DURING THE COLONIAL PERIOD, 1400–1700

Anne Bradstreet (1612–1672), "The Flesh and the Spirit"

BORN DURING THE REVOLUTIONARY WAR PERIOD, 1700–1800

Philip Freneau (1752–1832), "To a Honey Bee", "The Wild Honeysuckle"

BORN DURING THE PERIOD OF WESTWARD EXPANSION, 1780–1860

*Richard Henry Dana (1787–1879), "The Soul"
Fitz-Greene Hallack (1790–1867), "Red Jacket"
*William Cullen Bryant (1794–1878), "Thanatopsis", "The Battlefield", "Song of Marion's Men", "Hymn to the North Star", "To a Waterfowl"
Joseph Rodman Drake (1795–1820), "The American Flag"
Edward Coate Pinkney (1802–1828), "A Health"
*George Pope Morris (1802–1864), "Woodman, Spare That Tree"
*Ralph Waldo Emerson (1803–1882), "Each and All", "Concord Hymn", "The Snowstorm", "Compensation", "Forbearance"
Nathaniel Parker Willis (1806–1867), "April"
*Henry Wadsworth Longfellow (1807–1882), "Evangeline", "Paul Revere's Ride", "The Wreck of the Hesperus", "A Psalm of Life", "Nature", "The Arrow and the Song", "Hiawatha's Childhood",

"My Lost Youth", "The Builders", "Excelsior", "St. Francis'
Sermon to the Birds"
*John Greenleaf Whittier (1807–1892), "The Barefoot Boy", "Brown
of Ossawatomie", "The Eternal Goodness", "In School-Days",
"Barbara Frietchie", "Skipper Ireson's Ride"
*Edgar Allan Poe (1809–1849), "The Raven", "Annabel Lee", "The
Bells", "The Happiest Day"
*Oliver Wendell Holmes (1809–1894), "The Chambered Nautilus",
"Old Ironsides", "The Deacon's Masterpiece", "The Height of the
Ridiculous"
Jones Very (1813–1880), "The Earth", "The Latter Rain"
*John Godfrey Saxe (1816–1887), "How Cyrus Laid the Cable", "My
Familiar", "Solomon and the Bees", "The Head and the Heart",
"The Blind Man and the Elephant"
*Henry David Thoreau (1817–1862), "Sic Vita", "Winter Memories"
James T. Fields (1817–1881), "The Owl Critic", "Ballad of the
Tempest"
James Russell Lowell (1819–1891), "The Heritage", "The Present
Crisis", "Washington", "Not Only Armed Our Infancy", "To the
Dandelion", "Yossouf", "The First Snowfall"
*Walt Whitman (1819–1892), "Oh Captain! My Captain!", "A
Noiseless Patient Spider"
Herman Melville (1819–1891), "The Maldive Shark", "The College
Colonel", "The March into Virginia"
Julia Ward Howe (1819–1910), "The Battle Hymn of the Republic"
*Thomas Buchanan Read (1822–1872), "Sheridan's Ride", "Drifting"
George Henry Boker (1823–1890), "A Ballad of Sir John Franklin"
Bayard Taylor (1825–1878), "Bedouin Song", "America"
*Richard Henry Stoddard (1825–1903), "There Are Gains for All Our
Losses", "Abraham Lincoln"
John Townsend Trowbridge (1827–1916), "Midwinter", "The
Peewee"
Henry Timrod (1826–1867), "At Magnolia Cemetery"
Paul Hamilton Hayne (1830–1886), "In Harbor"
*Emily Dickinson (1830–1886), "The Railway Train", "The
Chariot", "Autumn", "Your Riches Taught Me Poverty",
"Because I Could Not Stop for Death", "I Never Saw a Moor"
Edmund Clarence Stedman (1833–1908), "The Hand of Lincoln"

*Phillips Brooks (1835–1893), "O Little Town of Bethlehem", "Christmas Everywhere"

*Thomas Bailey Aldrich (1836–1907), "The Ballad of Baby Bell", "A Turkish Legend", "Guilielmus Rex"

*Bret Harte (1839–1902), "John Burns of Gettysburg", "How Are You, Sanitary?", "Dickens in Camp", "The Reveille"

*Joaquin Miller (1841–1913), "Columbus", "Westward Ho!"

*Edward Rowland Sill (1841–1887), "Opportunity", "The Things That Will Not Die", "The Fool's Prayer"

Sidney Lanier (1842–1881), "Song of the Chattahooche"

*James Whitcomb Riley (1849–1916), "Little Orphant Annie", "When the Frost Is on the Punkin", "The Old Swimmin' Hole", "The First Bluebird"

*Eugene Field (1850–1895), "Wynken, Blynken, and Nod", "Little Boy Blue", "The Dreams", "Little Blue Pigeon"

*Ella Wheeler Wilcox (1850–1919), "Solitude", "As by Fire", "An Inspiration", "One Ship Drives East"

*Henry Van Dyke (1852–1933), "America for Me"

*Edwin Markham (1852–1940), "The Man with the Hoe", "How the Great Guest Came", "A Prayer", "Outwitted", "Preparedness"

Born during the Period of the Civil War, 1860–1870

Bliss Carman (1861–1929), "A Vagabond Song"

George Santayana (1863–1952), "There May Be Chaos Still", "A Minuet on Reaching the Age of Fifty"

Edwin Arlington Robinson (1869–1935), "Miniver Cheevy"

Born during the Period of Recovery, 1870–1900

Stephen Crane (1871–1900), "War Is Kind"

*Paul Laurence Dunbar (1872–1906), "Dawn", "The Dilettante: A Modern Type", "Conscience and Remorse", "The Master Player"

*Robert Frost (1874–1963), "Mending Wall", "A Prayer in Spring", "Stopping by Woods on a Snowy Evening", "The Road Not Taken"

*Carl Sandburg (1878–1967), "Evening Waterfall", "Fog"

*Sara Teasdale (1884–1933), "Wood Song", "Stars", "Barter"

William Rose Benet (1886–1950), "The Fawn in the Snow", "The Death of Robin Hood"

H.D. (1886–1961), "Evening"

T. S. Eliot (1888–1965), "Journey of the Magi", "The Wind Sprang Up at Four O'Clock"

Conrad Aiken (1889–1973), "All Lovely Things"

*Edna St. Vincent Millay (1892–1950), "Autumn Chant", "First Fig", "Recuerdo", "Portrait by a Neighbor"

Archibald MacLeish (1892–1982), "Mother Goose's Garland"

*Stephen Vincent Benet (1898–1943), "Christopher Columbus", "Hernando De Soto", "Pocahontas", "Captain Kidd", "George Washington", "John Adams", "Benjamin Franklin"

The High School Years: Some Important Considerations

T HE HIGH SCHOOL years present a special challenge for many homeschooling parents. Often the parents I speak to express real trepida-
tion about homeschooling through high school. Since my own experiences homeschooling older students have been rewarding, I want to
assure parents that it can be done, and it can be done well. Further, I
have found these years to be, in certain ways, the most pleasant time I
have had with my children.

Most ninth graders are still in the dialectical stage. They are concerned more with grasping intellectual argument than with presenting it
eloquently. Analysis has a place of primary importance.

LOGIC

Some parents may wonder about the absence of formal logic in my
curriculum. To grasp any universal truth, one must make inductions
from the particulars of experience. That means that there must be
particulars from which to draw the induction, and enough of them to
make valid inductions. If you lived in Southern California all your life,
did not travel or discuss trees with anyone, you would think that every
oak tree had small prickly leaves that came off erratically all year long. In
fact, in Minnesota, there are oak trees with large, smooth leaves that fall
off only in the fall. You need more experience before you can conclude
what oak trees are like and when they lose their leaves. The proper goal
of the high school curriculum is to provide such particulars. College is
the place to develop the universal considerations that come from these
particulars and to put a name to them.

The beginning of the study of logic involves simply becoming familiar with intellectual argument. Questions like "What is the main point in this paragraph?" and "How did the author arrive at this conclusion?" will teach students to recognize an argument and tell whether a conclusion follows from its premises. The seventh to ninth grader who works with argument in this way will have a wealth of experience for use in the abstract considerations of formal logic. He would be cheated of this natural, easy preparation if he rushed into technicalities. When the time is right, and with an appropriate background, those formal considerations come easily and with a certain real grasp. Then the student can attach the names and see that this or that argument is an instance of the middle not being properly distributed or that the error is an improper conversion of the universal affirmative.

The student should not only be acquiring particulars to be used later, he should also be developing certain habits of mind. Let me say a word here about the study of grammar. This study is important in the development of the intellectual life. Grammar is not necessary for learning how to write; good writing comes more from regular practice than from anything else. Grammar is an analytic exercise that involves putting one's mind to a whole (a small whole, true, but a whole) and seeing how each part of that whole functions with respect to every other part. It requires discipline because every word in the sentence must be explained specifically; there is no room for vague generalizations. It entails real attention to detail because every part must be taken account of. These are characteristics that the student needs to develop if he is to think well. If he learns to do these things with respect to grammar, he has received both a kind of formation that can be applied to other subjects and an experience of using these skills with respect to a matter that he can master. Learning grammar well is an essential component of the logical or dialectical stage of intellectual development.

In the tenth and subsequent grades, the student should continue both to study and to develop particular arguments as well as to practice analysis, but he should now concentrate on presenting a position well. We never stop analyzing the positions we encounter. There are always questions that need answers, and thoughtful consideration, separation and categorization are required to bring those answers to light. But we also need to learn how to present the answers persuasively.

THE RHETORICAL STAGE

The art of rhetoric, the third part of the classical Trivium, begins with an ability to assemble thoughts and ideas and present them well, both orally and in writing. The high schooler is able to pay particular attention to this kind of formation, so his stage of intellectual development can be called the rhetorical.

The rhetorical stage overlaps with the dialectical on one end and with the movement to subjects as subjects, which is the proper formality for the college student, on the other. It is characterized in the student by a discovery that he needs to know more and a resulting interest in and capacity for acquiring information. His imagination is active; there is a budding enjoyment, which should be fostered, of the poetical, in literature, art and music.

High-school-age students are ready to give themselves to high and noble things. Their growing love of the poetical is a sign of this newly felt response to the good, the true and the beautiful. We need to appeal to this desire in our students by making available to them objects that are proportionate to their desire. They are capable of nobility, and we should encourage them to pursue it.

APOLOGETICS

The most noble and most important object is the Catholic faith. While the most effective way of passing on the faith is to live it ourselves, it is also necessary to present the truth of the faith in ways that appeal to the intellect and to provide opportunities to live and witness to that faith. Training in Catholic apologetics, some opportunities and encouragement to testify to their faith, along with time and occasions for a deeper and stronger prayer life, will call forth the best that is in our children.

There are many sources that make an appeal to the intellect, showing the reasonableness of the faith. The Fr. Laux books, which I include in my curriculum, contain intelligible and thorough presentations of doctrine. *Of Sacraments and Sacrifice*, by Fr. Clifford Howell (31); *The Great Divorce*, by C. S. Lewis (6); *The Belief of Catholics*, by Fr. Ronald Knox (31); *To Know Christ Jesus*, by Frank Sheed (25); *Surprised by Truth*, edited by Patrick Madrid (21); and the *Catechism of the Catholic Church* (25) are all titles that spring immediately to mind as engaging texts that bring the faith to life. There are many others as well.

Catholic Apologetics, by Fr. Laux (53); *Following Christ in the World*, by Anne Carroll (49); *Biblical Apologetics*, by Fr. Frank Chacon and Jim Burnham (47); and *Catholicism and Fundamentalism*, by Karl Keating (25), are all good sources for training in apologetics. Opportunities for witnessing to the faith and using apologetic training are easily found in pro-life work. My family has prayed outside aborturies, participated in pro-life marches and also helped out at the local crisis pregnancy center. These have all been occasions of growth for my children. It is also beneficial to encourage young people to explain to others, whenever it comes up, what we believe and how we try to live those beliefs.

Once, at a local amusement park, two of my children (who have asked to be called Child A and Child B) went off to ride a roller coaster, arranging to meet the rest of us later, at a designated location. When we met again, I could see that the elder of the two, Child A, had had a wonderful time. She was glowing. I said, "That must have been a great roller coaster!" She said, "Oh, Mom, we were in line in front of a woman who was ranting about how this park won't let homosexuals dance together. I was worried about what Child B would think, and this lady was not trying to keep her opinions to herself, so I said loudly that I thought it was great not to allow homosexuals to dance together." I didn't think that was the end of the story, so I asked my daughter how the lady had responded.

"She asked what was wrong with homosexuals dancing together, so I explained that practicing homosexuality is wrong for many of the same reasons contraception is wrong, that the primary end of marriage is procreation, and that all these wrong things lead to abortion."

"So, what did she think about that?"

"She said that I was probably one of those people who stand outside abortion clinics making women feel bad, and I told her that while I do pray the Rosary outside the abortuary, that isn't what makes women feel bad. If you're doing the right thing and someone prays for you, you won't feel bad. It's because you already know that this is not good that public prayer makes you feel bad. And then I said, 'You sound like you work for Planned Parenthood', and she said, 'As a matter of fact, I do!' That was the end of the conversation."

Not all of my children would have had this conversation, because some of them are too shy to engage a stranger in a public debate. But I want all of them to be able to understand and articulate the connections my daughter expressed to that woman.

UNINTERRUPTED QUIET

Since youngsters of this age are still in formation, this period of their life should not be only, or even primarily, concerned with outside activities, however good those activities might be. In terms of both education and prayer life, high-school-age students need periods of uninterrupted quiet in which they can think and pray.

While it is true that you can lead a horse to water but you can't make him drink, it is also true that if you lead a thirsty horse to water, he usually *will* drink. Your child's prayer life is not unlike that. You cannot make your teenaged son or daughter contemplative and prayerful, but you can encourage him or her to be so by providing the time for daily Mass and weekly or monthly holy hours. You might ask a teenaged son to accompany his mother to holy hour, telling him he can protect her. Or he could go with Dad, as a special gift they give to God together. Think about ways to help your children make the faith their own, both intellectually and by pious practices.

THE FINE ARTS

The high-school-aged person is attracted to the noble in other fields as well. Literature, art and music are all areas where we can expose our children to beautiful work and express our own appreciation of that work. Young people will respond to classical music if it is presented to them. They can appreciate the art of Raphael, Michelangelo and Ruisdael if we make an effort to acquaint them with their works. Good literature is appealing in itself and should be read constantly by our older students. If they are given the opportunity to encounter the best and finest of the arts, they will be moved by it. I thought this was true before my children arrived at their present age; now I am sure, because I have seen it happen with my children and the children of my friends.

There is a certain truth to the adage "we are what we eat". When we eat healthy foods, we are healthier, because our bodies receive the kind of nutrition that enables them to grow and develop. When we eat junk food, the opposite happens; our bodies are starved for real nutrients. This is also true on a spiritual level. We *are* what we read and what we see and what we hear. Our imaginations are furnished by these objects. If this furniture is noble and beautiful, the faculty of imagination will be strengthened and ordered. Charlotte Mason, who is sometimes referred to as the pioneer of the homeschooling movement, says one "cannot measure the influence that one or another artist has upon the child's sense of beauty, his power of seeing, as in a picture, the common sights of life; he is more enriched than we know in having really looked at even a single picture." Additionally this is a great pleasure; once the child learns how to look at a picture or how to listen well to a piece of music, he will have a skill that will immeasurably enrich his life.

CONVERSATION: TRAINING IN RHETORIC

Exposure to copious numbers of high and noble objects, however, will not, by itself, bring about the good we desire for our children. It will help; it may even be a necessary component; but what is more essential is the time and conversation we give to our children. Adolescent children are in formation, and the best source for their formation is our own explanations of the way we live, why we make the choices we do, how we view the Church and the world. If, for example, you decide that your children are not going to watch a certain movie, explain to them why not. Say no, but use that opportunity to form their minds with respect to your understanding of what is important.

In my experience, if you do that faithfully, thoughtfully and regularly, your children will come to view the world as you do. They will learn the principles of your decisions and make them their own principles.

This kind of conversation often has to do with questions of moral behavior, as in the above example. But we should also encourage our children to have a right attitude toward their academic efforts through conversations in which we make a conscious effort to point out the truth and beauty in every subject. Foster a love of those things. In subjects like astronomy, natural history and literature, this is easy to do. Show your interest in these areas. You may not have time to do the observations or readings that your students are doing, but you can listen with attention to what they say and express your appreciation of the things they tell you about. Your reaction to the information they share will have a large effect upon their own response to that information.

The combination of poetical interests and recognition of his need for information gives the student of this age an ability to express himself in elegant and persuasive language.

Rhetoric is of three kinds: the political, the forensic and the ceremonial. These three kinds differ in their ends. The political aims at establishing whether a proposed course of action is expedient or inexpedient; the forensic, whether an action done was just or unjust; and the ceremonial, whether someone deserves praise or blame. To achieve these ends, the speaker has three means of persuasion. The first of these is his own character: he must represent himself as one who is worthy of belief. The second is his power to affect and control the emotions of his listeners, for their state of mind will greatly affect how receptive they are to his argument. And the third is the persuasive quality of the argument itself, for the premises must be likely and the procedure logical.

Knowing these things can help the student refine his communication skills. He will realize that to communicate effectively he must take into account the audience and its reaction to the speaker. It is worthwhile to spend some time thinking about who is in the audience and what they are likely to react to as well as about the argument itself. Also, the speaker's appearance and general demeanor will communicate credibility or the lack of it. A speaker must establish himself as a person worth listening to.

These communication skills will be very important in college, so our children need to practice them. We not only need to talk to our children and instruct them in how to speak and write well; we need to let them talk to us. We need to listen.

Parents often worry that they will not have the time to read what their children read and so will not be able to discuss the work with them. Ideally you should read, or should have read, the same material that your children are reading. If, however, that is not the case (and with a large family, it is often *not* the case), you are still able to discuss with them. Have them tell you the plot, ask about the characters, encourage them to articulate their understanding of the author's point of view. You know more than they do about reality, and that is the touch point of all such discussions.

In certain respects it can even be an advantage not to know the material firsthand, because your questions will be more searching and your child will know that your questions are real, coming from your desire for knowledge, rather than being simply an attempt to see if he "got it". Ask questions as though the people in the story were new neighbors whom your child had met and you had not. Ask the questions that would occur to you in that situation. Who are they? How many of them are there? How do they make their living? How are they related to each other? What are their values? How can you tell? What are they doing? How do they react to one another?

Not long ago one of my high school students read *The Count of Monte Cristo*. I have never read this book or even seen the movie, but I know that when there was an index of forbidden books, this book was on it! After some investigating, my husband and I decided that our daughter could read it, but that we would have to make sure she could see what was wrong with the book. We had a lovely, lengthy discussion. When we were done, I could have told you a lot about the plot and the characterizations in that book. I asked lots of questions, encouraging my daughter to describe the plot, the characters, how they related one to another, what they did and why they did it, until I felt I knew enough about the book to make some moral judgments. I could not tell my daughter, or you, how well written this work is—I have not read it and do not know. But I could point out that though the Count of Monte Cristo is sympathetically portrayed, his major motivation in the course of the story is revenge. My daughter did not see that as clearly as I did until we discussed it.

In this stage of intellectual formation, the manner in which ideas are expressed has central importance in the curriculum. Encouraging young people to discuss, keeping in mind the ends and means of rhetoric, is one way to capitalize on their natural gifts. There are also exercises that can contribute to elegant writing. Some of them are mentioned in my curriculum. However, I have found that while in the early years the best teaching device for learning to write is simply to have the children write regularly and at some length, in the high school years it is better to do a few papers well, working on writing and rewriting, than to do many papers poorly. Have the students write with attention to clarity, elegance and persuasion. Then rewrite, cut down, rephrase and rewrite again.

PHILOSOPHY AND THEOLOGY

During this period of formation, I try to keep in mind that the liberal arts we are studying, and preparing to study, are ordered to philosophy and theology. This kind of education is devoted to what is intrinsically worth knowing, for a man and for a Christian, whatever his way of life may be. Some of my students will go on in these areas, and some probably will not. But whether they do or not, to prepare for such an academic program is to prepare for any further learning one may intend as well as to prepare for a reasonable and Christian life even if one does not pursue the academic life.

Though not all of us are called to be philosophers and theologians, we are all called to think and to think well. We all need to make judgments about the true and the false. How many times have you listened to a debate or a speech or a sermon and thought that there was a great deal of irrelevant matter introduced? Or thought that it would help the whole discussion if someone would define his terms? Or, if the terms *were* defined, that everyone would abide by the definitions given? This is the sort of thing that we are all called to do and that we want to teach our children to do.

The kind of education I propose will help the student to do these things whether or not he goes on in philosophy and theology. If a student does pursue philosophy and theology, it will fit him for such studies.

My religion curriculum is intended both to teach the doctrine of the faith clearly and to provide background information that will make theology courses in college more immediately knowable, allowing the students to get involved right away in the heart of the matter.

Philosophy is also prepared for in our curriculum. To do philosophy well, one needs to have a certain amount of experience, so that the matter of judgment is present in the imagination of the student. Direct experience in many areas is most fruitful, but the indirect experience gained by reading good historical and fictional books is also valuable.

MATHEMATICS

Mathematics is important for the development of the high school student. This is an area where one has an opportunity to see a subject from the "top down". Most areas of knowledge, for us, proceed from effect to cause. We observe what goes on around us and draw conclusions from our experience about the nature of the things we observe. In mathematics we have the opportunity of seeing a subject as God sees all of reality, from cause to effect. One learns the principles of the science first and then draws the consequences from those principles.

Mathematics can be difficult to teach, both because of the material, which some of us have not thought about since our own high school days, and because it is easy to fall behind in the necessary corrections of daily lessons.

Here is a system that has helped me stay on top of the correction of the students' lessons: I tell my students to bring their lesson (or part of a lesson) to me as soon as it is done, promising to stop whatever I am doing long enough to correct the lesson. After I circle any errors, I hand it back. The students then go over their errors, reworking the problems, and bring the lesson to me again. I correct the reworked problems and note those that are still wrong. Those problems we go over together, later, when I am free to do so. But I find that they often get the problems right the second time through. If they do not, I know there is actually a problem with understanding the material and not just a problem with inattention. Those difficulties are the ones they need help with.

This system helps in several ways. The students know that I am actually going to look at their work as soon as it is done, and that in itself is helpful. They know that if they do not understand how to do something, we will catch it before a habit of doing it the wrong way develops. It also saves me time because I do not go over problems that they actually do know how to do; I only work on the ones that really are difficult for them.

There are some subjects where a lapse of time before the work is corrected is not significant. If you do not get around to reading an English paper for a number of days, it is not going to make much difference. This is not true in math, because if the student is doing something wrong, he will continue to do it wrong every day, developing bad habits, until someone tells him that it is wrong and shows him how to do it correctly. This is something I learned the hard way, having to back up one of my children a number of lessons, because there were several concepts he had just not understood, and I had not realized it.

In terms of the principles of the science, geometry precedes algebra, yet algebra is more suited to the powers of the ninth-grade student. Algebra can be done well by the student who is not yet ready to deal explicitly with universal principles. Geometry cannot be done as well by such a person. In tenth or eleventh grade, when geometry is studied and the universal considerations of the science are made clear, the student will see that the algebra he has been doing is in fact derived from geometrical truths.

In this way, algebra is like the catechism studied in the early grades. While there is at first some real understanding of the matter, there is much more memorization, which will later on be more fully understood.

THE AIM OF LIBERAL EDUCATION

In every subject, whether it proceeds from cause to effect or from effect to cause, the aim of liberal arts education is to give the student the principles of the subject studied in such a way that he will be able to make right judgments about that area of reality. That is why this kind of education is called *liberal* education. Liberal means "free"; a liberally educated man is a free man because he is able to direct his own life and is not dependent upon the judgments or understanding of others.

In this method of education one pays attention to the particular intellectual strengths of each child at every stage of his development and uses those strengths in every subject. This makes homeschooling easier, because one does not have to worry about finishing every book or course. If you help your child do what he is ready to do at that point of his intellectual development, he will profit from his work, whether he does all the chapters or not. Ordinarily it is better to finish what you start, but sometimes you cannot. And sometimes it is better to slow down and concentrate, practicing skills rather than acquiring more information.

This is true for all the stages of formation but perhaps especially for the high school years. It is much better to do fewer subjects and do them in more depth, than to do many subjects superficially. It is better to do a few papers and do them well, working on writing and rewriting, than to do many papers poorly. The student learns more by working on a paper or a subject until he has gotten it right than by covering a great deal of information. For one thing, he learns what real mastery is.

TAILOR YOUR CURRICULUM

As you arrive at the high school years, pinpoint your student's difficulties and work on them. For example, if you administer a diagnostic spelling test to your high schooler and discover that his spelling level is sixth or seventh grade, it would be best to work assiduously with him on this subject, even if that means not covering certain other areas. I know several families who had students in this position. One of those families did in fact work intensively on spelling for their first year of homeschooling, using *The Writing Road to Reading*. At the end of the year the high schoolers retook the diagnostic test and were thrilled to find that their spelling level was now eleventh grade, seventh month. There were probably other subjects that were not covered because of the amount of time spent on spelling. However, this was time well spent, because good spelling is a foundational skill. Also, the students learned valuable lessons about how to learn and saw that serious, focused, attention pays off.

If your child has particular areas of difficulty, clearly the homeschooling situation allows for more concentrated effort in those areas. If your child does not have particular problems but does have particular interests, the homeschooling situation allows him to delve more deeply into those interests.

Dorothy Sayers, in her description of the rhetorical stage of formation, says that

> The doors of the storehouse of knowledge should now be thrown open for them to browse about as they will. The things once learned by rote will be seen in new contexts; the things once coldly analyzed can now be brought together to form a new synthesis; here and there a sudden insight will bring about that most exciting of all discoveries: the realization that a truism is true. . . . Any child who already shows a disposition to specialize should be given his head: for, when the use of the tools has been well and truly learned, it is available for any study whatever.

My eldest daughter (Child A) loves Spanish history. She developed this love in high school and read an enormous amount on the subject. She did research projects and wrote papers and educated all of her family in the process. She had a wonderful time and learned more about this subject, and more about the learning process, than she ever would have in a traditional school.

In general I recommend planning a curriculum that pays attention to your child's stage of intellectual formation as well as to his particular interests and any weaknesses he may have. Concentrate on those areas that need most attention, and make time for special interests.

If the particular areas in which your children need special help, or take special interest, are outside your competence, get a tutor. You might go to the local junior college and talk to a counselor about finding an algebra tutor, for example.

What about the student who has neither special problems nor special interests? Such a student still profits from the tailored curriculum, because he does not go on to the next concept until the current one has been learned and because he knows that there is an interested and concerned adult who actually notices what has been learned and what has not.

COLLEGE

In addition to taking into account your child's special needs and interests, look at the college you think your child may attend, and tailor your curriculum to its requirements. As long as you use the dialectical skills your child has developed in the seventh to ninth grade and have the rhetorical skills of writing and oral presentation worked into your program, the specific courses covered can be chosen with a view to college entrance.

My own high school curriculum is, I think, a good preparation for any of the authentically Catholic colleges currently available. In this book I give an overview of recommended courses. I have included some study guides and other general information.

Academically, homeschooling provides an education as good as or better than most "traditional" schools. There are, of course, other considerations that must be taken into account in making the decision to homeschool, especially through high school.

TIME MANAGEMENT

For the last six years I have been teaching high school students, mostly my own children but also the children of friends and neighbors. One expects that once children get to this stage of life they will be independent learners, able to teach themselves. At least, that is what I expected, but it did not take long before I realized that this was not the case. Actually, the seventh or eighth grader seems better able to work independently, perhaps because the work is not quite so difficult. The older student needs instruction about what he is expected to do, and he needs a checkpoint. Most of us need an outside deadline lest the temptation to put things off be too great. This is even more true of the adolescent. He needs to know that on Thursday, for example, someone is going to be looking over his work. Without that practical motivation, Thursday after Thursday is likely to pass without the work being done.

We have had some youngsters come and do school with us all day and some once a week. In either case I would schedule uninterrupted time to work with the students. One day it occurred to me that this was not being done with my own older children; they were expected both to do the work and to provide their own motivation. Surely, if I could give this amount of attention to other people's children, I could give it to my own. So we began and found it works pretty well. Once a week we go over the coming assignments together so that any questions about procedure can be answered. Then the students cannot use the excuse, "But we didn't know how." Once or twice a week we also schedule time to go over their assignments. They do most of their subjects on their own, as well as any preparation for discussions. I correct work and tests and discuss with them. The students are getting their work done in a more timely manner now, and I am still able to work with my younger students, who need more one-on-one attention to daily work.

Lists are very helpful in the accomplishment of timely and thorough schooling. I have included an example of our weekly lists at the end of each high school section.

Sometimes this arrangement works best with an outside person. Perhaps you and another mother could arrange to trade off checking each other's children's work. Or perhaps you could take over the direction of someone else's child in a particular subject. High school is a good place for cooperation, because often it is a good idea for the student to experience someone other than his mother as "teacher" before going off to college (60).

Whatever you do, and allowing for the necessary flexibility life requires, I think a general plan will help your high schooler achieve his school goals. I have written syllabi to address that need, but you could just as well do your own. Take the material you want to cover, decide whether you will have your child do papers or write answers to questions or take quizzes and then divide the material you want to cover by the time you have available. There you have your general plan. You can change it as you need to, but you have a strategy to work with.

PHYSICAL ACTIVITY

Another consideration, particularly with boys, is providing an outlet for their excess energy. Boys need physical activity: sports or a job or a service project. But a high school is not necessary to supply this need. Look among your friends for those who might need the skill (or the physical strength) of your teen. When he reached this stage, my eldest son began working part time at a local car wash owned by friends from our parish and also golfed twice a week with his grandfather. Both of those activities were arranged because I saw the need, but they worked out well.

Adolescents need to be reminded that God has a specific plan for their lives. We all need to be reminded of this regularly, but teenage children are particularly susceptible to the kind of doubt and worry that makes it necessary to remind them of God's loving care for them.

Though we have a large number of homeschoolers in my area, there are no boys exactly the age of one of my boys. This son was bemoaning this fact once, loudly and persistently. Rather than, "This is your cross, honey, so take it up and carry it cheerfully", or "What's wrong with your sisters?", either of which I might have said, I thought about his loneliness and desire for companionship. "Why aren't there any boys his age for him to play with?" I wondered. "It really is rather strange, in terms of the large number of families and large number of children in each of those families, that there shouldn't be boys the right age."

As I reflected on that, it seemed to me that the right response to make to my son was something like the following. "I know it is hard to be without boys your age to play with. It *is* strange that there are plenty of girls here, but no boys. I can only conclude that it is not an accident. I mean, God could have had more boys your age here if He had wanted to. It is not as though He said, 'Sorry, I just couldn't manage it.' It must be part of His plan for you.

"There are certain qualities a young man develops when he is left to his own devices. He learns to use his imagination. He has more opportunity to think without distractions and to develop his intellectual capacity. He often learns how to get along with his family and how to be helpful to his parents and siblings in a way he wouldn't if he were constantly with friends. All of these qualities are very valuable and rather rare in the adult world. I wonder if God doesn't have a plan for you that will require these qualities. Remember, He could have arranged things differently, and He didn't. So use this time to develop those qualities that you wouldn't be able to otherwise.

"Your life will change. In a few years you will be off somewhere in the world using the talents you develop now. You will be busy then, living an active life. Right now you have an opportunity. Use it, and remember that it is part of God's plan for you."

So I said something like that. Whatever I said, it made a difference to my son. To be reminded that God does indeed have a specific plan for each of us is important. Instead of bewailing the circumstances we find ourselves in, we can direct ourselves, and our children, to the right use of those circumstances.

RAGING HORMONES

Sometimes homeschooling parents will think about sending their child back to a regular school when the child begins to exhibit "R.H." [Raging Hormones] behavior. While there are children who never react in this way, the fact is that some of them do—even homeschooled children. This is probably the worst time to send children away from home. The alienation the child feels from the family can be intensified by sending him away. If he stays home, he will realize that it is necessary to work out his differences, and thus he will learn a valuable lesson about life in the "real" world.

When people say that homeschooling does not prepare children for life, the homeschooling mother can reply that the earthly happiness of most people depends upon their ability to get along in a family. Homeschooling allows children to learn this very important skill.

There was a time when homeschooling through high school was a lonely business. There were not many people doing it, and there were many who thought it could not be done. That is no longer true. The Catholic homeschooling movement is still young, but there are now a significant number of families who have been homeschooling for enough years to have high-school-age children and beyond. We can

GRADUATION REQUIREMENTS

The minimum requirements for graduation from high school vary from state to state. The following guideline is for the minimum requirements in California. Check your own state's requirements.

English	4 years	40 units
Math	2 years	20 units
Social Studies	3½ years	35 units
Science (lab for 1 year)	2 years	20 units
Physical Education	2 years	20 units
Fine Arts or Foreign Language	1 year	10 units
Health	½ year	5 units
TOTAL		150 units

Total number of units required is 225, with the remainder being made up by electives. In terms of credits the number required is 22.5.

COLLEGE REQUIREMENTS

Requirements for the college bound, based upon the recommendations for Thomas Aquinas College: *

English	4 years	40 units
Algebra	2 years	20 units
Geometry	1 year	10 units
	More math is encouraged.	
History/Geography (Social Studies)	3 years	30 units
Science	3 years	30 units
	Astronomy and Natural History are encouraged.	
Language	2 years	20 units
	Preferably Latin, and preferably more than 2 years.	
TOTAL		150 units

*The recommendations of Thomas Aquinas College are used as an indicator. Call the college you are interested in to learn its course requirements.

look to these children to see the fruit of homeschooling right through high school. The children I know who were homeschooled until college are pleasant, happy, intellectually interested and academically competent. They do not have debauched cultural trappings to rid themselves of, as many traditionally schooled children often do. They have a head start on the path to a life centered in the holy Catholic Church and obedient to the will of their Savior.

COURSE RECOMMENDATIONS
Combining Minimum California State Requirements and
Course Recommendations for Thomas Aquinas College

NINTH GRADE

Religion
Grammar and Composition
Algebra I
American History
Earth Science
Art/Music
  TOTAL: 60 units
American Literature and Poetry (optional)
Latin I (optional)
  TOTAL: 80 units

TENTH GRADE

Religion
Geometry
English
Ancient History
Latin I or II
Readings in Natural History
  TOTAL: 60 units

ELEVENTH GRADE

Religion
Algebra II
English

European History
Latin II
Physical Education
    TOTAL: 60 units
Biology (optional)
    TOTAL: 70 units

TWELFTH GRADE

Religion
American Government
Chemistry
Health (half year)
Physical Education
    TOTAL: 45 units
Latin III (optional)
Advanced Math (optional)
British Literature (optional)
    TOTAL: 75 units

Total units: 225; with all optional courses, 285.

This suggested course of study is just that, a suggestion. It is an example of the kind of planning for the whole of the high school years that needs to be done.

GRADES AND GRADING INFORMATION

Susan, a close friend of mine, does not give grades in her homeschool. She says there is no point; her children never go on to the next concept until they have learned the previous one, so there would be only A's if she gave grades. I think her comment shows the problem we home-school parents have with grading. We usually do not go on until A work is being produced, and lower grades will not reflect the child's grasp of the concepts.

Nonetheless, grades are important in their own way. For some children, especially those who have previously attended school, grades provide motivation. There are those who object that since we want our children to love learning for its own sake, we should not encourage them to learn "for the grade". That is certainly true. Nevertheless, a grade can be a kind of objective reflection of the work done. One learns for the sake of learning, but work well done is acknowledged to be such, and there is a kind of honor attached to that.

Also, grades will be given and will matter at some point. Even if you have homeschooled and have not given grades through high school, grades will be assigned in college. It is easier to get used to this system of assessment before one gets to the point where it is of serious import.

Lastly, if a student is applying to another school for admission, grades will be expected. Certainly in high school, students should be given grades so that they will have a transcript to send to the colleges they are interested in attending.

Therefore, I recommend a system something like the following: pick assignments to grade, and tell the students that this assignment is going to be graded when it is turned in (they may still have to correct it). In math, grade the tests. In English, grade written assignments, especially those that the student does following explanation on your part. In history, grade papers and end of chapter questions such as those in *Old World and America*. In science, the little quizzes at the end of the chapter, as well as the answers to the questions throughout the chapter, may be graded. Basically, decide ahead of time what you want to grade, and let the students know. Then stick to it.

The following tables may help you in grading:

Letter	Grade	May be broken down thus:		
A	90–100	90–93 A–	94–97 A	98–100 A+
B	80–89	80–83 B–	84–86 B	87–89 B+
C	70–79	70–73 C–	74–76 C	77–79 C+
D	60–69	60–63 D–	64–66 D	67–69 D+
F	59 or lower	0–59 F		

GRADE POINT AVERAGES

A or A+	4.00	C	2.00
A–	3.75	C–	1.75
B+	3.50	D+	1.50
B	3.00	D	1.00
B–	2.75	D–	.75
C+	2.50	F	.00

The Rhetorical Stage

Tenth Grade Curriculum

Sources for items followed by a number in parentheses may be found at the back of the book in the list of suppliers.

Religion—*Mass and the Sacraments,* by Fr. John Laux (53); *Of Sacraments and Sacrifice,* by Fr. Clifford Howell (31); *Catholic Apologetics,* by Fr. John Laux (53); *From Baptist to Catholic Apologist,* by Tim Staples (47); the *Catechism of the Catholic Church* (25). There is a syllabus available for this course (36).

As in the previous texts of this series, the lessons in *Mass and the Sacraments* include well-chosen questions requiring careful analysis. The writing assignments are good and easy to do, since the outlines for requested papers are often given in the text. The topic of this book is interesting to students and can be made even clearer by supplementing the text with *Of Sacraments and Sacrifice,* which is out of print but quite easy to obtain. (Fr. Howell's book is excellent, except for the last chapter. We do not read the last chapter when using this book.) After reading these two texts, the student will know the essential elements of a sacrifice and be able to show that these elements are present in the Mass. He will also understand the relationship between the natural and the supernatural orders and be able to give the proximate and remote matter of each sacrament. Part two of the *Catechism,* pp. 277–420, may be referred to for additional information on the topics of the sacraments.

In *Catholic Apologetics,* particular attention should be paid to each of the five steps in the whole argument for the truth of the Catholic faith. Again, Fr. Laux' chapter questions are helpful. Some of these questions may be answered in writing, and some orally. Have the student write five papers while studying this text, one paper for each part of the argument. In this way the general argument for the reasonableness of our belief in the Catholic faith is reproduced by the student, and because each step in that argument has been the subject of a separate paper, the whole argument is clearly seen.

Before starting *Catholic Apologetics,* have the student listen to a tape by Tim Staples, one of the converts whose story is presented in the book *Surprised by Truth,* edited by Patrick Madrid (21). This tape, a recounting of Tim's journey to the Catholic Church, makes a big impression on high-school-age students. The tape sets the stage, or provides the context, for the students to see the importance of apologetic argument and also to see which issues tend to occur over and over again within that context.

The tape also provides an opportunity for the students to see the Church through the eyes of an apologist who is on fire for Christ and His Church. High-school-age students are ready to give themselves to the high and noble. Their growing love of the poetical in literature, music and art is a sign of this newly felt response to the good, the true and the beautiful. We need to appeal to this desire in the students by making available to them objects that are proportionate to their desire. They are capable of nobility, and we should encourage them. I think this tape is one way to do so.

Later on, in eleventh or twelfth grade, review much of this material and have the students read *Surprised by Truth.* Also use the booklet *Beginning Apologetics,* by Fr. Frank Chacon and Jim Burnham (47), which contains succinct arguments addressing the usual difficulties non-Catholics have with the faith. Once we have gone through a section, I have the students practice defending the doctrine of the Church by arguing against me, as I present the erroneous position. If your tenth grader is really interested, he might begin doing this now.

Mathematics—*Geometry,* by Harold Jacobs (20); or the geometry video course from Superstar Teachers High School Series (55).

Geometry is one of the disciplines in the Quadrivium. It is a subject, something studied not as a tool for other disciplines but as an end in itself. Euclid's *Elements,* the original geometry, is not easy to do at home. It is time intensive in terms of presenting the propositions and watching their presentation. However, studying geometry is important for both practical and theoretical reasons.

The PSAT test is offered to students across the country in October of their junior year in high school. If they do well on this test, they are eligible for the National Merit Scholarship competition. In any case, students who take the PSAT may regard it as a valuable opportunity to practice for the SAT or ACT, tests necessary for college entrance. For more information on these tests, contact the College Board (15).

The PSAT contains both algebra and geometry problems, and therefore the mathematics course for sophomore year should prepare the student in both areas. One strategy is to review the algebra from last year, doing a few lessons each week all year, while doing a full geometry course. If the student has mastery of the Saxon *Algebra I*, his algebraic skills will be sufficient.

Jacobs' *Geometry* is a traditional geometry program, employing deductive proofs. We skip the first chapter and begin in the second chapter, where the study of geometry begins. It is important to have this subject, done in this way, in the curriculum at some point. Most of the subjects we study proceed from effect to cause. We see the effects and proceed by reason to a knowledge of what the cause must be. Mathematics in general, and geometry in particular, provide a place in the intellectual life where one may start with the causes, or principles, of the science and proceed to the effects. This manner of knowing is the way that God knows. He knows all that He knows in terms of Himself, the cause of all that exists. When the student studies theology, it is helpful to have a paradigm of knowledge that proceeds from cause to effect, so that the manner of God's knowledge may be illustrated by something the student has experienced.

The video geometry program is simpler and not quite as thorough, but it does provide another way to study this subject that may be less intimidating to some students.

English—*Warriner's English Grammar and Composition, Fourth Course,* by John E. Warriner (21); or the Seton sophomore English course (49); *Analogies 1, Analogies 2, Analogies 3* from EPS (19); *The Harp and Laurel Wreath: Poetry and Dictation Selections for the Classical Curriculum,* edited by Laura Berquist (25)

In the sophomore year students should concentrate on writing skills and literary analysis. The grammar sections of *English Grammar and*

Composition are of secondary importance this year, especially if the student is studying Latin. Any foreign language study that involves translation will keep grammar skills fresh. The subjects for composition and analysis, which form the heart of the English program at this stage, may be found in any of the courses being studied. We use the ancient history course (see below) as the primary matter of writing and analysis, utilizing the composition sections of the *Warriner's* text as a guide to structure and procedure. The "General Questions for Works of Literature", which are included in the ninth-grade resource list, are used as a basis for literary discussion. *The Harp and Laurel Wreath: Poetry and Dictation Selections for the Classical Curriculum* has a section with terms to know for the study of poetry, poetry selections that illustrate those particular poetical features and study questions and answers.

An alternative to this would be to enroll in the Seton sophomore English course. Some part of every quarter is spent on writing skills. The other part of each quarter concentrates on literary analysis. *Animal Farm* and *The Tale of Two Cities* are both investigated with a view to theme, character development and conflict. There is a section on poetry analysis, as well as one that studies imagery, figures of speech and other poetical devices. The material in the Seton syllabus is excellent.

In either case, it is beneficial to add the study of analogies to your curriculum. The PSAT and SAT tests have a whole section of the verbal portion of the test just on analogies, so it is helpful for the student to have had some experience dealing with them. Further, doing analogies correctly involves critical thinking, which is both good for students and fun.

Ancient History and Literature—*The Founding of Christendom*, by Warren H. Carroll (10); and numerous supplementary texts (see the resource lists at the end of this section). There is a syllabus for this course (36).

In the sixth and seventh grades, my curriculum proposes a study of ancient history that is suitable to that stage of intellectual development. In high school it is appropriate to come back to the same subject in a manner suited to the older student.

The study of history is important for at least two reasons. A wide historical acquaintance supplies the student with certain causes of the present political and social order. It also provides vicarious experience. The necessary experience for political prudence is lacking in the young, but reading thoughtful historical works will in some measure supply that experience. Thus, a consideration of history prepares the student for the study of both ethics and politics. Even an understanding of the soul and the nature of man is clarified by examples from history.

However, it is important for the young to have a framework for their study of the more difficult texts of ancient history. It is also important that they see the Incarnation of our Lord as the central event of all history. *The Founding of Christendom* provides for both these necessities.

In addition to the starred texts in the "History and Literature List for Tenth Grade", found in the resource lists at the end of this section, one may incorporate certain literary selections that are set in this period of history or are connected in some other way. *Pygmalion*, by George Bernard Shaw (6), is a modern mythological tale, great fun to read and discuss alongside the ancient myth of the same name. The plays *Julius Caesar* and *Antony and Cleopatra,* both by William Shakespeare (6), are interesting to read in the light of the actual historical events on which they are based. *The Four Loves* and *The Weight of Glory,* by C. S. Lewis (6), provide some experience with philosophical thought in a manner fitted to the young. The syllabus mentioned above incorporates those works and also contains a poetry supplement, which discusses the primary terms necessary for the study of poetry, for example, rhythm, rhyme, assonance, alliteration, onomatopoeia, imagery, simile, metaphor and personification.

Latin—*Latin I* or *Latin II*, by Fr. Robert Henle (21); and *Latin Grammar* (21). There is a syllabus available for *Latin I* (36).

Latin I is an excellent text. The student continually reviews the material he has already learned and moves on from this foundation to a more complex treatment of the subject. If your student has already completed *Latin I, Latin II* continues the same approach, with appropriate review. These texts do not move as quickly as some others I have used over the years, and I like them better for that reason. The material seems actually to sink in permanently.

Science—Readings in natural history: *King Solomon's Ring*, by Konrad Lorenz (6); *The Insect World of J. Henri Fabre*, by Edwin Way Teale (57); *A+ Projects in Biology*, by Janice VanCleave (24). There is a syllabus for this course (36).

The Insect World of J. Henri Fabre is presently out of print. However, a good library should have it in its stacks. (Also, if you have access to the Internet, abebooks.com is a used-book store that carries many out-of-print titles.) There are other suggestions for natural history readings in the resource list at the end of the tenth-grade section.

Natural history is important in the intellectual development of children because it encourages wonder, an attitude of mind that characterizes the lifelong learner. Natural history also familiarizes the child with the living creature as living, for he sees the animal performing its proper operations. This study prepares the student for the study of philosophy.

Additionally, and more proximately, natural history prepares the student for the study of biology. Students appreciate biology more and do better in their biology courses if they have considered living animals before they start dissecting dead ones. Even if students do not dissect specimens, most biology texts consider the parts of the living creature without much reference to the end to which those parts are ordered, namely, the life of the living being. Natural history supplies for that deficiency.

Read *King Solomon's Ring*, a delightful book about Dr. Lorenz' experiences raising animals. Have the student note how Dr. Lorenz prepares for behavioral experiments. Read *The Insect World*, which contains chapters from Fabre's great entomological works, and discuss his mode of procedure. With this background, have the student undertake two natural history projects. The first project should be shorter and less ambitious than the second. It could be as simple as setting out various dishes of food for birds in order to observe their feeding habits. The second project should be longer and more involved. After each project, have the student write a report that incorporates the proposal for the study, the method followed, the data acquired, and the conclusion reached. *A+ Projects in Biology* has a number of suggestions for projects.

Sample Weekly Schedule for Tenth Grade

Name	Week 1	Date

MONDAY

Math	Geometry: Introduction; Algebra: half of lesson 68.
English	Analogies: pp. 1–3.
Latin	Read introduction, pp. 1–5. Do the assignment and exercises 1, 2, and 3. Write down all vocabulary words.
History	Make a time line (if you have not done so).
Science	Start a notebook for your natural history information. Read fifteen pages of *King Solomon's Ring*.
Religion	Look over your text. Read the table of contents. Read chap. 1, pp. 1–3. Do no. 1 on p. 8.

TUESDAY

Math	Geometry: lesson 1; Algebra: finish lesson 68.
English	Analogies: pp. 4–9.
Latin	Read pp. 9–15. Do the assignment and exercises 4–7.
History	Start map of the Mediterranean area and the Holy Land. Label the important political and physical features.
Science	Read fifteen pages of *King Solomon's Ring*.
Religion	Read pp. 3–6. Prepare questions 1–7 on p. 9.

WEDNESDAY

Math	Geometry: lesson 2; Algebra: start lesson 69.
English	Analogies: pp. 10–13.
Latin	Read pp. 15–19. Do the assignment and exercises 8–12.
History	Finish map.
Science	Read fifteen pages of *King Solomon's Ring*.
Religion	Discuss work from Monday and Tuesday with Mom.

<u>THURSDAY</u>

Math	Geometry: lesson 3; Algebra: finish lesson 69.
Latin	Do exercises 13 and 14. Review all vocabulary.
History	Read pp. 148–59, chap. 7. Enter all dates on time line.
Science	Read fifteen pages of *King Solomon's Ring*.
Religion	Read chap. 1, pp. 6–8. Prepare questions 1–10.

<u>FRIDAY</u>

Math	Geometry: lesson 4.

Grade Ten Resource Lists

HISTORY AND LITERATURE

Most of these books are available in your library if you would like to borrow them. Barnes and Noble bookstores carry many of them if you want to purchase them. American Home-School Publishing (4) also carries a number of them. The books starred with an asterisk are those used or suggested in the ancient history syllabus from Mother of Divine Grace School (36).

GENERAL BOOKS FOR THE STUDY OF ANCIENT HISTORY

The Holy Bible*	
The Founding of Christendom*	Warren H. Carroll
History of Western Civilization: A Handbook*	William H. McNeill
Art of Ancient Greece*	Claude Laisne
The Anchor Atlas of World History	
The Everlasting Man	G. K. Chesterton
Fifteen Decisive Battles of the World*	Edward Shepherd Creasy
The Oxford History of the Roman World	Boardman, Griffin and Murray
The Oxford History of Greece and the Hellenistic World	Boardman, Griffin and Murray
The Romans	Donald Dudley
A History and Description of Roman Political Institutions	Frank Frost Abbott
Society and Politics in Ancient Rome	Frank Frost Abbott
Parallel Lives*	Plutarch

(Note: Plutarch's "Lives" are an important source of information for many of the major figures of the following time periods, but the material is rather racy in parts. Read it with your students, or use an edited version.)

BOOKS FOR THE STUDY OF ANCIENT MYTHOLOGY

Mythology*	Bullfinch
Mythology	Edith Hamilton

*Metamorphoses**   Ovid
  (Read only with supervision.)
  (The following five titles are introductory retellings.)
Till We Have Faces ["Cupid and Psyche"]   C. S. Lewis
*The Wonder Book**   Nathaniel Hawthorne
*Greek Myths**   Ingri and Edgar d'Aulaire
*Jason and the Golden Fleece**   Padraic Colum
Tales of Greek Heroes   Roger Lancelyn Green

EARLY GREECE, 2500–499 B.C.

Art of Ancient Greece   Claude Laisne
*Parallel Lives**   Plutarch
*The Book of Daniel**
*The Iliad**   Homer
*The Odyssey**   Homer
*The Children's Homer**   Padraic Colum
  (An introductory retelling.)
*The Theben Plays**   Sophocles
  (Includes *Antigone, Oedipus Rex, Oedipus at Colonus*)
The Clouds   Aristophanes
  (Please note: Aristophanes' other plays need editing before they are suit-
  able for the young. This play, *The Clouds*, is not really suitable for the
  young either, because it is about the philosophies and philosophers of
  Aristophanes' time and is not very intelligible until you know something
  about those people and the positions they held, but it is the most acces-
  sible of Aristophanes' plays.)
Agamemnon   Aeschylus
Eumenides   Aeschylus
Prometheus Bound   Aeschylus
Fables   Aesop

SPEECH FOUND IN *The World's Great Speeches*
*The Funeral Oration**   Pericles

THE PERIOD OF THE PERSIAN WARS, 499–457 B.C.

*Fifteen Decisive Battles of the World**	Edward Shepherd Creasy
*The Histories**	Herodotus
*Parallel Lives**	Plutarch
*The Book of Esther**	
Electra	Euripides
*Antigone**	Sophocles
Oedipus Rex	Sophocles
Oedipus at Colonus	Sophocles
A Day in Old Athens	William S. Davis

THE PERIOD OF THE PELOPONNESIAN WARS, 457–404 B.C.

*Art of Ancient Greece**	Claude Laisne
*Fifteen Decisive Battles of the World**	Edward Shepherd Creasy
*Parallel Lives**	Plutarch
*History of the Peloponnesian Wars**	Thucydides
*A History of My Times**	Xenophon
*Anabasis**	Xenophon
*The Exploits of Xenophon**	Geoffrey Household
*Memorabilia**	Xenophon
The Dialogues	Plato

SPEECHES FOUND IN *The World's Great Speeches*

*On His Condemnation to Death**	Socrates
*On the Union of Greece to Resist Persia**	Isocrates

THE PERIOD OF THE RISE OF MACEDON, 404–336 B.C.

*Art of Ancient Greece**	Claude Laisne
*Parallel Lives**	Plutarch
The Philippics	Demosthenes
The Categories	Aristotle
The Prior and Posterior Analytics	Aristotle
The Physics	Aristotle
Concerning the Soul	Aristotle
The Nicomachean Ethics	Aristotle

The Metaphysics	Aristotle
The Poetics	Aristotle
The Rhetoric	Aristotle

SPEECHES FOUND IN *The World's Great Speeches*

*On the Crown**	Demosthenes
*The Second Oration against Philip**	Demosthenes

THE HELLENISTIC KINGDOMS, 323–51 B.C.

*Art of Ancient Greece**	Claude Laisne
Universal History	Polybius
(a Greek writing about the Roman conquest of Greece)	
The Elements	Euclid
On Floating Bodies	Archimedes
On Conic Sections	Apollonius
Alexander the Great and the Hellenistic World	Andrew Burn

THE EARLY HISTORY OF ROME, 753–508 B.C.

*The History of Rome from Its Foundation**	Livy (books I–V)
The Aeneid	Virgil

THE ROMAN REPUBLIC, 509-133 B.C.

*Parallel Lives**	Plutarch

THE CONQUEST OF ITALY, 509-265 B.C.

*The History of Rome from Its Foundation**	Livy (books VI–X)

THE PUNIC WARS, 264-241 B.C. AND 218-201 B.C.

*The History of Rome from Its Foundation**	Livy (books XXI–XXX)
*The Rise of the Roman Empire**	Polybius
Swords against Carthage	Friedrich Donauer

ROMAN EXPANSION IN THE EAST, 200–133 B.C.

*The Rise of the Roman Empire**	Polybius

SPEECHES FOUND IN *The World's Great Speeches*

*To His Soldiers**	Hannibal

DECAY OF THE ROMAN REPUBLIC, 133–30 B.C.

The Standard Bearer, A Study of Army Life in the Time of Caesar	Albert Carlton Whitehead
Caesar's Army: A Study of the Military Art of the Romans	Harry Pratt Judson
*Parallel Lives**	Plutarch
*Commentary on the Gallic War**	Julius Caesar
On Friendship	Cicero
Children of Ancient Gaul	Louise Lamprey
Swords in the North	Paul Lewis Anderson
For Freedom and for Gaul	Paul Lewis Anderson
A Slave of Cataline	Paul Lewis Anderson
Pugnax the Gladiator	Paul Lewis Anderson
On Land and Sea with Caesar	Reuben Field Wells
With the Eagles	Paul Lewis Anderson
With Caesar's Legions	Reuben Field Wells
Roman Life in the Days of Cicero	Alfred John Church

SPEECHES FOUND IN *The World's Great Speeches*

*First Oration Against Catiline**	Cicero
*The Fourth Philippic**	Cicero
*To the Conspirators**	Catiline
*To His Troops**	Catiline
*On the Treatment of the Conspirators**	Julius Caesar
*The Catilinarian Conspirators**	Cato, the Younger
*Oration on the Dead Body of Julius Caesar**	Mark Antony

The Roman Empire, 30 b.c.–a.d. 410

The History of the Decline and Fall of the Roman Empire	Edward Gibbon; abridged edition by Rosemary Williams
*Parallel Lives**	Plutarch
The Annals of Imperial Rome	Tacitus
On Britain and Germany	Tacitus
Lives of the Caesars	Suetonius
Antiquities of the Jews	Josephus

(history of the Jews from creation through a.d. 66)

Jewish War	Josephus

(includes an account of the destruction of the Temple)

The History of the Church	Eusebius
Letters from a Stoic	Seneca
On the Natural Faculties	Claudius Galen
Natural History	Pliny, the Elder
Letters	Pliny, the Younger
A Day in Old Rome	William S. Davis
Children of Ancient Rome	Louise Lamprey
The Common People of Ancient Rome	Frank Frost Abbott
The Roman's World	Frank Gardner Moore
Lucius, Adventures of a Roman Boy	Alfred John Church
Augustus Caesar's World	Genevieve Foster
(introductory)	
*Helena**	Evelyn Waugh

Philosophers to Know

Early Greece, 2500–499 b.c.

Thales of Miletus	c. 640–c. 546
Anaximander	c. 611–547
Anaximenes	c. 600–c. 540
Pythagoras	c. 582–c. 500
Heraclitus	c. 535–c. 475
Parmenides	c. 515–450
Anaxagoras	c. 500–427

The Period of the Persian Wars, 499–457 B.C.

Zeno of Elea	c. 490–c. 430
Empedocles	492–432

The Period of the Peloponnesian Wars, 457–404 B.C.

Socrates	c. 469–399
Democritus	c. 460–c. 370
Plato*	428–348
Diogenes Laertius	c. 412–c. 323

The Period of the Rise of Macedon, 404–336 B.C.

Aristotle	384–322

The Hellenistic Kingdoms, 323–51 B.C.

Epicurus	c. 342–270

Decay of the Roman Republic, 133–30 B.C.

Lucretius	c. 96–c. 55
Cato the Younger	95–46

The Roman Empire, 30 B.C.–A.D. 410

Seneca	c. 4 B.C.–A.D. 65
Epictetus	A.D. c. 50–c. 125
Marcus Aurelius	A.D. 121–180

Church Fathers to Know

St. Ignatius of Antioch	30–107
St. Polycarp	65–c. 155
St. Justin Martyr	110–165
St. Irenaeus	120–202
St. Clement of Alexandria	c. 150–215
Tertullian	c. 150–220
Origen	c. 185–c. 254
St. Athanasius	293–373
St. Gregory of Nyssa	335–395
St. John Chrysostom	c. 347–407
St. Augustine of Hippo	354–430

ADDITIONAL BOOKS FOR THE STUDY OF NATURAL HISTORY

The various books by Fabre from which the selections in *The Insect World of J. Henri Fabre* were taken (unfortunately, all presently out of print):

The Life of the Fly	*The Sacred Beetles and Others*
The Life of the Caterpillar	*The Mason-Wasps*
The Life of the Grasshopper	*The Mason-Bees*
The Life of the Scorpion	*The Glow Worm and Other Beetles*
The Life of the Weevil	*Bumble Bees and Others*
The Hunting Wasps	

Other books by Fabre, such as:

Animal Life in Field and Garden
Social Life in the Insect World
The Wonders of Instinct
Our Humble Helpers

The Handbook of Nature Study	Anna Botsford Comstock
Walking Catfish and Other Aliens	Charles Roth
Animal Architects	Russell Freedman
The Spider	John Crompton
The Ways of the Ant	John Crompton
The Snake	John Crompton
A Hive of Bees	John Crompton
The Herring Gull's World	Niko Tinbergen
Curious Naturalists	Niko Tinbergen
The Amateur Naturalist	Gerald Durrell
Nature Discoveries with a Hand Lens	Richard Headstrom
Adventures with a Microscope	Richard Headstrom
Man Meets Dog	Konrad Lorenz
Animal Navigation	Ronald M. Lockley
The Alien Animals: The Story of Imported Wildlife	George Laycock
The Swiss Family Robinson	Rev. Johann Wyss
All Creatures Great and Small	James Herriot
(and other books by the same author)	

Eleventh Grade Curriculum

Sources for items followed by a number in parentheses may be found at the back of the book in the list of suppliers.

Religion—*An Introduction to the Bible*, by Fr. John Laux (21); Topic Tabs (11); the *Catechism of the Catholic Church* (25); *Dei Verbum* (*Dogmatic Constitution on Divine Revelation*), in *Vatican Council II: The Conciliar and the Post-Conciliar Documents*, vol. 1, edited by Austin Flannery, O.P. (51). A syllabus for this course is now available (36).

Start the year by having the student insert Topic Tabs in his Bible. This great Bible reference system gives instant access to the Bible verses that are most often required in apologetic work. While inserting the tabs, the student has an opportunity to recall the material he learned last year as well as get an overview of Scripture, which is the focus of this year's curriculum.

An Introduction to the Bible, by Fr. John Laux, is the basic text for this course. It provides an excellent introduction to Scripture study. During the course of the year, each book of the Bible is introduced in the text, read by the student and commented on in the text. Both the textual introductions and the commentary are helpful. The *Catechism of the Catholic Church* has additional material that is appropriate for the student's study of Scripture. Part one, section one, article three (nos. 101–41) should be studied in detail. *Dei Verbum* is also important to read for a fuller understanding of the role of Scripture in the life of the Church. Though *An Introduction to the Bible* was written before the Second Vatican Council, the teaching of the Church with respect to Scripture has not changed since the Council, and reading these three texts in conjunction with one another makes the continuity of doctrine in the Church apparent. Draw the student's attention to the footnotes in *Dei Verbum*. The references to the Fathers and Doctors of the Church are a further affirmation of the unchanging character of Church teaching.

Mathematics—*Algebra II*, by John Saxon (48); or *Algebra II* from Keyboard Enterprises (27)

The Saxon text continues the study of algebra. It presents the material in an orderly manner and reviews the concepts regularly. As in the last text, if the student does the lessons consistently and completely, redoing any problems that have been done incorrectly, he will be able to work through this text. The homeschool packet comes with tests, and I recommend doing a certain number of them to check on the mastery level of the student. Sometimes students answer the more difficult questions by referring to the text. Then they think they understand something they do not. The tests will reveal such a situation.

There is a solutions manual available that will help you help your student through any tough problems.

If you think more help than a solutions manual is needed, Keyboard Enterprises has an Algebra II class on video that students I know have used successfully. The explanations given on the tape are clear and cogent.

English—Various selections read in conjunction with European history; papers in history; *The Harp and Laurel Wreath: Poetry and Dictation Selections for the Classical Curriculum,* edited by Laura Berquist (25); or the Seton junior English course (49). A syllabus integrating the suggestions in this section with a historical study of England and Spain is available (36).

Integrate the study of historical fiction, biography, poetry, plays and novels with your study of European history this year. *The Song at the Scaffold,* by Gertrude von le Fort (13); selections from *The Idylls of the King,* by Alfred Lord Tennyson (6); *Henry V*, by William Shakespeare (6); *Kennilworth,* by Sir Walter Scott (61); *Come Rack! Come Rope!,* by Msgr. Robert Hugh Benson; *The Gunpowder Plot,* by Hugh Ross Williamson; *The Ballad of the White Horse,* by G. K. Chesterton (33); *Pride and Prejudice,* by Jane Austen (6); and *Murder in the Cathedral,* by T. S. Eliot (6), are works we have used. The sections titled "Europe at the Same Time" in the history and literature lists from the ninth-grade resource list have other suggestions as well. Notice the differences in the manner of presentation in each of these types of writing. Use the "General Questions for the Study of Literature", also found in the ninth-grade resource section, for discussions. If a more structured literature study is desired, Progeny Press (44) has a number of study guides for works that could be used in this class. Have your student write papers, perhaps four, that come out of your discussions with him. *The Harp and Laurel Wreath: Poetry and Dictation Selections for the Classical Curriculum* contains a section on the various meters used in poetry, what it means to scan a poem and how to scan, along with numerous poetry selections, study questions and answers.

European History—Choose an area of interest, and then pick titles in that area from the list at the end of this section; see also *The Ultimate Geography and Timeline Guide*, by Maggie Hogan and Cindy Wiggers (21).

Though the student's interest should be consulted in deciding on the country and era to be studied, I suggest that some amount of time, perhaps a whole semester, be given to the study of English history and a similar period of time to Spanish history. One possibility for such a course would be to use Churchill's *The History of the English-Speaking Peoples,* edited by Henry Steele Commager (4, 57), and *The Lives of the Kings and Queens of England*, by Antonia Frazer (6), as the basic texts for first semester. Intersperse four other texts, roughly one every four weeks, that expand information given in the framework text. *Richard the Third: The Great Debate,* by Paul Murray Kendall (6); *Robert Southwell: A Unit Study on English History, Poetry and the Catholic Faith,* by Philip Healy and Lesley Payne (21); *Edmund Campion,* by Evelyn Waugh (50); and *Bloody Mary,* by Carolly Erickson (6), are books I would recommend.

In the second semester, use *A History of Medieval Spain,* by Joseph O'Callaghan (6), as the initial text. This is a large and somewhat difficult text, but it is an excellent source for information that is hard to obtain elsewhere. Use selections from it, and also read *Characters of the Inquisition,* by William Thomas Walsh (53); *Isabella of Spain,* by William Thomas Walsh (31); and *Columbus and Cortez, Conquerors for Christ,* by John Eidsmoe (26).

Assign a paper or two through the year, the topic to be chosen by the student. Evaluate the paper with respect to elegance of expression as well as content.

A wide historical acquaintance is important because it supplies the student with knowledge of two sorts. On the one hand, certain causes of the present political and social order come to light. The Constitution of the United States, for example, did not spring into being from nothingness. There was a tradition, a way of thinking, that was formed in England prior to the revolution. A study of English history illuminates American history.

The study of Spanish history from the Spanish point of view modifies the picture of Europe that many students have. There is a bias toward the English point of view in most available materials, a bias that a study of Catholic Spain will modify. For this reason I think this is a fruitful study.

Additionally, the histories of these two countries involve events about which Catholics should be fully informed, events that are often misinterpreted, misrepresented or misunderstood. Include the English Reformation, Mary Tudor and Elizabeth I in your study of English history. When someone starts talking about "Bloody Mary", your student should be able to respond with the facts. The Spanish Inquisition is another area where misinformation abounds. Read material that is well documented and researched.

The other kind of knowledge that history contributes to is universal and is itself of two sorts. The necessary experience for political prudence is lacking in the young, but reading thoughtful historical works will in some measure supply that experience. Thus, a consideration of history prepares the student for the study of both ethics and politics. Even an understanding of the soul and the nature of man is clarified by the examples of history.

There are many good reasons for spending time teaching and learning history. History gives a sense of perspective. It supplies material for right judgment. It makes it possible to see the present in the light of the past, so that the part is seen in the light of the whole. Rightly done, as I said in the introduction, history is a preparation for both philosophy and theology. It is a suitable matter for the student to practice his newly developing intellectual skills upon, and it supplies experience, inductions for the cultivation of judgment.

Your history course can accomplish all of these goals, but the materials you use are going to make a big difference in how well they are achieved. This is so important that I would like to tell you what I have learned about evaluating texts. Then, if you prefer a course of study different from the one I have recommended, you will know what to look for.

When you are evaluating materials for your curriculum, look for material that is not ideologically motivated. That is, you don't want something with "an axe to grind" (a particular view of women, or oppression, or government) that colors all of the content. For those who object that all information is colored in some way, I can say only that I have seen big internal differences between texts.

When my eldest daughter wanted to do a study of Spanish history, we needed to locate texts to use. (You would be surprised at how hard it is to find good Spanish history texts.) We finally found three texts, which we compared to one another. One of them saw all Spanish history from the viewpoint of the Muslims. It was so blatantly pro-Muslim that the whole of the work was invalidated. Every particular event mentioned in this text that was also mentioned in the others said that the Muslims were in the right and the Spanish Catholics were wrong. The other texts sometimes agreed with that judgment, but not often.

A good text will present original sources whenever possible, using material that was written close to the time of the events. It won't draw too many conclusions, leaving that exercise to the reader. When it does draw a conclusion, it will acknowledge that there are other positions possible but will give reasons why this seems to be the best understanding of the events.

Paul Murray Kendall's *Richard the Third* is a good example of this kind. Mr. Kendall, in thinking Richard was a good man, is unlike most people. But he cites materials from the time of Richard, points to their inconsistency with the usual view of his conduct, suggests alternative understandings and acknowledges that his is not the only point of view. The reader can tell that he is being asked to consider the same material the author has considered; he is not simply given the author's judgment. To approach history that way, the author must be more committed to the truth than to his own position, and he must recognize that such a subject cannot be known the way that subjects of the sciences can be.

A good text will also avoid egregious errors, such as informing the reader that annulment is "another name for divorce". Or that Philip II was said to be a chaste man, but, since that is impossible, he must have had mistresses. Or that the Reformation was inspired by the fact that the Catholic Church chained up the Bible. All of these positions are statements that I have actually seen in so-called history books!

There are certain standard difficulties that texts often have. When checking out a text, look at these areas before you make a decision about whether to use it.

The Reformation is a good era to look at in measuring a text. If the facts are presented well there, the rest of the work is likely to be good. Another test case is the so-called "Black Legend" of early Spanish colonization of the New World. Many texts ignore the good the Spanish did and the truly high motives of the missionaries, in favor of dwelling on the wicked practices of some of the Spanish governors, who acted in defiance of the King's orders. Also suspect are American history materials that discuss only the so-called En-lightenment as a source of thought for the founding fathers and ignore the legacy of common law and Christianity. And any text that discusses the Dark Ages as a time of intellectual poverty, ignoring St. Thomas, the University of Paris, St. Bonaventure and St. Albert, doesn't know what it is talking about.

In general, it is Catholicism that suffers at the hands of Protestant or secular history, and it is there that you look in evaluating the usefulness of a given text. This does not mean that only texts written by Catholics are any good. Sometimes non-Catholic authors and historians are gifted and accurate in their presentations. *The Children of the New Forest*, by Captain Frederick Marryat, for example, is an enjoyable fictional history of the time of the Roundheads and Charles II. Captain Marryat was not a Catholic, but his presentation of the Catholics in his book is fair and accurate as far as it goes.

The Ultimate Geography and Timeline Guide has a section for the high school student that complements any history program.

Latin—*Latin II*, by Fr. Robert Henle (21); *Latin Grammar* (21); or *Latin III*, by Fr. Robert Henle (21)

Both *Latin II* and *Latin III* are excellent texts. The student continually reviews the material he has already learned and moves on to a more complex treatment of the subject. If your student has already completed *Latin II, Latin III* continues the same approach, with appropriate review. These texts do not move as quickly as some others I have used over the years, and I like them better for that reason. The material seems actually to sink in permanently. I usually have the students spend two years on *Latin I* and two years on *Latin II*. They move through the text slowly and thoroughly.

Physical Education—Any reasonable form of regular physical activity.

I include this in the curriculum because many states require two years of physical education for graduation. One can have a regular walking program or take up golf or swimming. Irish step dancing is another form of exercise that would fulfill this requirement.

Biology—*Life Science: All Creatures Great and Small*, by Michael J. Spear (11); *Biology: The Easy Way* (Barron's Educational Series, Inc.) (28); *Insects* (Golden Guide) (24); *How to Make Insect Collections* (24); Dissection Kit #1 or #2 (24); *The Anatomy Coloring Book*, by Wynn Kapit and Lawrence M. Elson (45); *Darwin's Black Box*, by Michael Behe (6); *Defeating Darwinism by Opening Minds*, by Phillip E. Johnson (46); *Humani Generis* (51); *Lab Science: The How, Why, What, Who 'n' Where Book*, by Barbara Edtl Shelton (20); or *Biology for Christian Schools*, by William Pinkston, Jr. (8, 49)

Life Science: All Creatures Great and Small could be used with younger students, and the junior in high school will find it quite easy. Therefore he can be expected to master the information in the book. The basic notions of the discipline of biology are included in the text. *Biology: The Easy Way* has a somewhat more detailed and comprehensive content. It could be used as an alternative primary text, or it could be used to expand the concepts discussed in *Life Science: All Creatures Great and Small*. The *Life Science* text has a discussion of insect collections early in the year. At that time, have your student collect and mount twelve insect specimens, displaying them according to an order he determines. Then have him write a paragraph about each insect, describing what he knows about the life of the insect, or what he can reasonably deduce about its life from its form. (For example, this insect has wings, so it probably flies.) After writing about each separate insect, he should write a short paper describing the similarities and differences of the twelve specimens.

In a later chapter animals are discussed, from the simple to the more complex. Either dissection kit mentioned above could be used at this time. The first kit contains the tools and equipment necessary for dissection, as well as a preserved frog, earthworm, and grasshopper to dissect. The second kit has the same equipment and eight preserved specimens for dissection—a fetal pig, frog, perch, crayfish, grasshopper, earthworm, clam and starfish.

The various animal systems come up in the second half of the text, and the *Anatomy Coloring Book* helps the student visualize those systems. The coloring book is very detailed in its depiction and in its descriptions of the systems.

At the end of the year, with all of this background, students find *Darwin's Black Box* exciting to read. It builds upon the information they have been studying and makes a convincing case against Darwinian evolution. *Defeating Darwinism* is another text that speaks cogently and interestingly to this issue. The encyclical *Humani Generis* speaks specifically about evolution and should be familiar to all Catholic students.

Lab Science: The How, Why, What, Who 'n' Where Book has many additional suggestions for and information about the lab portion of your science curriculum.

For those who prefer a textbook, *Biology for Christian Schools* is the best I am familiar with. It does contain some anti-Catholic statements, however, so you will need to preview the material before handing it to your student. However, these errors can be turned to advantage by spending time discussing them with your student as they arise in the text, thus helping him see both the errors and the truth clearly. We do not want to shield our children from all knowledge of error or of contrary positions. We want them to be formed first in the truth and then exposed to error in a careful, prudent and guided manner. Their grasp of the truth will be strengthened by this way of proceeding. All apologetic work involves knowing the alternative positions.

Test Preparation—*8 Real SATs* (45); *Word Flash* (20); *Analogies 1, Analogies 2, Analogies 3* (19)

The PSAT is offered in October of each year. Juniors in high school who participate in the PSAT and do very well become eligible for the National Merit Scholarship competition. Further, college-bound students often take the SAT in the spring of their junior year in high school, so that they can apply for college admissions early in their senior year. In either case the student should prepare for the tests. If *Analogies 1, 2,* and *3* were studied last year, they should be reviewed prior to the test. If they were not included in the curriculum last year, they should be now. *Word Flash* is an excellent text for helping increase vocabulary knowledge. The only test preparation program available that comes from the College Board (15), the organization that produces the tests themselves, is *8 Real SATs,* which also includes two practice PSAT tests. I have found that taking practice tests, one every week, under conditions that simulate actual test-taking conditions, is very helpful to students. Going through the completed tests, checking the answers and correcting the errors, is even more helpful, because there is no substitute for knowing the answers. These practice tests are a way of learning what needs to be learned.

Sample Weekly Schedule for Eleventh Grade

Name	Week 1	Date

MONDAY

Math	Lesson 1.	
English	Read first twenty pages of your book. Do first analogies quiz.	
European History	Make a time line (if you have not done so).	
Science	Read chap. 1.	
Religion	Read introductory material. Who is the author? What is the title? The subtitle? Look over the table of contents.	
Latin	Review all declensions and conjugations from last year.	

TUESDAY

Math	Lesson 2.
English	Read next twenty pages. Analogies: go over first quiz with me.
Latin	Pp. 305–6. Read; do the assignment and exercises.
History	Start map of Europe. Do the outline of the whole and draw the political lines.
Science	Do chap. 1 review.
Religion	Read and outline pp. 1–6. Define "inspiration" and "inerrancy".

WEDNESDAY

Math	Lesson 3.
English	Read next twenty pages. Analogies: take next quiz.
Latin	Pp. 307–8. Do exercises 3–6.
History	Finish map.
Science	Read chap. 2.
Religion	Pp. 7–10. Discuss with me.

THURSDAY

Math	Lesson 4.
English	Read next twenty pages.
Latin	Pp. 309–11. Do the assignment and exercises 7–9. Study all vocabulary.
History	Read pp. 148–59, chap. 7. Enter all dates on time line.
Science	Do chap. 2 review.
Religion	Pp. 11–17. Prepare questions 1–10.

FRIDAY

Math	Lesson 5.

Grade Eleven Resource Lists

ADDITIONAL OR ALTERNATIVE HISTORY READINGS

An "L" after the author's name indicates that the library or used-book sources will be your best bet for securing this title; "IP" indicates that the book is currently in print; "*" indicates an especially enjoyable book.

RUSSIAN HISTORY

Peter the Great, His Life and World	Robert K. Massie	IP*

HISTORICAL FICTION

The Death of Ivan Ilych	Leo Tolstoy	IP
War and Peace	Leo Tolstoy	IP
The Brothers Karamazov	Fyodor Dostoyevsky	IP

FRENCH HISTORY

Louis and Antoinette	Vincent Cronin	L*
Louis XI: The Universal Spider	Paul Murray Kendall	IP*
Saint Louis	Margaret Labarge	L
To the Scaffold: The Life of Marie Antoinette	Carolly Erickson	L*
History of the French Revolution	Jules Michelet	IP
Joan of Arc	Mark Twain	IP
Joan of Arc	Hilaire Belloc	IP
The Two Lives of Charlemagne	Einhard and Notker the Stammerer	IP
The Life of Charlemagne	Einhard	L
Louis IX, Most Christian King of France	Margaret Wade Labarge	IP
The Old Regime and the French Revolution	Alexis de Tocqueville	L
Citizen	Simon Schama	IP*

HISTORICAL FICTION

The White Company	Sir Arthur Conan Doyle	IP
The Song of Roland		IP
The Count of Monte Cristo	Alexandre Dumas	IP

ITALIAN HISTORY

The Borgias	Ivan Cloulas	L*
Fall of the House of Borgia	E. R. Chamberlin	IP
The Civilization of the Renaissance	Jacob Burckhardt	IP

HISTORICAL FICTION

The Count of Monte Cristo	Alexandre Dumas	IP
The Betrothed	Alessandro Manzoni	IP
Much Ado about Nothing	William Shakespeare	IP

GENERAL MEDIEVAL

Chronicles of the Crusades	Joinville and Villehardouin	IP

ENGLISH HISTORY

A History of the English-Speaking Peoples	Winston Churchill	L*
Churchill's History of the English-Speaking Peoples	Henry Steele Commager, editor	L*
The Lives of the Kings and Queens of England	Antonia Fraser	IP
History of the Kings of Britain	Geoffrey of Monmouth	IP
Eleanor of Aquitaine and the Four Kings	Amy Kelly	IP
The War of the Roses	Elisabeth Hallam	IP
Richard the Third: The Great Debate	Paul Murray Kendall	IP*
Richard the Third	Charles Ross	IP
Catherine of Aragon	Garrett Mattingly	IP
The Six Wives of Henry VIII	Antonia Fraser	IP*
How the Reformation Happened	Hilaire Belloc	IP
The Beginning of the English Reformation	Hugh Ross Williamson	L
Bloody Mary	Carolly Erickson	IP*
Queen Elizabeth	Theodore Maynard	L

Robert Southwell: A Unit Study on English History, Poetry and the Catholic Faith	Philip Healy and Lesley Payne	IP*
Saint Robert Southwell and Henry Garnett: A Study in Friendship	Philip Caraman, S.J.	IP
Edmund Campion	Evelyn Waugh	IP*
The Gunpowder Plot	Hugh Ross Williamson	IP
The Last of the Royal Stuarts	Herbert Vaughn	IP

HISTORICAL FICTION

Beowulf		IP
Ivanhoe	Sir Walter Scott	IP*
Kenilworth	Sir Walter Scott	IP
The Talisman	Sir Walter Scott	L
The Children of the New Forest	Frederick Marryat	IP
The White Company	Sir Arthur Conan Doyle	IP*
King John	William Shakespeare	IP*
Richard II	William Shakespeare	IP*
Henry IV, Part I	William Shakespeare	IP*
Henry V	William Shakespeare	IP*
Scottish Chiefs	Jane Porter	IP
Mary Queen of Scots	Antonia Fraser	IP*
The Black Arrow	Robert Louis Stevenson	IP
Sun Faster! Sun Slower!	Meriol Trevor	L
Come Rack! Come Rope!	Msgr. Robert Hugh Benson	IP

SPANISH HISTORY

OLD WORLD

Butler's *Lives of the Saints*: Hermenegild Isidore of Seville Dominic Vincent Ferrar		IP
A History of Medieval Spain	Joseph O'Callaghan	IP*
Philip II	William Thomas Walsh	IP*
Isabella of Spain	William Thomas Walsh	IP*
Characters of the Inquisition	William Thomas Walsh	IP*

St. Teresa of Avila	William Thomas Walsh	IP*
The Emperor Charles V	Karl Brandi	L
Tree of Hate	Philip Wayne Powell	L*
Isabella of Spain: The Catholic Queen	Warren Carroll	IP*
The Conquest of Granada	Washington Irving	L

NEW WORLD

Columbus and Cortez, Conquerors for Christ	John Eidsmoe	IP*
Christopher Columbus's Book of Prophecies	Kay Brigham	IP
Cortez of Mexico	Ronald Syme	L
The Conquest of New Spain	Bernal Diaz	IP
Our Lady of Guadalupe and the Conquest of Darkness	Warren Carroll	IP
California Missions (A Pictorial History)	(Sunset Publ. Corp.)	IP*
Junipero Serra	Don Nevi	L

MODERN MEXICO

Blood Drenched Altars: A Catholic Commentary on the History of Mexico's Revolution	Francis C. Kelly	IP
Mexican Martyrdom: Firsthand Experiences of the Religious Persecution in Mexico	Wilfred Parsons, S.J.	IP*
The Mexican Revolution and the Catholic Church	Robert Quirk	IP
The Cristero Rebellion	Jean Meyer	L
The Holy War in Los Altos	James Tuck	L
Padre Pro	Fanchon Royer	L
Blessed Miguel Pro: 20th Century Martyr	Ann Ball	IP

HISTORICAL FICTION

El Cid	Racine	IP
Don Quixote	Miguel Cervantes	IP
The Song of Roland		IP
The Pit and the Pendulum (for a contrasting view of the Inquisition)	Edgar Allan Poe	IP
The Last Crusader	Louis de Wohl	L*
The Custer Legacy	Bruce Clark	IP

Twelfth Grade Curriculum

Sources for items followed by a number in parentheses may be found at the back of the book in the list of suppliers.

Religion—*Following Christ in the World*, by Anne Carroll (49); *Surprised by Truth*, edited by Patrick Madrid (21); *Beginning Apologetics*, by Fr. Frank Chacon and Jim Burnham (47)

Following Christ in the World covers many timely issues and practical considerations from a Catholic viewpoint. There are references to the encyclicals and to the magisterial teaching of the Church. This course reviews topics covered in earlier classes, such as the immortality of the soul and the divinity of Christ. It also introduces new material that all Catholics should be familiar with, such as liberal capitalism and the social encyclicals, war and peace and justice in the marketplace. It contains a small section of philosophical terms and concepts that whets the student's appetite for more.

Both *Beginning Apologetics* and *Surprised by Truth* are helpful to read alongside the primary text. We have found the following procedure to work well with *Beginning Apologetics*. On Monday have the student read one chapter. On Tuesday have him look up the Scripture references in the text. On Wednesday have him defend the position while you take the part of the adversary, and on Thursday have the student write an essay on the subject in question. (We call these 45-minute essays.)

Mathematics—*Advanced Math*, by John Saxon (48), or *Exploring Creation with Physics*, by Jay Wile (59); *The Joy of Mathematics* by Theoni Pappas (17)

Advanced Math is the next in the Saxon series. It is difficult but quite thorough. It covers trigometric and inverse functions, conic sections, rational roots and more. A solutions manual is available and, at least in my house, needed. *Exploring Creation with Physics* is an extensive, user-friendly text written specifically for the homeschool situation. Dr. Jay Wile, the author, is willing to provide support via e-mail, regular mail, the internet, fax or phone. The text is written in a conversational style that is easy for the student to read and understand.

A third alternative for mathematics in the senior year is to review the algebra course from last year and use interesting and supplemental texts like *The Joy of Mathematics*. This is an additional text I recommend for all seniors, whatever their primary text, because it addresses some of the concepts that encourage wonder in the student. The golden mean, Zeno's paradox, the magic square, tessellations and Pascal's triangle are all discussed.

If your child is going to college, it is important to continue with some kind of mathematics through high school. College level mathematics courses will be much easier and less time consuming if the algebraic skills acquired earlier are not forgotten. Additionally, this is where mathematics gets even more interesting.

British Literature—See list in resource section; *The Harp and Laurel Wreath: Poetry and Dictation for the Classical Curriculum*, edited by Laura Berquist (25); or the Seton twelfth grade English course (49)

Pick any ten of the books on the resource list, read them and write three shorter papers on three of the books and one ten-page paper comparing two of them. You may compare the characterizations, the plot, the artistic expertise, the authors' philosophical judgments or any other aspect of the books. The general questions for works of literature in the ninth-grade resource list may be used. The analysis expected of the student is consonant with his abilities at this level. In other words, the work expected of the student should be more advanced than in previous years. He should exhibit more subtlety in understanding, more discrimination in the interpretation of texts and more attention to language in his papers. There should be some study of British poetry as well. A number of such poems, along with terms to know for the study of poetry, are included in *The Harp and Laurel Wreath: Poetry and Dictation for the Classical Curriculum*. If you find *The Prose and Poetry of England* (57), use it.

The Seton course is very good, using the excellent, out-of-print *Prose and Poetry of England* as the text.

American Government—*Summa Theologiae*, by St. Thomas Aquinas (31, 46); *The Timetables of History* (45); *The American Revolutionaries: A History in Their Own Words*, by Milton Meltzer (20); *Common Sense,* by Thomas Paine (4); *The Declaration of Independence* (20); *The Federalist Papers*, by Alexander Hamilton, James Madison and John Jay (20); *The Anti-Federalist Papers*, edited by Ralph Ketcham (20); *The Constitution of the United States* (20); *Quadragesimo Anno*, an encyclical by Pope Pius XI (51); *Democracy in America,* by Alexis de Tocqueville (20); or *American Government and Economics in Christian Perspective*, by Laurel Hicks, George T. Thompson, Michael R. Lowman and George C. Cochran (1)

Start with question 91 of the *Summa*. (Stella Maris Catalog [51] has an English edition of selections from the *Summa* that is inexpensive and contains these sections.) Read and discuss all six articles. This is the context within which the foundation of our country should be considered. Next read question 105, article 1, for consideration of the merits of various forms of government. Have your student write summaries of the argument in the articles as he goes through them.

Construct a time line of the prominent events of the period of the Revolution up to the 1840s. Use the *Timetables of History* (or other sources) for this project. This will give a framework for the upcoming discussions.

Then have the student read *The American Revolutionaries* to give him an overview of the situation in America at the time of the Revolution. The material in this text comes from firsthand accounts. *Common Sense* could be studied next. It is one of the important documents of that period, since it did much to promote a declaration of independence from England. At this point ask for two papers, both written in the first person, one from an ordinary citizen of revolutionary leanings, and the other from such a person with Tory sympathies.

Now read the *Declaration* itself. (The Elijah Company [20] carries a *Documentary History of the United States* that contains both the *Declaration* and the Constitution.) Have the student outline the document so that the claims of the young country are clear. Then the *Federalist* and the *Anti-Federalist Papers* should be read in an alternating sequence. When the controversial questions that occupied the early framers of the Constitution are clear to the student, have him read the Constitution carefully, part by part. Have him write a summary of each part and discuss it with him.

Quadragesimo Anno contains an account of Catholic social teaching; it deals explicitly with labor, capitalism and socialism. Having read the Constitution carefully, the student is in a position to reflect on it in the light of the teachings of the Church. Discuss this text thoughtfully; it is not easy for the high school student, but it can be done.

Lastly, have the student read chapters 4–18 in *Democracy in America*. Alexis de Tocqueville wrote this text in the 1840s, after traveling extensively in the United States. He gives the reader a clear account of how the Constitution has worked up to that point. He also makes astute observations about the present course of the country and what he expects to happen in the coming years.

As a final assignment, have the student write a paper on one of the topics he considered in the readings from the *Federalist* and *Anti-Federalist Papers*. He should lay out the question he chooses, present both sides of the issue, tell how the Constitution treats the issues and make a judgment about it.

If a textbook approach is preferred, *American Government and Economics in Christian Perspective* is well done. It presents the Constitution clearly and thoroughly. The student has the opportunity to work through the Constitution part by part, seeing each part in its inception and, through discussion, in the developments that have taken place in its interpretation. The student tests and reviews may be used for reinforcement and motivation, if they are helpful for your student. This is not a Catholic text, but it is Christian and is written by people with a grasp of their subject.

Language—Latin: *Latin III* or *Latin IV*, by Fr. Robert Henle (21), with *Winnie ille Pu* (6), *Lingua Latina* (28), *Caesaris Bellum Helveticum* (6). Spanish: *Spanish: The Adventure Begins*, published by Power-glide Language Courses (45)

If *Latin III* was completed last year, go on to translation, starting with easier material (*Winnie ille Pu, Lingua Latina*) and then doing the translations in *Caesaris Bellum Helveticum* before moving on to *Latin IV*.

If Latin has become fairly easy and the declensions and conjugations are second nature, learning another language might be an alternative at this point. Any of the Romance languages would be easy to learn after Latin. The Power-glide courses are said to be very effective. I have not used them yet, because we usually keep working on Latin, but those I know who have used them are very pleased with the results.

Chemistry—*The Visual Dictionary of Chemistry,* by Jack Challoner (6); *Chemistry: Concepts and Problems: A Self-Teaching Guide,* by Clifford C. Houk and Richard Post (6); *Solutions 12,* by Ronald Marson (21); *Lab Science: The How, Why, What, Who 'n' Where Book,* by Barbara Edtl Shelton (20); or *Exploring Creation with Chemistry,* by Jay Wile (59); *The Chemical History of a Candle,* by Michael Faraday (6)

The Visual Dictionary of Chemistry, published by Dorling-Kindersley, has excellent pictures that students find helpful in their first experiences with a chemistry lab. *Chemistry: Concepts and Problems: A Self-Teaching Guide* gives a useful overview of the subject. It does not provide the same detail or conversational style of *Exploring Creation With Chemistry,* but it is quite easy to use and does address the important concepts of introductory chemistry. *Solutions 12* is one of the TOPS units and provides instruction in very simple chemical experiments. *Lab Science: The How, Why, What, Who 'n' Where Book* has additional resource suggestions for lab equipment and procedures. With these materials a very satisfactory chemistry course can be constructed.

If a ready made course is preferable, *Exploring Creation with Chemistry* is thorough and easy to use. It was designed specifically for homeschoolers. The student is taken step by step through the standard material for a high school chemistry class. Dr. Wile provides support for the homeschooling family; you can write, e-mail, fax or call with your questions, and he will respond. There are experiments included in the text that are actually possible to do at home, and Dr. Wile has provided a list of necessary equipment you can purchase from him for a reasonable price. I have not used this course yet, but I plan to with my next chemistry student.

The Chemical History of a Candle is a delightful book that makes the connection between chemistry and biology very clear and, even more importantly, shows that the study of chemistry is ordered to the understanding of reality. Michael Faraday always insisted that he was a natural philosopher, a lover of wisdom, rather than a scientist. This text testifies to the truth of that appellation. The six lectures contained in the book are directed to discovering what happens when a candle burns. As the argument proceeds, one discovers that there is a relation between the combustion of a candle and a living kind of combustion that goes on in the human being. Reading this book is one of the highlights of the school year.

Health—*Casti Connubii*, an encyclical by Pope Pius XI (51); *Catechism of the Catholic Church* (25)

Casti Connubii is an outstanding document on the subject of Christian marriage. The Catholic teaching on marriage, the relationship between the spouses and the importance of children is very clear and understandable, and the prohibition of birth control, divorce and adultery is equally clear. The portions of the *Catechism* that treat of marriage show that the understanding of the Church on the nature of marriage has not changed. These readings will reinforce the material in the religion curriculum for this year.

Physical Education—Any reasonable form of regular physical activity.

I include this in the curriculum because many states require two years of physical education for graduation. One can have a regular walking program or take up golf or swimming. Irish step dancing is another form of exercise that would fulfill this requirement.

Sample Weekly Schedule for Twelfth Grade

Name   Week 1   Date

MONDAY

Math	Lesson 1.
English	Read first third of *Beowulf*.
Government	P. 748. Read the first article. Make an outline.
Chemistry	Read the introduction and lecture 1 of *The Chemical History of a Candle*.
Religion	Read introductory material. Who is the author? What is the title? The subtitle? Look over the table of contents.
Latin	Review all declensions and conjugations from last year.

TUESDAY

Math	Lesson 2.
English	Read second third of *Beowulf*.
Latin	Read *Winnie ille Pu* all week. Write out your translation.
Government	Read and outline the second article. Discuss with me.
Chemistry	Read the first experiment, write it out or do it.
Religion	Read chap. 1 today and tomorrow.

WEDNESDAY

Math	Lesson 3.
English	Finish *Beowulf*.
Latin	See Tuesday.
Government	Read and outline the third article. Discuss with me.
Chemistry	Discuss the readings and the experiment with me.
Religion	Finish chap. 1.

THURSDAY

Math	Lesson 4.
English	Discuss *Beowulf* with me.
Latin	See Tuesday.
Government	Read and outline the fourth article. Discuss with me.

Chemistry   Read lecture 2.
Religion   Discuss chap. 1.

FRIDAY

Math   Lesson 5.

Grade Twelve Resource List

BRITISH LITERATURE

Beowulf *	
Sir Gawain and the Green Knight *	
Ecclesiastical History of the English People	Bede the Venerable
"The Parson's Tale" * (from *The Canterbury Tales*)	Geoffrey Chaucer
The Ballad of the White Horse *	G. K. Chesterton
Ivanhoe *	Sir Walter Scott
The White Company *	Sir Arthur Conan Doyle
A Man for All Seasons *	Robert Bolt
The Life of St. Thomas More *	William Roper
The Merchant of Venice *	William Shakespeare
Men of Iron	Howard Pyle
The Black Arrow	Robert Louis Stevenson
Henry V *	William Shakespeare
A Midsummer Night's Dream *	William Shakespeare
Diary of Samuel Pepys	Samuel Pepys
Gulliver's Travels	Jonathan Swift
Robinson Crusoe	Daniel DeFoe
The Life of Samuel Johnson	James Boswell
The Vicar of Wakefield	Oliver Goldsmith
Treasure Island	Robert Louis Stevenson
Adam Bede	George Eliot
Silas Marner *	George Eliot
Middlemarch	George Eliot
Pride and Prejudice *	Jane Austen
Emma *	Jane Austen
David Copperfield *	Charles Dickens
Oliver Twist	Charles Dickens
The Warden *	Anthony Trollope
Barchester Towers	Anthony Trollope
The Moonstone *	Wilkie Collins

The Woman in White	Wilkie Collins
Apologia pro Vita sua	John Henry Cardinal Newman
"The Wreck of the *Deutschland*"	Gerard Manley Hopkins
The Path to Rome	Hilaire Belloc
The Count of Monte Cristo	Alexandre Dumas
Les Misérables	Victor Hugo
*The Adventures of Sherlock Holmes**	Sir Arthur Conan Doyle
The Everlasting Man	G. K. Chesterton
Murder in the Cathedral	T. S. Eliot
*Brideshead Revisited**	Evelyn Waugh
*Out of the Silent Planet**	C. S. Lewis
*Perelandra**	C. S. Lewis
That Hideous Strength	C. S. Lewis

A Final Word

Is the Trivium, then, a sufficient education for life? Properly taught, I believe that it should be. At the end of the Dialectic, the children will probably seem to be far behind their coevals brought up on old-fashioned "modern" methods, so far as detailed knowledge of specific subjects is concerned. But after the age of 14 they should be able to overhaul the others hand over fist. Indeed, I am not at all sure that a pupil thoroughly proficient in the Trivium would not be fit to proceed immediately to the university at the age of 16, thus proving himself the equal of his medieval counterpart. . . .

—Dorothy Leigh Sayers

Appendix

THIS BOOK is primarily about resources to use in constructing a curriculum suitable for your child and your family. I would like to propose briefly some suggestions about what *not* to use.

When I was thirteen I read Tolstoy's *Anna Karenina*. That is, I read the words. I thought I had read the story, but I did not realize until ten years later that reading the words is not necessarily the same as reading the story. I was too young to understand Anna, because I did not have the experience required to read the book profitably. I knew it was about an adulterous woman, but I did not see the full gravity of Anna's sin and the kind of consequences that are only to be expected in such a situation.

In college I read *War and Peace*, also by Tolstoy, and thought I was in a position to compare these two works. After all, I said to myself, I had read them both. Then I went back to *Anna Karenina* and found a work that had a richness I had completely missed. It was not about the external actions of a sinful woman but about the internal and gradual corruption of a soul and about possible alternative behaviors, embodied in other characters.

Reading that book when I was thirteen was a mistake on my part. I should have been reading other books, more suitable to my age, that would have prepared and disposed me to read *Anna* well later on. Further, I thought for ten years that I had read one of the "great" books, when I had completely missed the point. Fortunately, I read it again, but not before I had made some very foolish comparisons between this book and *War and Peace*.

In Ecclesiastes we read, "For everything there is a season, and a time for every matter under heaven" (Qo 3:1). This experience is something I try to keep in mind when planning the curriculum of my children. There is a right time for thinking about subjects and a right way to think about them at a given time. This right time depends on more than the ability to perform the action. The student may be able to read the words, but understanding comes with maturity, and maturity comes from experience and a reflection on experience that requires a certain amount of time.

There is often a temptation, when planning curriculum, to include material that is too difficult. We want to see the students moving on to the next stage of development. We want them to excel, and we do not want them to miss out on the "classics". But when we include difficult material before the students are ready to do it, they will not do it well. They may or may not realize that the material is too hard for them, but the chances are good that they will not enjoy it. They are also apt to make the mistake that I made and think that they have understood something when they have not. This is not necessarily a question of intelligence. It is a question of maturity.

One might think, for example, that reading Plato's *Dialogues* at length in early adolescence would whet the appetite for more in subsequent years when one is actually ready to do philosophy. Unfortunately, my experience is that doing difficult material of this kind before a student is ready to think about it in the right way tends to make him less likely to do it well, or at all, later on. Partly, this is because he thinks he has already done it, and partly it is because the work does not engage his interest until it speaks to an experience the student has had himself.

The questions raised in Plato's *Meno* are really interesting to someone who has considered the nature of learning. Or even for someone who has not yet thought about it but who has had experiences of different types of learning and can reflect on how learning takes place. Reading the *Meno* too early does not dispose a student to read it well later; he is inclined to think it is uninteresting or silly. Or he may like it, but he will not yet have given much thought to how virtue is taught, and thus he will not bring to a consideration of the dialogue the essential ingredient. If you want your student to read the *Meno* intelligently, at the right time of life, you would be better advised to have him read lots of history, with examples of virtuous fathers and their offspring. Plutarch's *Lives* would be fine, if you want to use classical literature, but William Thomas Walsh's books would also do well. It is the acquaintance with history and wondering why virtuous fathers often do not have virtuous children that is advantageous.

I live in a college community, one where the great books of Western civilization are read as a matter of course. Such books are taken seriously, and the general opinion is that one's education is not complete without an acquaintance with them. Yet, the considered view among many of those who deal on a daily basis with college students is that the best students are not those who come to the college already having read the books included in the program. Rather, for the most part, the best students are those who have read history, literature and natural history and who have done basic astronomy, as well as Latin or another inflected language. A reasonable study of these disciplines will make the harder courses easy when the time comes.

These studies are better preparation for the difficult considerations appropriate to college students than attempts to do the college material itself would be. The study of history expands the experience of young people vicariously, and great literature presents truths about reality that they would not be apt to see themselves. Natural history, the study of animals and plants, makes students aware of the workings of nature, which prepares them for a philosophical study of nature. These are the types of materials that we should include in our curriculum, because they equip the student to do more difficult studies by helping him acquire experience and by encouraging reflection on that experience.

We should also allow time for reflection, time for the young to wonder about reality and to investigate their areas of interest. A curriculum can be too difficult because it does not allow the student enough time really to think, as well as by its use of material that is not proportioned to his abilities.

One might ask, then, what happens to the classical curriculum this book is supposed to consider? How can one have a classical curriculum without reading the classics? The answer is that one cannot have a classical curriculum in the fullest and most perfect sense until one has students who are capable of the kind of abstract thinking required for a study of the subjects of the Trivium: grammar, logic, rhetoric; and the Quadrivium: arithmetic, geometry, music and astronomy. To do these subjects fully, one needs to be able to read Martin of Denmark and Thomas of Erfert on speculative grammar, Aristotle on the *Prior* and *Posterior Analytics* and *Rhetoric*, Euclid's *Elements*, Plato's *Timaeus* and Ptolemy's *Almagest*. Further, these studies are ordered to philosophy and theology, which involve reading Plato's *Dialogues*, Aristotle's *Physics*, *De*

Anima, Ethics and *Metaphysics,* St. Augustine's *City of God,* the *Summa Theologiae* of St. Thomas Aquinas and various other treatises.

These are hard subjects, really exciting, but abstract. Even more than *Anna Karenina,* they require preparation: experience, maturity and a disposing formation.

It is the disposing formation that occupies our attention as home-schooling parents. This formation, because it is a preparation for a classical education, can in an extended sense be said to be classical education. It is not classical education in the fullest sense, but it may still be truly called classical, both because it leads to such an education and because it employs the method of such an education. It is this beginning of a classical education that we should keep in mind as we design our children's course of studies.

There is a beginning to the study of grammar that involves learning the vocabulary and forms of language and parsing sentences. Memory and observation characterize this stage of formation, which distinguishes the student up to sixth grade. The freshman in college who studies speculative grammar is employing those same powers, but in an abstract consideration. He will be better off for having worked on grammar earlier in the way that was commensurate with his talents at that time.

Similarly, there is a beginning to the study of logic that involves simply becoming familiar with intellectual argument. As I mentioned earlier, students at this stage of formation should work on recognizing the argument present in the material they use in their studies. Making outlines of the discussion in the text or even highlighting the topic sentence in every paragraph of a speech or essay will draw the student's attention explicitly to the progression of the author's thought. He will see whether the conclusion drawn follows from the premises given. Such exercises are a natural preparation for formal logic.

The science of rhetoric begins with an ability to assemble thoughts and ideas and present them well. This requires attention to the power of language, and that requires a certain experience of good and bad rhetoric. The study of poetry (not poetry in translation) and the reading of various authors who intend to convince their audience of a particular position are very helpful in seeing why what Aristotle says in the *Rhetoric* is true.

This is the classical curriculum for children as Dorothy Sayers envisions it in her landmark essay, "The Lost Tools of Learning". Such an education is about formation rather than information and depends more on the method used with the texts than on which particular texts are used. One still looks for good texts, and some texts are better than others, both in themselves and for a particular child. There are a number of subjects that should be addressed in every curriculum, primarily those subjects mentioned above. Every curriculum should include the truths of the faith at each stage of development. Chances are good that your student will not like all these disciplines equally, but he should nonetheless develop the different powers of the soul. All of this having been said, it is still true that the formation of this education comes chiefly from the method employed in the study of the subjects.

This formation develops habits of thought that make it possible to use information rightly. A consideration of what kind of logical study is appropriate for the seventh- to ninth-grade student will illustrate the difference between the two modes of "classical education". Students in these years are ready to think about argument. They can see that this premise either does or does not follow from that one. But it is a mistake to assume that this means they are ready for the abstract considerations required for formal logic. Before they start thinking about whether the universal affirmative converts universally they should have followed arguments in which that relationship is illustrated.

The junior high and high school student who has looked at and thought about a number of intellectual arguments will be in a stronger position to study formal logic when the time comes. Picking a speech from a period in history that is of interest, outlining it, laying the outline aside for a few days and then using it to reproduce the speech helps the student think about the argument present in the speech. Jumbling the order of the outline and then later trying to reduce the confusion to the best possible sequence also enables him to think about what comes first and why.

After a number of such exercises, the student can write a paper defending a controversial position, using the techniques he has learned by his close examination of various speeches. Further, his attention can be directed to the argument present in whatever materials he is using for his school subjects. Does this follow from that? Where is this said? Is there an implication here? What are the four major sentences in this four-paragraph essay? Asking these kinds of questions in every subject is the way to form the intelligence. The subjects provide material for that formation, and discussion and analysis form the heart of the curriculum.

Such a preparation will make the theoretical treatment of logic in Aristotle, or even in a textbook about formal logic, much more intelligible and therefore more fruitful for the student. For a parent designing a classical curriculum, it is better to concentrate on exercises like those mentioned above than to buy a textbook about teaching logic to your children.

If you do this, you will both prepare your children to think about the harder and more abstract subjects when they are ready to do so, and you will be helping them develop the habits of thought that enable them to think well about any subject they choose when they want to know more about it. They will have the "tools of learning" and can go on to study the Trivium and the Quadrivium, or any other area of interest, in its fullness.

The goal of the high school curriculum is to help the student express himself elegantly and persuasively. Doing this requires practice; in terms of writing it means writing and rewriting, cutting down, rephrasing and rewriting again. It also means encouraging discussion, where the student tries to present a sequenced position about his understanding of a text. What the subject matter of the papers is or what the discussion centers on may vary from student to student. Your curriculum may reflect your interests and those of your students, but the method is essential and should remain the same for all students of this age.

My point is that we should not think that a classical curriculum for older students, a curriculum that prepares them for thinking about high and noble things, depends on doing Greek and Roman classical texts exclusively, or even predominantly. Nor is it helpful to assign excessively difficult texts. In fact, such texts may be detrimental to intellectual development, and all really difficult texts should be chosen carefully for their suitability and used in moderation, leaving plenty of time for reflection.

A friend who taught swimming to small children found that at a certain age the children would begin to retain what they had learned from one summer to the next and could build on the previously acquired skills. Before that point, they would have to start over each summer, getting used to the water and learning to float anew. She finally began to say to the parents who asked her to teach swimming to their very young children, "I'll be happy to accept your money and play with your children, but if it is learning to swim that you have in mind, I advise you to wait for a few years."

Patience is a virtue that is employed in many ways in the raising of children, including the development of their curriculum. The tools of learning are acquired by concentrating, at each stage, on the areas of development that are appropriate to that stage. It is not essential to use ancient authors to have this kind of a classical curriculum. What is essential is that the children do what is appropriate at each stage of learning. They should memorize at the grammatical stage. This strengthens and makes docile their imagination so that in the next stage of learning, the logical, they will have the help of a trained imagination in following and constructing arguments. In turn, it is essential to this education that when the children are capable of grasping and marshaling arguments, they should practice doing so. If they do, then the last stage, the rhetorical, can be given to articulating those arguments elegantly, in the service of the truly noble. This formation will give them the tools of learning, a formation that may be truly called classical and that will dispose them to a formal study of the highest and best subjects at the proper time.

Suppliers

1. A Beka Publications
   Box 18000
   Pensacola, FL 32532–9160
   800–874–3592
   (Please note that not all of this supplier's texts are recommended. Unfortunately, most of their history texts and some science texts contain errors with respect to the doctrine and historical background of the Catholic Church.)

2. Acorn Naturalists
   17300 E. 17th Street, #J–236
   Tustin, CA 92680
   800–422–8886
   Fax 800–452–2802

3. Addison-Wesley Longman
   10 Bank Street
   White Plains, NY 10606–1951
   800–447–2226
   Fax 800–333–3328

4. American Home-School Publishing
   5310 Affinity Court
   Centerville, VA 20120–4145
   800–684–2121
   Fax 800–557–0234

5. Any educational supply store

6. Any good bookstore

7. Bethlehem Books Distribution Center
   10194 Garfield Street, South
   Bathgate, ND 58216
   800–757–6831
   www.bethlehembooks.com

8. Budgetext
   Attn: Order Department
   P.O. Box 1487
   Fayetteville, AR 72702–1487
   888–888–2272
   Fax 800–642–2665

9. Calvert School
   Department 2CAT
   105 Tuscany Road
   Baltimore, MD 21210
   410–243–6030

10. Canticle Communications
    P.O. Box 711809
    San Diego, CA 92171
    800–859–8415
    Fax 619–514–3695

11. Catholic Heritage Curricula
    18252 Little Fuller Road
    Twain Harte, CA 95383–9753
    800–490–7713
    Fax 800–490–7713

12. Catholic Home Educator
    P.O. Box 787
    Monrose, AL 36559–0787

13. Catholic Home-Schoolers' Bookshelf
    2399 Cool Springs Road
    Thaxton, VA 24174
    540–586–4898

14. Catholics United for the Faith
    827 North 4th Street
    Steubenville, OH 43952
    614–28FAITH

15. College Board SAT Program
    P.O. Box 6200
    Princeton, NJ 08541–6200
    609–771–7600

16. Common Sense Press
    P.O. Box 1365
    8786 Highway 21
    Melrose, FL 32666
    904–475–5757
    Fax 904–475–6105

17. Dale Seymour Publications
    P.O. Box 5026
    White Plains, NY 10602–5026
    800–872–1100
    Fax 800–551–7637

18. Dossier [Catholic Dossier]
    P.O. Box 591120
    San Francisco, CA 94159–1120
    800–651–1531

19. Educator's Publishing Service
    31 Smith Place
    Cambridge, MA 02138–1000
    800–225–5750
    Fax 617–547–0412

20. Elijah Company
    1053 Eldridge Loop
    Crossville, TN 38558
    888–235–4524
    Fax 615–456–6384

21. Emmanuel Books
    P.O. Box 321
    New Castle, DE 19720
    800–871–5598
    Fax 302–325–9515

22. Greenleaf Press
    3761 Highway 109N, Unit D
    Lebanon, TN 37087
    800–311–1508
    615–449–4018

23. Hayes School Publishers, Inc.
    321 Pennwood Avenue
    Pittsburgh, PA 15221–3389
    800–245–6234

24. Home Training Tools
    2827 Buffalo Horn Drive
    Laurel, MT 59044–8325
    800–860–6272
    Fax 406–628–6454

25. Ignatius Press Distribution Center
    P.O. Box 1339
    Fort Collins, CO 80522
    800–651–1531

26. John Eidsmoe
    2648 Pine Acres
    Pikeroad, AL 36064
    334–270–1789

27. Keyboard Enterprises
    5200 Heil, #32
    Huntington Beach, CA 92649
    714–840–8004

28. Kolbe Academy
    1600 F Street
    Napa, CA 94559
    707–255–6499
    Fax 707–255–1581

29. Konos Helps
    P.O. Box 274
    New London, PA 19360–0274
    610–255–0199

30. Lifetime Books
    3900 Chalet Suzanne Drive
    Lake Wales, FL 33853–7763
    800–377–0390
    Fax 941–676–2732

31. Loomes Theological Book Sellers
    Old Swedish Covenant Church
    320 North 4th Street
    Stillwater, MN 55082
    612–430–1092

32. Lost Classics Book Company
    P.O. Box 3429
    Lake Wales, FL 33859–3429
    888–611–2665
    Fax 941–676–1707

33. Marygrove College Press
    BWH Distribution Center
    610 West Elm Avenue
    Monroe, MI 48161

34. Memoria Press
    P.O. Box 5066
    Louisville, KY 40255–0066
    502–458–5001

35. Metropolitan Museum of Art
    Special Service Office
    Middle Village, NY 11381–0001
    800–662–3397 Inquiries
    800–468–7386 Orders

36. Mother of Divine Grace School
    P.O. Box 1440
    Ojai, CA 93023
    805–646–5818
    Fax 805–646–0186

37. Neumann Press
    Rt. 2, Box 30
    Long Prairie, MN 56347
    800–746–2521

38. Office of Educational Programs
    National Museum of American Art
    Smithsonian Institution
    Washington, D.C. 20560

39. Opera World
    Box 800
    Concord, MA 01742
    800–99OPERA

40. Our Father's House
    5530 South Orcas
    Seattle, WA 98118
    206–725–9026

41. Our Lady of the Rosary School
    116–1/2 North Third Street
    Bardstown, KY 40004
    502–348–1338
    Fax 502–348–1943

42. Our Lady of Victory School
    103 E. 10th Avenue
    P.O. Box 819
    Post Falls, ID 83854
    208–773–7265
    Fax 208–773–1951

43. Prentice Hall Publishing Company
    4350 Equity Drive
    Columbus, OH 43228
    800–848–9500, ext. 408

44. Progeny Press
    200 Spring Street
    Eau Claire, WI 54703–3225
    715–833–5261

45. Rainbow Re-Source Center
    8227 Ulah Road
    Cambridge, IL 61238
    888–841–3456
    Fax 309–937–2983

46. Roman Catholic Books
    P.O. Box 2286
    Fort Collins, CO 80522

47. Saint Joseph Radio
    P.O. Box 2983
    Orange, CA 92669
    714–744–0336
    Fax 714–744–1998

48. Saxon Publishers
    1320 West Lindsey Street
    Norman, OK 73069
    800–284–7019

49. Seton Home Study School
    1350 Progress Drive
    Front Royal, VA 22630
    540–636–9996

50. Spalding Education Foundation
    2814 West Bell Road, Suite 1405
    Phoenix, AZ 85023
    602–866–7801
    Fax 602–866–7488

51. Stella Maris Catalog
    P.O. Box 11483
    Fort Worth, TX 76110
    800–772–5928

52. Stone Tablet Press
    12 Wallach Drive
    Fenton, MO 63026
    314–343–4244

53. TAN Publishers
    P.O. Box 424
    Rockford, IL 61105
    800–437–5876

54. The Back Pack
    Used Textbook Dealers
    P.O. Box 125
    Ernul, NC 28527
    919–244–0728

55. The Teaching Company
    7405 Alban Station Court
    Suite A107
    Springfield, VA 22105–2318
    800–832–2412
    Fax 703–912–7756

56. Timberdoodle
    E1510 Spencer Lake Road
    Shelton, WA 98584
    360–426–0672

57. Used-book stores

58. Wilcox-Follett Company (Best known as)
    Follett Educational Service, Used Textbooks (Now)
    5563 S. Archer Avenue
    Chicago, IL 60638
    800–621–4272

59. Wile, Dr. Jay
    Apologia Educational Ministries
    808 Country Club Lane
    Anderson, IN 46011
    765–649–4076

60. Mother of Divine Grace School provides a teaching service, as do
    the other schools listed here. Students may send in work to their
    consultant, who will correct it and send it back.

61. More Than Books
    146 McClintock Way
    Kanata, Ontario K2L 2A4
    Canada
    613–592–5338
    (This company carries many of the materials recommended. They
    are a useful resource for Canadian homeschoolers.)

62. St. Francis Books
    41 Janedale Crescent
    Whitby, Ontario L1N 6Z5
    Canada
    905–579–5457

Notes

Notes

Notes

Notes